Good
Housekeeping

Family Italian
COOKBOOK

Butternut Squash and Pesto Rotini (recipe page 86)

Family Italian
COOKBOOK

185 Trattoria Favorites to Bring Everyone Together

HEARST BOOKS

New York

HEARST BOOKS
New York

An Imprint of Sterling Publishing
387 Park Avenue South
New York, NY 10016

GOOD HOUSEKEEPING

Rosemary Ellis	*Editor in Chief*
Courtney Murphy	*Creative Director*
Susan Westmoreland	*Food Director*
Samantha B. Cassetty, MS, RD	*Nutrition Director*

Book Designer: Anna Christian
Project Editor: Sarah Scheffel
Cover Designer: Jon Chaiet

Photography Credits on page 255

Library of Congress Cataloging-in-Publication Data

Good housekeeping family Italian : 185 trattoria favorites to bring everyone together.
    pages cm
"Rosemary Ellis, editor in chief"—Title page verso.
Includes indexes.
ISBN 978-1-61837-118-8
1. Cooking, Italian. I. Ellis, Rosemary. II. Good housekeeping. III. Title: Family Italian.
    TX723.G6293 2014
    641.5945—dc23
                        2013031716

10 9 8 7 6 5 4 3 2 1

The Good Housekeeping Cookbook Seal guarantees that the recipes in this cookbook meet the strict standards of the Good Housekeeping Research Institute. The Institute has been a source of reliable information and a consumer advocate since 1900, and established its seal of approval in 1909. Every recipe has been triple-tested for ease, reliability, and great taste.

Good Housekeeping is a registered trademark of Hearst Communications, Inc.

www.goodhousekeeping.com

For information about custom editions, special sales, premium and corporate purchases, please contact Sterling Special Sales Department at 800-805-5489 or specialsales@sterlingpublishing.com.

Distributed in Canada by Sterling Publishing
c/o Canadian Manda Group, 165 Dufferin Street
Toronto, Ontario, Canada M6K 3H6

Distributed in Australia by Capricorn Link
(Australia) Pty. Ltd.
P.O. Box 704, Windsor, NSW 2756 Australia

Manufactured in China

ISBN 978-1-61837-118-8

Grilled Eggplant Caponata (recipe page 218)

Lentil Stew with Butternut Squash (recipe page 49)

Contents

Foreword **9**

Introduction **10**

1 Antipasti & Other Appetizers **19**

2 Salads & Soups **39**

3 Pizzas, Panini & Frittatas **59**

4 Best-Loved Pastas **81**

5 Risotto, Polenta & Other Grains **125**

6 Fish & Shellfish **145**

7 Poultry & Meat **165**

8 Vegetables & Sides **203**

9 Dolci Desserts **221**

Metric Equivalents **242**

Index **243**

Index of Recipes by Icon **250**

Photography Credits **255**

Peach Crostata (recipe page 233)

Foreword

Growing up in an Italian-American family, I learned the pleasures of the table early. I especially loved Sunday dinners: multi-course affairs with simple food—a pasta, roasted lamb or pork with vegetables, a platter of broccoli rabe or another green, a salad course, and then fruit. Whether my grandmother or mother prepared the feast, it was always unpretentious and satisfying. But what really made these meals special was the company: Friends and family gathered around the table to relax and enjoy each other. There was always a carafe of wine for the grownups—and lots of laughter.

In the *Family Italian Cookbook*, we share 185 truly delicious recipes that will turn family suppers into celebrations—Italian style! Some are no-fuss timesavers, others require a little more love and attention, but every dish is just right for good times at the table with those you love. Tasty antipasti like bruschetta or prosciutto wrapped around melon slices are a fun way to start a meal. And when paired with a rustic soup or simple Italian salad, homemade pizza, veggie-filled frittatas, or hot and crusty panini make a quick and easy meal everyone will enjoy.

Our mouthwatering mains are sure to bring everyone to the table, whether you serve a classic like lasagna, chicken Parmesan, or osso bucco, or repertoire-expanding dishes like Leg of Lamb with Mint Pesto or Linguine with Frisée, Bacon, and Egg. Pair them with creamy polenta or one of our Italian takes on green beans (with hazelnuts), asparagus (with gremolata), or escarole (with white beans) and dinner is served. Then relax around the table with slices of our flourless chocolate cake or a few biscotti, paired with espresso or maybe some sweet wine and you'll experience the pleasures of being Italian!

To make meal-planning easy, each recipe is paired with icons indicating quick-and-easy, low-cal, and heart-healthy options plus make-ahead and slow-cooker dishes too. And to help you shop, we open with an overview of classic Italian ingredients you'll want on hand, from balsamic vinegar to authentic Parmigiano-Reggiano. Tips on essential techniques will have you grilling pizza and making perfect al dente pasta like a true Italian. Wishing you and yours happy times around the dinner table!

—Susan Westmoreland
Food Director, *Good Housekeeping*

Introduction

When you want to prepare wholesome and delicious meals that bring your family together, take it from us: Nothing entices people to the table like Italian cuisine. Even simple Italian fare—a heaping bowl of pasta, a juicy chicken roasted with fresh Italian herbs, or a pot of homemade minestrone with crusty bread—is sure to please all comers.

In the *Family Italian Cookbook*, we've collected 185 of our all-time favorite recipes, so that you and yours can enjoy simple Italian home-style cooking at its best. When it comes to mouth-watering main courses, this cookbook is filled with inspiring choices. Your family will clamor for seconds of the timeless classics, including Northern-Style Lasagna, Veal Parmigiana, and Risotto Milanese. Here, too, are new takes on familiar dishes, like Sicilian Tuna with Puttanesca Sauce; sophisticated dinner options, such as Balsamic Roasted Pork with Berry Salad; and wonderful casual choices, be it Chicken and Pesto Stacks or Eggplant and Ricotta Baked Ziti. The delectable side dishes—Crispy Parmesan Broccoli and Balsamic-Glazed Baby Carrots, among others—are ideal accompaniments to the entrées. And, finally, wow them with one of our luscious Italian-style desserts: Walnut Biscotti, Chianti-Roasted Pears, and Ganache Tart with Salted Almond Crust are sure to impress.

To help ensure your success, throughout the book, we provide advice on essential techniques, from roasting peppers to chopping fresh herbs, plus recipes for basics like pesto and marinara sauce that you'll use again and again. And, because wholesome, top-quality ingredients are another key to successful Italian cooking, a glossary of the basics follows.

Essential Italian Ingredients

The following products are essential to great Italian cooking. We use them generously in the recipes that follow, so stock up! Throughout the book, you'll find boxes about other key Italian ingredients, along with easy recipes for home-made sauces and condiments.

✦ **Olive oil:** Used in Mediterranean cooking since antiquity, olive oil is fundamental to Italian cuisine. You'll see it's the primary cooking oil called for in *Family Italian*, and it's used in vinaigrettes and brushed on our bruschetta, too. Pressing tree-ripened olives produces the prized liquid. It's flavor, color, and fragrance depend on the region of origin and the quality of the harvest.

Extra-virgin olive oil comes from the first pressing; it is the highest quality and therefore the most expensive, although a range of prices are available. Its luscious fruity flavor and aromatic bouquet make it ideal for salad dressings and for drizzling over finished dishes.

Regular olive oil (sometimes called pure olive oil) is from subsequent pressings. The light golden oil has a milder fruity flavor and is a good budget choice for cooking. For more tips on choosing and storing, see "Selecting Olive Oil," at right.

✦ **Vinegar:** Derived from the French *vin aigre*, meaning "sour wine," vinegar is made by bacterial activity that converts fermented liquids such as wine or cider into a weak solution of acetic acid, which give it its sour taste. Red and white wine vinegars have been used in Italian cooking for centuries in everything from pickles to marinades to salad dressings. The more expensive vinegars are produced by an ancient process that slowly turns the wine sour, instead

SELECTING OLIVE OIL

Here's how to pick the best bottle.

✦ **Go for extra virgin.** It's made from the first press of olives, so it has the most antioxidants and flavor. Look for an oil that's cold-pressed, meaning no heat was used during processing. If that's too pricey, opt for an inexpensive extra virgin or regular olive oil for cooking, then splurge on a high-quality one for drizzling.

✦ **Watch out for "imported from Italy."** Italy and its neighbors Spain and Greece are the biggest olive oil producers, and their strict quality standards mean you'll get a better product. Seek out the words "made in" (as in "made in Italy") for a guarantee that the oil comes from that country. Some mass-produced extra-virgin oils say "imported from Italy" on the front label, but if you turn the bottle around you may find info that says it's a blend of olives from several countries.

✦ **Buy dark-colored bottles** and keep them in a dark, cool place, since light and heat can turn oil rancid. Olive oil is best used within six months, but it can last up to two years if stored properly.

of by inoculating them with fast-acting bacteria. Herb vinegars, made by steeping fresh herbs such as tarragon or rosemary in vinegar, are also popular in Italy, as are fruit vinegars based on everything from figs to berries.

Balsamic vinegar: Everyone's favorite Italian vinegar is balsamic, a dark and pungently sweet vinegar made from white Trebbiano grape juice. The process for making balsamic vinegar, cooking and aging fresh grape must (juice), has been handed down from generation to generation in Italy since the eleventh century. Artisanal balsamic vinegar is famous for its syrupy consistency and sweet tangy flavor, which is achieved by aging it in several varieties of progressively smaller wooden barrels over decades. This precious condiment is best reserved for drizzling over meat or berries; in Italy, it is sometimes served after dinner as a digestive. Commercial balsamic vinegar typically consists of a small amount of artisanal vinegar mixed with wine vinegar and caramel color. It lends a sweetness and depth of flavor to vinaigrettes, sauces, and more.

✦ **Pasta:** The Chinese may have invented noodles, but Italians have turned pasta into a favorite worldwide. In this book, we often use dried Italian-style pasta rather than fresh, since it's readily available and easy to turn into a quick meal. Made from flour and water, dried pasta is not only more economical but lower in fat than fresh pasta; it's a good match for robust, strong-

WHOLE-WHEAT AND MULTIGRAIN PASTA

As delicious as traditional semolina pasta is, it doesn't pack the fiber punch of whole-wheat or multigrain, which provide 5 to 7 grams of fiber per serving (2 ounces, uncooked), compared with regular pasta's 2 grams.

Either can make a great substitute—it just depends on what you're preparing. The nutty flavor of whole-wheat pasta pairs nicely with garlicky greens and simple tomato- and vegetable-based sauces, while the milder taste of multigrain pasta marries well with tomato-based meat and fish sauces.

When shopping, look for "whole grain" or "whole wheat" on the packaging and the Whole Grain Council's stamp on the label (tomato and spinach pastas don't count as whole grain). The ingredients should include whole wheat, oats, and/or flax seed. Store these pastas as you would the regular kind—in a dry place at a cool room temperature. But note that their extra bran can cause them to go rancid faster than semolina pastas, so shop where there's high product turnover and use within six months of purchase.

flavored sauces. For creamy or light-bodied sauces, homemade or prepared fresh pasta is also an excellent choice. Made with eggs, fresh pasta has a silky surface and a delicate texture. Store it in the refrigerator up to one week, or freeze up to one month.

For the best taste and texture, buy dried pasta made from durum wheat flour or semolina flour. Or, to up your fiber quotient, consider whole-wheat or multigrain pasta (see "Whole-Wheat and Multigrain Pasta," page 12). Store dried pasta in a cool, dry, dark place for up to one year and whole-wheat pasta for up to six months. Don't store pasta on your countertop in clear containers: Although it looks attractive, exposing pasta to light destroys riboflavin, a key nutrient in pasta.

✦ **Polenta:** The Italian term for cornmeal, polenta comes in many colors and grinds. Coarse, stone-ground yellow polenta has a rich, nutty taste thanks to the flecks of germ that remain in the meal. White polenta has sweeter, flowery undertones. Fine-ground, quick-cooking polenta will save busy cooks time in the kitchen.

Coarse: This rough-cut polenta keeps its strong starchy flavor and texture during cooking. It mixes easily with other ingredients while its grittier texture has a rich, distinctive taste.

Medium: For smoother, creamier dishes, use a medium-ground polenta with a sand-like consistency. Medium-grind lends itself to easy molding once the polenta is cooked.

Fine: This floury, finely ground meal makes an ideal baking ingredient. The crumb has a crunch similar to shortbread and an inviting golden color.

✦ **Rice:** Arborio, Carnaroli, and Vialone Nano are all types of round, short-grained rice grown in northern Italy. All are used to prepare risotto,

FREEZING AND REHEATING CASSEROLES

Cool the baked pasta or polenta in casserole pan, uncovered, at least 30 minutes in refrigerator or until just warm. Wrap tightly with heavy-duty foil; label and freeze up to 3 months.

At least 24 hours but no more than 2 days before reheating, place your frozen casserole in the refrigerator to thaw slightly.

To reheat in a conventional oven, unwrap the casserole. Loosely cover it with foil and bake according to the recipe's reheating instructions until the center reaches 160°F (check with an instant-read thermometer).

To reheat in a microwave, unwrap the casserole; cover the top with waxed paper, tucking it under the dish (make sure it's microwave-safe) to keep in place, or use plastic wrap and turn back a corner to vent. Heat in microwave according to the recipe's heating instructions, first on Low until ice crystals are gone and you can easily insert knife into center of casserole. Then cook on High until food is heated through and the internal temperature of your casserole is 160°F on an instant read thermometer.

a rich, creamy dish often amplified with vegetables, seafood, or cheese that's popular on Italian restaurant menus. The traditional method of preparing risotto is not complicated, but it does require a bit of time. The goal is to make the rice absorb enough hot broth until it swells and turns the rice into creamy yet still slightly firm grains, which requires the slow addition of broth and continual stirring. We offer two convenient twists on this labor-intensive method: Risotto Milanese plus seafood and vegetable risottos made in the microwave (pages 126 to 130) and Butternut Squash Barley Risotto prepared in a slow cooker (page 131).

✦ **Beans:** Italians use an abundance of fiber-rich beans in everything from soups and stews to pastas and salads. When Italian favorites like fresh fava (broad beans), cannellini (white kidney beans), and garbanzo beans (chickpeas) are not available, most Italian cooks will use dried beans. These keep for about one year, but since they are not stamped with a "sell-by" date, purchase them from bulk bins or a grocery store with a high turnover rate.

To save time, you can use canned beans in the recipes in this book instead. They're a boon to busy cooks because they don't require soaking or further cooking, and some people find them easier to digest than freshly cooked dried beans. Different brands vary in texture and sodium content, so stock up on your favorite label. Canned beans should be rinsed and drained under cold water before being used. This quick rinse refreshes their flavor and removes some of the sodium added during the canning process.

✦ **Cheese:** Cheese has been made since prehistoric times in Italy, but until recent times, very few Italian cheeses beyond the most famous—Parmesan, mozzarella, and gorgonzola—were known outside Italy. These days, salty hard cheeses like Pecorino-Romano and luscious soft cheeses like fresh ricotta and mascarpone are readily available at supermarkets. If you want to venture beyond the options outlined below, visit a specialist cheese shop or Italian delicatessen to sample a selection of artisan cheeses. Italians use cheese as an accent to enhance the flavor of a dish, not to make it taste cheesy. So, do as the Italians do and use cheese in moderation.

Fontina: An Italian cow's milk cheese that's been made in the Aosta Valley in the Alps for more than 800 years, classic Fontina d'Aosta is smooth-textured and mildly pungent, while other versions that are sold in the U.S. are typically aged less and are therefore milder.

Gorgonzola: Made from cow's milk, this Italian blue cheese has a creamy texture and milder flavor. Young Gorgonzola dolce is the softest and most mild, though it is still quite tangy, while aged versions are firmer and have a more assertive flavor.

Mascarpone: Technically not a cheese, mascarpone is a mild clotted cream with a thick creamy texture similar to France's crème fraîche. It is delectable served alongside fresh fruit and is a key ingredient in classic versions of the beloved Italian dessert tiramisù.

Mozzarella: One of the best melting cheeses, in Southern Italy, mozzarella is often made from water buffalo milk and hand-formed into balls. You can find fresh (and also smoked) mozzarella at specialty food stores. In the U.S., mozzarella is often factory-produced from whole or partially skimmed cow's milk.

Parmesan: Although there are many Parmesans, there is only one authentic Parmigiano-Reggiano, Italy's premier grating cheese. Protected by Italian law, it can be made only in a geographically defined area around Parma, Italy. Its rich, complex flavor and extremely granular, dry texture are the result of at least fourteen months of aging. Buy it by the wedge and grate just before serving, or shave it with a vegetable peeler.

Homemade Ricotta

With only three ingredients and less than 30 minutes, you can have homemade ricotta—for half the price of store-bought cheese.

ACTIVE TIME: 5 minutes
TOTAL TIME: 25 minutes plus standing
MAKES: about 2 cups

Cheesecloth
8   cups whole milk, or 4 cups whole milk and 4 cups reduced-fat (2%) milk
1   teaspoon salt
2   tablespoons lemon juice

1. Line large strainer with four layers cheesecloth and place in large bowl; set aside.

2. In heavy-bottom 4-quart saucepan, heat milk and salt to boiling on medium-high, stirring occasionally to prevent scorching.

3. Stir in lemon juice; cover pot and remove from heat. Let stand 5 minutes. With slotted spoon, gently transfer curds from saucepan to strainer. Drain 3 minutes. Discard whey.

4. Transfer to clean bowl, cover, and refrigerate up to 1 week.

EACH 2-TABLESPOON SERVING: About 50 calories, 4g protein, 0g carbohydrate, 4g total fat (2g saturated), 0g fiber, 16mg cholesterol, 60mg sodium ☺ ♥ ▤

Pecorino-Romano: A hard grating cheese that's akin to Parmesan, it has a slightly salty, piquant taste that pairs beautifully with robust tomato sauces. Italian Pecorino-Romano is made from sheep's milk.

Provolone: This southern Italian cow's milk cheese has a firm texture and a mild, smoky flavor that's terrific melted in a panini. It features a golden brown rind and comes in a variety of shapes, though the squat pear shape is most recognizable.

Ricotta: The traditional version of this soft, fresh Italian cheese is prepared from the whey collected after making other cheeses. The whey is cooked a second time with coagulants to produce a mild, granular cheese. The ricotta sold in American supermarkets is usually a blend of whey and cow's milk, either partially skimmed or whole. It's easier than you might think to make your own; see our recipe at left.

Ricotta Salata: This is a pressed, lightly salted Sicilian sheep's milk cheese with a slightly crumbly, firm texture. It's delicious grated over pasta or shaved onto salads.

✦ **Olives:** Olives are the fruit of the olive tree, cured, salt-brined, or pickled for consumption. A huge variety of olives are found in different regions throughout Italy, from Puglia's plum-sized Cerignola, which is picked green, to the purplish Gaeta found in Lazio to small, aromatic Taggiasca olives from northern Liguria. Their flavor depends not only on the type of fruit, but on their ripeness and processing method. Olives picked fresh or green, early in the season, have a slightly bitter, tangy flavor and dense texture. When left on the tree to mature, they become softer and milder tasting. While each type of olive has its own particular flavor it can be difficult to source specific varieties outside of Italy.

Happily, many are interchangeable. If you can't find good Italian black olives, substitute the more readily available Kalamata olive—this is what we call for in many of the recipes in this book. Green Sicilian olives can be found in most delis or in supermarkets that have an olive bar. Our Antipasti Platter and Spiced Citrus Olives call for mixed olives: Purchase a pre-selected assortment at your supermarket or deli or experiment with mixing your own.

Avoid buying pitted olives, which can be bitter and will never have the flavor of olives preserved with their pits intact. To pit them, put the olives on a work surface, place the flat side of a large knife on top of one olive, and press down to lightly crush the olive; remove and discard the pit. When cooking with olives, it's preferable to add them at the last minute; cooking olives a long time accentuates their bitterness. Because the strength and flavor of olives varies, always taste one before you add so you can adjust the quantity accordingly. Marinated olives are best eaten on their own, as part of an antipasti platter.

✦ **Fresh tomatoes:** Italy would not be Italy without its markets, where a panoply of fresh-picked vegetables still lure cooks on a daily basis. But Italians love their tomatoes best of all and use them to full effect in everything from pastas and pizzas to antipasti and salads. Here's how to pick and prepare the best of the crop.

Select firm tomatoes with unblemished skin, a red wine–like aroma, and vibrant color that's lighter at the stem end then at the bottom. The color graduation is a sign that the tomato has ripened naturally, rather than artificially with ethylene gas—which usually results in a telltale uniform color. Keep in mind that with

Oven-Dried Tomatoes

Use these to brighten up spreads, pasta sauces, pizza toppings, and more.

ACTIVE TIME: 5 minutes
TOTAL TIME: 4 hours 35 minutes plus cooling
MAKES: 18 ounces

4	pounds ripe plum tomatoes, each cut lengthwise in half
2	tablespoons olive oil
¼	teaspoon salt
¼	teaspoon freshly ground black pepper
5	garlic cloves, each cut in half
4	sprigs fresh thyme, torn

1. Preheat oven to 300°F. Line two 15½" by 10½" jelly-roll pans with parchment.

2. In large bowl, mix tomatoes, oil, salt, and pepper. Arrange tomatoes, cut sides up, on pans. Scatter with garlic cloves and thyme.

3. Bake 4 hours and 30 minutes or until tomatoes have collapsed and begun to brown, rotating pans between oven racks halfway through roasting.

4. Cool tomatoes on parchment on wire rack. Transfer to resealable plastic bag and store in refrigerator up to 1 week. (For longer storage, transfer tomatoes to jar with tight-fitting lid. Pour in enough oil to cover by ¼ inch. Cover and refrigerate up to 1 month.)

EACH OUNCE: About 35 calories, 1g protein, 5g carbohydrate, 2g total fat (0g saturated), 1g fiber, 0mg cholesterol, 40mg sodium ☺ ♥ ▬

heirloom tomatoes, which can be pink, yellow, black, purplish, or even green when they hit their flavor peak, redness doesn't necessarily equal ripeness.

Store tomatoes stem-side up, away from heat or direct sunlight, and use them within four days. Do not refrigerate: At temperatures below 55°F, the water in the tomato expands and the sugars convert to starch, creating an unpleasant mealy texture.

Peel off the tomato's skin before making a sauce or canning, since the skin can toughen during long cook times. The best removal method: Submerge the tomato in boiling water for 15 seconds, then pop it in a bowl of ice water to cool—the skin should slip right off when you cut away the core.

✦ **Canned Tomatoes:** Although fresh, ripe tomatoes are essential to many Italian specialties, canned tomatoes are appropriate for many cooked dishes, from sauces to stews. Canned San Marzano tomatoes, an heirloom variety of plum tomatoes are considered by many cooks to be the best tomatoes for sauces in the world. Compared to the more commonly canned Roma tomato, they have more flesh than juice (and fewer seeds), providing a sweeter, more concentrated flavor that is also less acidic. When cooked, these tomatoes deliver a depth of flavor and a satisfying fruity quality that is not too cloyingly sweet. Whole, peeled canned San Marzano tomatoes are available at many supermarkets or in specialty food shops, so when you see them, stock up. When crushed tomatoes are called for, consider pulsing whole San Marzanos in your food processor to create your own puree.

CHOPPING FRESH HERBS

There's nothing like a sprinkling of fresh herbs to brighten a dish. To chop parsley, mint, cilantro, or other small leaves, strip the leaves from the stems and pile them on a cutting board. Cut the herbs into small pieces by holding the tip of the blade against the board and rocking the handle up and down.

To slice basil, sage, or other large leaves, stack them, then tightly roll them up lengthwise, cigar style. Place on a cutting board and cut crosswise with a large sharp knife into thin or thick slices. Known as *chiffonade*, this technique can also be used for dark leafy greens like Swiss chard or kale.

✦ **Herbs:** Italians make skillful use of a wide variety of herbs, most notably basil, oregano, mint, and parsley. Most fresh herbs are highly perishable, so buy in small quantities. To store them for a few days, immerse the roots or stems in 2 inches of water. Cover with a plastic bag and refrigerate. If a recipe calls for fresh herbs and you only have dried, use a third of the amount listed (e.g. for 1 tablespoon of fresh parsley, substitute 1 teaspoon dried).

Antipasti & Other Appetizers

Antipasti literally means "before the pasta" and refers to both hot and cold hors d'oeuvres. The components of traditional antipasti platters vary from region to region, but they can include everything from cured meats, cheeses, and olives to pickled vegetables and smoked fish.

In this chapter, we offer a selection of traditional Italian antipasti, such as Roman-Style Artichokes, with a bread crumb and Pecorino cheese stuffing, and Prosciutto with Melon, a fantastic flavor pairing you have to experience to appreciate. Spiced Citrus Olives and Giardiniera, pickled vegetables, also make their appearance on authentic antipasti platters. For quick and easy entertaining, we've also included an updated antipasti platter that features a Mediterranean hummus, fresh mozzarella, and breadsticks and fresh vegetables for dipping.

Our party-perfect crostini, bruschetta, and lasagna toasts all feature savory toppings on small pieces of Italian bread. Or for more finger food, try our Savory Tartlets (in three flavors) or Tomato and Mozzarella Bites (served on skewers).

Honeyed Figs and Brie pair cheese and fresh fruit to perfection, as does Roasted Apricots and Pistachios, which is topped with crumbled goat cheese. Or make your own fresh ricotta (page 15)—it's easier than you might think—and serve it simply with some rustic bread and freshly ground black pepper. Or try it baked, as a first course, with a tomato-vinaigrette-tossed side salad.

Tomato and Mozzarella Bites (recipe page 31)

Roasted Prosciutto-Wrapped Asparagus

This classic Italian finger food requires only three ingredients. Use medium-sized asparagus spears because they are easier to handle. You can oven-steam the asparagus in advance, then roast the wrapped spears just before serving.

ACTIVE TIME: 30 minutes
TOTAL TIME: 50 minutes
MAKES: 12 antipasto servings

24 medium asparagus spears (1½ pounds), trimmed
¼   cup boiling water
12 thin slices prosciutto (8 ounces), each cut lengthwise in half
½   cup freshly grated Parmesan cheese

1. Preheat oven to 400°F. Place asparagus and water in large roasting pan (17″ by 11½″); cover pan with foil. Place in oven and let steam until tender, 10 to 15 minutes. Transfer asparagus to paper towels to drain; pat dry. Wipe pan dry and leave oven on.

2. On waxed paper, place 1 prosciutto strip; sprinkle with 1 teaspoon Parmesan. Place asparagus spear on end of prosciutto strip. Roll prosciutto around asparagus spear, slightly overlapping prosciutto while rolling to cover most of spear. Repeat with remaining asparagus, prosciutto, and Parmesan.

3. Place wrapped asparagus in roasting pan (it's all right if spears touch) and roast until asparagus is heated through and prosciutto just begins to brown, about 10 minutes.

EACH SERVING (2 SPEARS): About 80 calories, 8g protein, 1g carbohydrate, 5g total fat (2g saturated), 1g fiber, 21mg cholesterol, 315mg sodium ☺ 🖤

Antipasti Platter

For a fast and tasty party appetizer, try this bountiful platter, which includes hummus, a Middle Eastern chickpea puree borrowed from Italy's Mediterranean neighbors.

TOTAL TIME: 15 minutes
MAKES: 6 first-course servings

1   container (8 ounces) prepared hummus
8   ounces smoked mozzarella cheese, thickly sliced
4   ounces thinly sliced salami
2   bunches radishes with tops, trimmed
1   small fennel bulb (8 ounces), cut into thin wedges
2   large carrots, peeled and sliced diagonally
½   cup mixed olives
Breadsticks and/or your favorite crackers

Spoon hummus into serving bowl. Arrange hummus and remaining ingredients on large tray or cutting board.

EACH SERVING: 280 calories, 15g protein, 16g carbohydrate, 18g total fat (8g saturated), 5g fiber, 44mg cholesterol, 625mg sodium ⚪

QUICK AND EASY ANTIPASTI

Antipasti follow the Italian philosophy of cooking: uncomplicated food made with the freshest, highest-quality ingredients, lovingly prepared and simply presented. Eight classics to try:

+ Cut a thin slice off the top (stem end) of cherry tomatoes. Scoop out and discard the seeds using a melon baller or teaspoon. Fill with flaked Italian tuna packed in olive oil or with a mixture of softened goat cheese, chopped basil, extra-virgin olive oil, salt, and ground black pepper.

+ Spread ricotta over thin slices of Italian bread; arrange on a cookie sheet, drizzle with extra-virgin olive oil, and sprinkle with salt and ground black pepper. Bake in a preheated 450°F oven about ten minutes or until the cheese bubbles.

+ Fill pitted dates with chunks of Parmesan or Pecorino-Romano cheese.

+ Wrap thinly sliced smoked salmon around breadsticks.

+ Prepare a tray of assorted cured meats, such as salami, mortadella, soppressata, pancetta, prosciutto, coppa, and bresaola.

+ Marinate small whole mushrooms, jarred roasted red peppers, canned quartered artichoke hearts, or small fresh mozzarella balls (bocconcini) in a mixture of extra-virgin olive oil, wine vinegar, sliced fresh basil, crushed red pepper, and salt.

+ Serve small bowls of assorted pickled vegetables such as pearl onions, sweet or sour pickles, carrots, cauliflower, pepperoncini, and olives.

+ Thickly slice large balls of fresh mozzarella and ripe tomatoes. Arrange on a platter, overlapping in concentric circles, alternating the tomatoes and cheese, and tucking fresh basil leaves between the slices. Finish the dish by drizzling with high-quality extra-virgin olive oil and sprinkling with coarse sea salt and ground black pepper.

Spiced Citrus Olives

Spiced Citrus Olives

Sweet fennel and warm spices are a perfect match for briny olives and bright citrus.

TOTAL TIME: 10 minutes plus marinating

MAKES: 2½ cups or 20 antipasto servings

1   lemon
1   orange
2   cups mixed olives
¼   cup olive oil
2   teaspoons fennel seeds
½   teaspoon crushed red pepper
¼   teaspoon ground coriander
¼   teaspoon ground cumin

1. From lemon, with vegetable peeler, peel 3 strips peel; then squeeze 1 tablespoon juice. From orange, with vegetable peeler, peel 3 strips peel; then squeeze 2 tablespoons juice.

2. In bowl, combine peels, juices, olives, oil, fennel seeds, crushed red pepper, coriander, and cumin. Refrigerate for 1 hour, or up to 1 week, before serving.

EACH 2-TABLESPOON SERVING: About 50 calories, 0g protein, 1g carbohydrate, 5g total fat (1g saturated), 0g fiber, 0mg cholesterol, 191mg sodium ☺ ♥ ▭

Giardiniera

This pickled assortment of vegetables is often served as part of an antipasti platter.

ACTIVE TIME: 1 hour

TOTAL TIME: 1 hour 20 minutes plus chilling

MAKES: 5 cups or 20 antipasto servings

½   small head cauliflower, cut into small flowerets (1½ cups)
1   large red pepper, cut into 1-inch pieces
1   cup peeled and thickly sliced carrot (2 large)
2   large stalks celery, thickly sliced
½   (5-ounce) jar green olives, drained
½   cup sugar
2¼ cups distilled white vinegar
¾   cup water
1   tablespoon kosher, canning, or pickling salt
¼   teaspoon mustard seeds
⅛   teaspoon crushed red pepper

1. In large bowl, combine cauliflower, red pepper, carrot, celery, and olives. In nonreactive 4-quart saucepan, combine sugar, vinegar, water, and salt; heat to boiling over high, stirring occasionally. Reduce heat to low.

2. In large container with lid, place mustard seeds and crushed red pepper; pack vegetables into container and pour hot syrup over, making sure vegetables are completely covered.

3. Allow giardiniera to cool, then chill for 3 hours before serving. Refrigerate pickles in an airtight container for up to 1 week.

EACH ¼-CUP SERVING: About 35 calories, 0g protein, 8g carbohydrate, 0g total fat (0g saturated), 1g fiber, 0mg cholesterol, 443mg sodium ☺ ▭

Roman-Style Artichokes

This stuffed vegetable recipe is best prepared in the spring and summer when artichokes are in season.

ACTIVE TIME: 45 minutes
TOTAL TIME: 1 hour 35 minutes plus cooling
MAKES: 8 first-course servings

2	tablespoons fresh lemon juice
8	medium artichokes
1½	cups loosely packed fresh mint leaves, chopped
1	cup fresh bread crumbs (from 2 slices)
1	cup plain dried bread crumbs
½	cup freshly grated Pecorino-Romano cheese
3	tablespoons extra-virgin olive oil
2	garlic cloves, finely chopped
½	teaspoon salt
¼	teaspoon ground black pepper

1. Fill large bowl with cold water and 1 tablespoon lemon juice.

2. Prepare artichokes as described in "Artichoke Selection and Prep," opposite. As you finish with each artichoke, place stems and trimmed artichokes in bowl of lemon water to prevent both from browning.

3. In deep 12-inch skillet or nonreactive 8-quart Dutch oven, heat *1 inch water* to boiling over high. Stand artichokes in boiling water and add stems; return to boiling. Reduce heat to medium-low; cover and simmer 30 to 40 minutes or until knife inserted in bottom of artichoke goes in easily. Drain artichokes.

4. Meanwhile, in medium bowl, combine remaining 1 tablespoon lemon juice, mint, fresh and dried bread crumbs, Romano, oil, garlic, salt, and pepper. Preheat oven to 400°F.

5. When artichokes are cool enough to handle, pull out prickly center leaves; with teaspoon or melon baller, scrape out fuzzy chokes (without cutting into hearts) and discard. Finely chop stems; stir into mint mixture.

6. Stand artichokes on 15½" by 10½" jelly-roll pan, stem sides down. For each artichoke, pull leaves to open slightly; spoon scant ½ cup mint mixture into center cavity. Bake 20 to 25 minutes or until stuffing is golden and artichokes are heated through.

EACH STUFFED ARTICHOKE: About 185 calories, 7g protein, 24g carbohydrate, 8g total fat (2g saturated), 1g fiber, 5mg cholesterol, 440mg sodium

ARTICHOKE SELECTION AND PREP

There's nothing like the slightly nutty flavor and tender texture of fresh artichokes. When shopping, look for artichokes that are compact, firm, and heavy for their size. They're at their peak in April and May. In spring and summer, choose those with an even green color. In fall and winter, it's okay to buy artichokes with touches of light brown or bronze on the outer leaves, caused by frost (which doesn't affect the flavor). Artichokes range in size from baby (2 to 3 ounces) to jumbo (15 to 20 ounces), but size is not a sign of maturity; they're all fully grown when picked. Cooked or raw, they keep for a week in the refrigerator.

TO PREPARE ARTICHOKES FOR COOKING:

1. With sharp knife, cut 1 inch straight across the top. Cut off the stem so the artichoke can stand upright. Peel the stem.

2. Pull off the outer dark green leaves from the artichoke bottom. With kitchen shears, trim the thorny tips of the leaves.

3. Spread the artichoke open and carefully cut around the choke with a small knife, then scrape out the center petals and fuzzy center portion with a teaspoon and discard. Rinse the artichoke well. (You can remove the choke after cooking, but you have to wait till the artichoke cools a bit.)

Crostini Platter

These crostini—with your choice of white bean, tuna and tomato, or caramelized onion and goat cheese topping—are party perfect. You can toast the bread up to a week before you need it. Just store it in a tightly sealed container at room temperature until you're ready to spread on one or more of the tasty toppings (which can all be made ahead of time too).

TOTAL TIME: 20 to 25 minutes

MAKES: 40 crostini

1   baguette (10 ounces)

Preheat oven to 400°F. Cut bread into ½-inch-thick slices; reserve ends for making bread crumbs. Arrange slices on two cookie sheets. Toast in oven 8 to 10 minutes or until golden brown, rotating pans between upper and lower oven racks halfway through. Cool on wire rack.

White Bean Topping

From *1 lemon*, grate ½ teaspoon peel and squeeze 2 tablespoons juice. In food processor with knife blade attached, pulse lemon peel and juice with *2 cans (15 to 19 ounces each) white kidney beans* (cannellini), rinsed and drained; *1 tablespoon olive oil; ¼ teaspoon ground cumin; 1 small crushed garlic clove; ¼ teaspoon salt; and ½ teaspoon ground black pepper* until well blended but still slightly chunky. (Refrigerate in airtight container up to 2 days, if you like.) Spread about 1 tablespoon bean mixture on each piece toasted bread. Sprinkle with *smoked paprika*.

EACH CROSTINO: About 45 calories, 2g protein, 8g carbohydrate, 1g total fat (0g saturated), 1g fiber, 0mg cholesterol, 95mg sodium ◎ ☺ ♥ ▤

Tuna and Tomato Topping

Drain *2 cans (6 ounces each) white tuna packed in olive oil* into medium bowl. Chop *⅓ cup pitted Kalamata olives, ¼ cup loosely packed fresh parsley leaves,* and *1 tablespoon drained capers*; add to bowl with *1 tablespoon olive oil* and mix with fork until evenly distributed. (Topping can be prepared early in day and stored, refrigerated, at this point.) Just before serving, toss in *16 thinly sliced grape tomatoes*. Place about 1 tablespoon tuna mixture on each piece toasted bread, gently pressing mixture together without mashing tuna.

EACH CROSTINO: About 40 calories, 3g protein, 4g carbohydrate, 1g total fat (0g saturated), 0g fiber, 2mg cholesterol, 80mg sodium ◎ ☺ ♥ ▤

Caramelized Onion and Goat Cheese Topping

In deep 12-inch nonstick skillet, heat *2 tablespoons olive oil* over medium 1 minute. Add *2 jumbo onions (1 pound each)*, halved and thinly sliced; cover and cook 20 minutes, stirring occasionally. Uncover and cook 20 minutes longer or until onions are very tender and deep golden in color, stirring occasionally. Stir in *2 teaspoons fresh thyme leaves, ¼ teaspoon salt,* and *½ teaspoon ground black pepper.* (Refrigerate in airtight container up to 2 days, if you like. Reheat onion mixture when ready to assemble crostini.) Top toasted bread with onion mixture. Dollop with *6 ounces soft goat cheese* (1 level teaspoon cheese per crostino).

EACH CROSTINO: About 45 calories, 2g protein, 6g carbohydrate, 2g total fat (1g saturated), 1g fiber, 2mg cholesterol, 75mg sodium ◎ ☺ ♥ ▤

Tomato and Ricotta Salata Bruschetta

Garlicky toast topped with tomatoes and cheese is a favorite Italian starter. Ricotta salata is a Sicilian sheep's milk cheese that has been pressed, salted, and dried. It can be found at Italian markets and specialty food shops. Goat cheese makes a great alternative.

ACTIVE TIME: 20 minutes
TOTAL TIME: 25 minutes

MAKES: 16 toasts

1	loaf (8 ounces) Italian bread, cut on diagonal into ½-inch-thick slices
8	garlic cloves, each cut in half
1	pound ripe plum tomatoes, seeded and cut into ½-inch pieces
1	tablespoon finely chopped red onion
1	tablespoon chopped fresh basil
4	ounces ricotta salata or goat cheese, cut into ½-inch pieces
2	tablespoons extra-virgin olive oil
2	teaspoons balsamic vinegar
¼	teaspoon salt
¼	teaspoon coarsely ground black pepper

1. Preheat oven to 400°F. Arrange bread slices on jelly-roll pan. Bake until lightly toasted, about 5 minutes.

2. Rub one side of each toast slice with cut side of garlic.

3. Meanwhile, in medium bowl, gently toss tomatoes, onion, basil, cheese, oil, vinegar, salt, and pepper until combined.

4. To serve, spoon tomato mixture onto garlic-rubbed side of toast slices.

EACH BRUSCHETTA: About 170 calories, 2g protein, 9g carbohydrate, 4g total fat (1g saturated), 1g fiber, 6mg cholesterol, 236mg sodium ♥

TUSCAN WHITE BEAN BRUSCHETTA: Proceed as directed in steps 1 and 2 above. Rinse and drain *1 can (15 to 19 ounces) white kidney beans* (cannellini) and place in medium bowl. Using fork, lightly mash, along with *1 tablespoon fresh lemon juice*. Stir in *1 tablespoon olive oil, 2 teaspoons chopped fresh parsley, 1 teaspoon chopped fresh sage*, and *¼ teaspoon each salt and ground black pepper*. Spoon mixture over garlic-rubbed side of toasts. Sprinkle each toast with *1 teaspoon chopped fresh parsley*.

EACH BRUSCHETTA: About 140 calories, 2g protein, 4g carbohydrate, 1g total fat (0g saturated), 7g fiber, 0mg cholesterol, 77mg sodium ♥

Lasagna Toasts

These open-faced sandwiches topped with fresh tomato, zucchini, basil, and cheese invite you to enjoy all the flavors of lasagna in a flash—you bake them in your toaster oven!

ACTIVE TIME: 15 minutes
TOTAL TIME: 35 minutes
MAKES: 4 toasts

4	large slices (½ inch thick) Italian bread
1	medium zucchini (8 ounces), cut into ¼-inch chunks
1	garlic clove, crushed with garlic press
1	tablespoon olive oil
4	ripe plum tomatoes (12 ounces), chopped
⅜	teaspoon salt
½	teaspoon ground black pepper
¼	cup packed fresh basil leaves
1	cup part-skim ricotta cheese, stone-bought or homemade (page 15)
¼	cup freshly grated Pecorino-Romano cheese
4	ounces fresh mozzarella cheese, sliced

1. Preheat toaster oven to 450°F. Toast bread 5 to 10 minutes or until golden.

2. In microwave-safe medium bowl, combine zucchini, garlic, and oil. Microwave on High 4 minutes, stirring once. Add tomatoes and ¼ teaspoon each salt and pepper; cover with vented plastic wrap and microwave on High 3 minutes.

3. Meanwhile, thinly slice basil leaves; reserve half for garnish. In small bowl, combine half of basil, ricotta, Romano, and remaining ⅛ teaspoon salt and ¼ teaspoon pepper.

4. Divide ricotta mixture among bread slices and spread evenly. Using slotted spoon, divide tomato mixture among bread slices; top with mozzarella slices.

5. In single layer on foil-lined toaster-oven tray (working in batches if necessary), bake toasts 8 to 10 minutes or until tomato mixture is heated through and mozzarella is melted and lightly browned. Garnish with reserved basil and cut into quarters to serve.

EACH ¼ TOAST: About 80 calories, 5g protein, 6g carbohydrate, 4g total fat (2g saturated), 1g fiber, 12mg cholesterol, 138mg sodium ☺ ♥

Baked Ricotta with Tomato Vinaigrette

For an elegant first course, these ricotta triangles are served with a side salad—a delightful alternative to the more common medallions of goat cheese on greens.

ACTIVE TIME: 15 minutes
TOTAL TIME: 1 hour 15 minutes
MAKES: 12 first-course servings

1 to 2 lemons

1   container (32 ounces) part-skim ricotta cheese, or 2 recipes Homemade Ricotta (page 15)

¾   teaspoon salt

⅜   teaspoon ground black pepper

½   teaspoon Dijon mustard

¼   cup olive oil

4   ripe plum tomatoes (12 ounces), coarsely chopped

1   bag (5 to 6 ounces) baby greens

1. Preheat oven to 375°F. From lemons, grate 1 teaspoon peel and squeeze 3 tablespoons juice. Set aside. Spray 9-inch glass or ceramic pie plate with nonstick cooking spray.

2. In medium bowl, stir lemon peel, ricotta, ½ teaspoon salt, and ¼ teaspoon pepper until blended. Spread ricotta mixture evenly in prepared pie plate. Bake 1 hour or until cheese is lightly browned. Let stand 10 minutes to allow cheese to set. Slice into 12 wedges.

3. Meanwhile, in medium bowl, whisk together lemon juice, Dijon, and remaining ¼ teaspoon salt and ⅛ teaspoon pepper. Whisk in olive oil in slow steady stream until blended. Stir in chopped tomatoes.

4. To serve, divide salad greens among serving plates; place 1 ricotta wedge alongside each portion. Top with tomato vinaigrette.

EACH SERVING: About 155 calories, 9g protein, 6g carbohydrate, 11g total fat (4g saturated), 1g fiber, 23mg cholesterol, 245mg sodium

Savory Tartlets with Three Fillings

To streamline the prep time for these two-bite tartlets, start with store-bought shells. Choose your filling, then do your prep while the oven preheats and the shells are baking.

ACTIVE TIME: 35 minutes
TOTAL TIME: 40 minutes

MAKES: 30 tartlets

30 mini phyllo (filo) pastry shells
Choice of tartlet filling (see below)

1. Preheat oven to 350°F. Line 18″ by 12″ jelly-roll pan with parchment paper.

2. Arrange shells in single layer in prepared pan. Bake 5 to 7 minutes or until golden brown. Cool completely in pan on wire rack.

3. Finish tartlets as instructed in filling recipe.

Creamy Spinach-Leek Filling

In 8-inch skillet, melt *1 tablespoon butter or margarine* on medium heat. Add *1 cup thinly sliced leek* (white part only) and *1/8 teaspoon each salt and black pepper.* Cook 6 minutes or until tender, stirring often. Add *1 1/2 cups packed baby spinach* and *1/4 teaspoon chopped thyme leaves.* Cook until spinach just wilts, stirring. Stir in *1 tablespoon chopped dill;* cool slightly. Finely chop mixture; divide among shells. In bowl, whisk *1 large egg* with *1/3 cup heavy cream, 1/8 teaspoon freshly grated nutmeg,* and *1/8 teaspoon salt* until smooth. Divide among shells. Bake 8 minutes or until just set. Garnish with *dill.*

EACH TARTLET: About 35 calories, 1g protein, 3g carbohydrate, 3g total fat (1g saturated), 0g fiber, 11mg cholesterol, 35mg sodium ☺ ♥ ▦

Herbed Goat Cheese Filling

Separate white and green parts of *1 green onion;* finely chop separately. In medium bowl, with fork, mix white part of onion, *4 ounces softened goat cheese, 1/2 teaspoon finely chopped thyme leaves, 1/4 teaspoon crushed fennel seeds,* and *1/8 teaspoon each salt and black pepper.* In small bowl, combine *1 seeded and chopped tomato, 3 tablespoons finely chopped pitted Kalamata olives, 1 teaspoon olive oil, 1/2 teaspoon balsamic vinegar,* green part of onion, and *1/4 teaspoon black pepper.* Divide cheese mixture among shells. Top with tomato mixture. Garnish with *basil* and *parsley.*

EACH TARTLET: About 35 calories, 1g protein, 2g carbohydrate, 2g total fat (1g saturated), 0g fiber, 2mg cholesterol, 45mg sodium ☺ ♥ ▦

Ricotta and Roasted Pepper Filling

In food processor with knife blade attached, combine *¾ cup ricotta cheese, 1 roasted red pepper, 3 tablespoons freshly grated Parmesan cheese, ⅛ teaspoon smoked paprika, ⅛ teaspoon cayenne (ground red) pepper,* and *⅛ teaspoon each salt and black pepper.* Pulse mixture until smooth. Transfer to resealable plastic bag; refrigerate up to 3 days, if desired. In 8-inch skillet, combine *1 tablespoon olive oil, 2 tablespoons blanched almonds,* and *⅛ teaspoon salt.* Cook over medium heat 7 minutes or until golden, stirring. With slotted spoon, transfer to paper towels. To same skillet, add *1 tablespoon capers*, patted dry. Cook 1 to 2 minutes or until crisp, stirring. Transfer to paper towels to cool, then chop. Snip one corner of ricotta-filled bag; pipe into shells. Top with almonds, capers, and *snipped chives.*

EACH TARTLET: About 40 calories, 2g protein, 3g carbohydrate, 3g total fat (1g saturated), 0g fiber, 4mg cholesterol, 55mg sodium ☺ ♥ ▭

Tomato and Mozzarella Bites

These skewers borrow the flavors of a Caprese salad to create a cocktail party treat. For photo, see page 18.

TOTAL TIME: 10 minutes

MAKES: 20 appetizer servings

2	tablespoons olive oil
2	tablespoons white balsamic vinegar
¼	teaspoon dried oregano
¼	teaspoon salt
¼	teaspoon ground black pepper
20	mini fresh mozzarella balls *(ciliegini)*
20	grape tomatoes
40	fresh basil leaves

1. In large bowl, whisk oil, vinegar, oregano, salt and pepper; add mozzarella balls and toss until coated with vinaigrette.

2. Onto each of 20 short skewers, thread 1 tomato, followed by 1 basil leaf, 1 mozzarella ball, and 1 more basil leaf.

EACH SERVING: About 95 calories, 5g protein, 1g carbohydrate, 8g total fat (4g saturated), 0g fiber, 23mg cholesterol, 47mg sodium ◕ ☺

Honeyed Figs and Brie

Dried figs are great in winter, but supple fresh figs are a luxury from summer to early fall. Just sink your teeth into their velvety skin for the delicate crunch of tiny seeds in sweet, tender flesh. Use them quickly: They last only a day or two in the fridge.

TOTAL TIME: 10 minutes

MAKES: 6 first-course servings

4 ounces Brie, cut into 6 small wedges
12 fresh figs, each cut in half
¼ cup pure honey
1 tablespoon water
4 sprigs fresh thyme
¼ teaspoon ground black pepper

1. Arrange Brie wedges on large plate in single layer. Arrange fig halves on top, cut sides up.

2. In small saucepan, heat honey, water, and thyme to boiling. Cook 1 minute.

3. Drizzle honey mixture over figs; sprinkle with black pepper.

EACH SERVING: About 180 calories, 5g protein, 31g carbohydrate, 6g total fat (3g saturated), 3g fiber, 19mg cholesterol, 120mg sodium

Fig and Walnut Cheese Balls

Perfect for cocktail parties or as a hostess gift, these sweet-and-savory delights can be made up to a week ahead. Hold off on covering them with nuts until just before you're ready to present them so the nuts stay crisp and fresh.

TOTAL TIME: 20 minutes plus chilling

MAKES: 3 cheese balls or 24 servings

2   packages (8 ounces each) Neufchâtel cheese

1   cup dried Calimyrna figs (5 ounces), stems removed, finely chopped

1   cup freshly grated Parmesan cheese

2   tablespoons honey

½   teaspoon ground black pepper

1   cup walnuts, toasted and finely chopped

1. In medium bowl, with mixer on medium speed, beat Neufchâtel 1 minute or until fluffy. Reduce speed to low; beat in figs, Parmesan, honey, and pepper.

2. Divide cheese mixture into 3 equal portions and place each on separate sheet of plastic wrap. Shape each portion into ball; fold plastic up to enclose. Refrigerate until chilled and firm, at least 1 hour or overnight. Roll chilled cheese balls in chopped walnuts.

3. To serve, if cheese balls have been refrigerated overnight, let stand 30 minutes at room temperature or until soft enough to spread.

EACH 1-OUNCE SERVING: About 120 calories, 5g protein, 7g carbohydrate, 9g total fat (4g saturated), 1g fiber, 18mg cholesterol, 155mg sodium

Artichoke and Mint Dip

You can prepare this refreshing summer spread in just a few minutes. Serve it with toasted Italian bread and raw vegetables.

TOTAL TIME: 10 minutes

MAKES: 3 cups

1	lemon
2	cans (13¾ to 14 ounces each) artichoke hearts, drained
½	cup freshly grated Pecorino-Romano cheese
½	cup light mayonnaise
¼	cup loosely packed fresh mint leaves, plus additional chopped mint for garnish
3	tablespoons olive oil

Toasted Italian bread slices, grape tomatoes, and yellow peppers for serving

1. From lemon, grate 1 teaspoon peel and squeeze 1 tablespoon juice.

2. In food processor with knife blade attached, blend lemon peel and juice, artichoke hearts, Romano, mayonnaise, mint, and oil until smooth. If not serving right away, refrigerate up to 3 days.

3. To serve, spoon mixture into dip bowl; garnish with chopped mint. Arrange toast and vegetables alongside.

EACH 2-TABLESPOON SERVING: About 50 calories, 2g protein, 2g carbohydrate, 4g total fat (2g saturated), 0g fiber, 4mg cholesterol, 110mg sodium ◔ ☺ ♥ ▭

Spring Pea Dip

Sweet peas pair with savory Parmesan in this luscious dip.

ACTIVE TIME: 20 minutes
TOTAL TIME: 25 minutes

MAKES: 1 cup

1	pound fresh peas in the pod, or 1 cup thawed frozen peas
¼	cup loosely packed fresh mint leaves, chopped
¼	teaspoon salt
¼	teaspoon ground black pepper
⅓	cup part-skim ricotta cheese, store-bought or homemade (page 15)
2	tablespoons freshly grated Parmesan cheese

Assorted spring vegetables for dipping, such as cucumber spears, yellow and red pepper strips, and baby carrots

1. Shell peas, if necessary: Run thumb along length of seam to open pod and release peas.

2. In 1-quart saucepan, heat *1 inch water* to boiling over high; add peas and heat to boiling. Reduce heat to medium; cover and cook 3 minutes or just until peas are tender. Drain peas and rinse under cold running water; drain well.

3. In food processor with knife blade attached, puree peas with mint, salt, and pepper. Transfer to small bowl; stir in ricotta and Parmesan. Serve dip, with vegetables, or cover and refrigerate to serve later.

EACH 2-TABLESPOON SERVING: About 40 calories, 2g protein, 4g carbohydrate, 2g total fat (0g saturated), 2g fiber, 4mg cholesterol, 110mg sodium ◔ ☺ ♥ ▭

Spring Pea Dip

Roasted Apricots and Pistachios

Roasting brings out fruit's inherent sweetness. This recipe combines succulent roasted apricots, toasted pistachios, and tangy goat cheese to create a luscious first course.

ACTIVE TIME: 5 minutes
TOTAL TIME: 25 minutes

MAKES: 4 first-course servings

8	fresh apricots, halved
1	tablespoon sugar
½	cup salted pistachios, toasted and chopped
2	ounces goat cheese, crumbled
1	tablespoon chopped fresh mint leaves

1. Preheat oven to 350°F.

2. Place apricot halves on foil-lined jelly-roll pan, cut sides up; sprinkle with sugar. Place pistachios on small baking pan.

3. Bake apricots 20 minutes or until tender and browned. Toast pistachios in same oven, 5 to 7 minutes, watching carefully to prevent burning. Turn pistachios onto plate to cool while apricots finish roasting.

4. Divide goat cheese among hot apricots; sprinkle with mint and pistachios.

EACH SERVING: About 170 calories, 7g protein, 16g carbohydrate, 10g total fat (3g saturated), 3g fiber, 7mg cholesterol, 119mg sodium

LET'S TALK APRICOTS

They can be as small as a pea or the size of a baseball—and white, pink, or even black. But the tart-sweet gems we most love are those with their namesake blushing-orange hue, which are available in June and July. Select plump, juicy-looking orange-yellow fruit; ripe apricots will yield to gentle pressure.

Ripen hard fruit in a paper bag for a day or two. Amazing in jams and tarts like rustic Italian crostatas, apricots also pair deliciously with pork and lamb. The pits (poisonous until roasted) can flavor sweets and liqueurs.

Prosciutto with Melon

The marriage of sweet, ripe melon and salty prosciutto is a classic combination. Imported prosciutto di Parma or San Daniele, available at Italian grocers and specialty food markets, are milder than the domestic varieties of this ham.

TOTAL TIME: 10 minutes

MAKES: 4 first-course servings

1   small honeydew melon or medium cantaloupe, chilled

4   ounces prosciutto, thinly sliced

Ground black pepper for sprinkling

1. Cut melon in half through stem end and remove seeds. Cut each half into 4 wedges; slice off rind.

2. Arrange 2 melon wedges on each plate; arrange prosciutto alongside melon. Sprinkle pepper on each serving.

EACH SERVING: About 150 calories, 9g protein, 22g carbohydrate, 4g total fat (1g saturated), 2g fiber, 23mg cholesterol, 548mg sodium ✓ ☺

LET'S TALK CANTALOUPE

Thin slices of prosciutto paired with juicy cantaloupe wedges is an Italian delight. Named for a castle in Italy, the true cantaloupe is a European melon that isn't readily available here. American "cantaloupes" are actually muskmelons but make for a luscious substitution available from June through September. Choose cantaloupes that are heavy for their size, have a sweet, perfumy fragrance, and yield slightly to pressure at the blossom end. Avoid melons with soft spots. Store unripe cantaloupes at room temperature, ripe melons in the fridge. Just before serving, cut in half and remove the seeds.

Salads & Soups

In Italy, salads tend to be a simple celebration of fresh greens and vegetables that change as the seasons do, tossed with a vinaigrette or extra-virgin olive oil, lemon juice, and a sprinkling of salt. We've included simple recipes for green salads featuring arugula, escarole, and other Italian greens that are just right for the Italian *L'insalata*, or salad course. But, as this chapter demonstrates, an endless array of Italian ingredients can be the basis for heartier salads, including grilled vegetables, toasted bread, fresh figs, beans and cheese, and cured meat, chicken, and tuna.

If you're looking for a main-dish salad, try our takes on panzanella salad, a traditional bread-and-tomato salad; we've added grilled chicken to one and cannellini beans and fennel to another to make them more substantial. For a refreshing summer salad, choose Tomato and Mozzarella Salad, topped with plenty of fresh basil, or our flavorful grilled interpretation of Caesar salad.

Soups can be refreshing, too: Make Chilled Tuscan-Style Tomato Soup or Summery Vegetable Soup, which can be served cold or hot. Many beloved Italian soups are rustic fare and an easy vehicle for delivering an abundance of vegetables: Mixed Vegetable Minestrone takes advantage of whatever veggies are in season, and Lentil Stew with Butternut Squash includes fiber-rich legumes as well. Pasta e Fagioli with Sausage and Chicken and Escarole Soup not only stick to your ribs, they're easy on your wallet, too.

Chilled Tuscan-Style Tomato Soup (recipe page 52)

Mixed Winter Greens

For a simple side salad, top an assortment of bitter greens with toasted slivered almonds and freshly shaved Parmesan cheese.

TOTAL TIME: 15 minutes
MAKES: 12 side-dish servings

CLASSIC BALSAMIC VINAIGRETTE

¼ cup balsamic vinegar

2 tablespoons pure honey

1 tablespoon Dijon mustard

¼ teaspoon salt

¼ teaspoon ground black pepper

½ cup extra-virgin olive oil

1 head escarole, chopped (6 cups)

2 small heads or 1 large head (14 ounces total) radicchio, sliced

5 ounces arugula

½ cup slivered almonds, toasted

3 ounces Parmesan cheese

1. Make vinaigrette: In small bowl, with wire whisk or fork, stir together vinegar, honey, Dijon, salt, and pepper. Add oil in slow, steady stream, whisking constantly until well blended.

2. In large bowl, combine escarole, radicchio, arugula, almonds, and vinaigrette. Toss until evenly coated. Divide salad among plates. With vegetable peeler, shave Parmesan directly onto each serving.

EACH SERVING: About 170 calories, 5g protein, 7g carbohydrate, 14g total fat (3g saturated), 2g fiber, 6mg cholesterol, 200mg sodium ●

Arugula and Olive Salad

Arugula partners with some classic antipasti ingredients in this satisfying salad.

TOTAL TIME: 10 minutes
MAKES: 4 first-course servings

6 ounces baby arugula

2 roasted red peppers, store-bought or homemade (see page 69), thinly sliced

¼ cup halved pitted Kalamata olives

Classic Balsamic Vinaigrette (at left)

1 ounce Parmesan cheese

In large bowl, combine arugula, roasted red peppers, olives, and 3 tablespoons balsamic vinaigrette. Toss to coat. Divide among serving plates. With vegetable peeler, shave Parmesan cheese into paper-thin slices over salads.

EACH SERVING: About 125 calories, 4g protein, 5g carbohydrate, 10g total fat (2g saturated), 1g fiber, 6mg cholesterol, 380mg sodium ● ☺

Tomato and Mozzarella Salad

For the best flavor, don't refrigerate this simple summery salad.

TOTAL TIME: 20 minutes

MAKES: 4 side-dish servings

3   pounds tomatoes, cut into 1½-inch chunks

8   ounces lightly salted, small fresh mozzarella balls *(bocconcini)*, each cut in half, or 1 package (8 ounces) fresh mozzarella cheese, cut into ½-inch chunks

1   cup loosely packed fresh basil leaves, chopped

3   tablespoons extra-virgin olive oil

¾   teaspoon salt

¼   teaspoon coarsely ground black pepper

In large bowl, toss tomatoes, mozzarella, basil, oil, salt, and pepper until evenly mixed.

EACH SERVING: About 160 calories, 7g protein, 9g carbohydrate, 12g total fat (5g saturated), 1g fiber, 22mg cholesterol, 255mg sodium ⊘

LET'S TALK BOCCONCINI

Italian for "little mouthfuls," *bocconcini* are small balls of mozzarella that can be found in gourmet shops and in the dairy case of some supermarkets. They are packed in whey or water and are sometimes tossed with herbs and spices, such as basil, black pepper, and crushed red pepper. If you buy the kind with flavorings, adjust the seasonings called for in the recipe accordingly.

Escarole Frisée Salad

Fresh parsley is an unexpected and delicious salad addition—perfect with this red wine and caper vinaigrette.

TOTAL TIME: 10 minutes

MAKES: 6 side-dish salads

2   tablespoons extra-virgin olive oil

1   tablespoon red wine vinegar

1   tablespoon capers, rinsed and chopped

¼   teaspoon salt

⅛   teaspoon ground black pepper

1   head escarole (8 ounces), chopped

1   head frisée (8 ounces), chopped

1   cup fresh flat-leaf parsley leaves

¼   cup finely chopped roasted yellow pepper, store-bought or homemade (page 69)

1. In large bowl, whisk together oil, vinegar, capers, salt, and pepper.

2. To same bowl, add escarole, frisée, parsley, and yellow pepper; toss to combine.

EACH SERVING: About 60 calories, 1g protein, 3g carbohydrate, 5g total fat (1g saturated), 3g fiber, 0mg cholesterol, 190mg sodium ⊘ ☺ ♥

Panzanella Salad with Grilled Chicken

This Florentine bread and tomato salad is popular in the summer when tomatoes are at their peak. For a fresh and flavorful twist, we added chicken breasts to the mix and tossed the ingredients on the grill.

TOTAL TIME: 30 minutes

MAKES: 4 main-dish servings

2	tablespoons red wine vinegar
1	garlic clove, crushed with garlic press
¾	teaspoon salt
½	teaspoon coarsely ground black pepper
¼	cup olive oil
4	ounces country-style bread (¼ small loaf), cut into ¾-inch-thick slices
2	red peppers, each cut lengthwise into quarters
1	red onion, cut into ½-inch-thick slices
1	pound skinless, boneless chicken-breast halves
2	pounds ripe plum tomatoes, cut into 1-inch chunks
¼	cup loosely packed small fresh basil leaves or 2 tablespoons chopped leaves

1. Prepare outdoor grill for direct grilling over medium heat.

2. Meanwhile, in large bowl, whisk together vinegar, garlic, ½ teaspoon salt, ¼ teaspoon black pepper, and 2 tablespoons oil until blended; set vinaigrette aside.

3. In jelly-roll pan, brush bread, red peppers, and onion slices with remaining 2 tablespoons oil to lightly coat both sides; sprinkle with remaining ¼ teaspoon each salt and pepper.

4. With tongs, place bread, red peppers, onion, and chicken on hot grill grate. Cover grill and cook bread about 3 minutes or until lightly toasted, turning over once. Cook peppers and onion about 8 minutes or until lightly browned and tender, turning over once. Cook chicken about 12 minutes or until meat thermometer inserted horizontally into breast registers 165°F, turning over once. As bread, vegetables, and chicken are done, transfer to cutting board. Cut bread, chicken, peppers, and onions into ½-inch pieces.

5. Into vinaigrette in bowl, stir tomatoes, basil, bread, peppers, onion, and chicken; toss to combine. Scoop into bowls to serve.

EACH SERVING: About 405 calories, 32g protein, 33g carbohydrate, 17g total fat (3g saturated), 6g fiber, 66mg cholesterol, 690mg sodium ✓ ☺

TIP: *If your grill grate isn't large enough to handle all the grilled ingredients for the salad at once, start with the bread and vegetables, and finish with the chicken.*

Grilled Caesar Salad

Grilling romaine or other sturdy greens that grows in a head (like endive, radicchio, or chicory) adds a rich "meaty" flavor that will enhance any salad.

ACTIVE TIME: 10 minutes
TOTAL TIME: 15 minutes
MAKES: 4 side-dish servings

2	tablespoons olive oil
4	ounces Italian bread, cut into ½-inch-thick slices
¼	cup light mayonnaise
¼	cup freshly grated Parmesan cheese
3	tablespoons fresh lemon juice
1	teaspoon anchovy paste, or 2 anchovy fillets, mashed
¼	teaspoon coarsely ground black pepper
1	garlic clove, cut in half
1	package (18 to 22 ounces) hearts of romaine, each head cut lengthwise in half

1. Prepare outdoor grill for direct grilling over medium heat.

2. Use 1 tablespoon oil to lightly brush bread slices on both sides. Place bread on hot grill grate, and cook 2 to 3 minutes or until toasted, turning slices over once. Transfer to plate; cool until easy to handle.

3. Meanwhile, in small bowl, whisk together mayonnaise, Parmesan, lemon juice, anchovy paste, pepper, and remaining 1 tablespoon oil.

4. When bread is cool, lightly rub both sides of each slice with cut garlic clove. Cut bread into ½-inch cubes.

5. Place romaine halves on hot grill grate and cook 4 to 5 minutes or until lightly browned and wilted, turning over once. Divide romaine among salad plates; drizzle with dressing and sprinkle with croutons to serve.

EACH SERVING: About 245 calories, 7g protein, 20g carbohydrate, 14g total fat (3g saturated), 3g fiber, 10mg cholesterol, 420mg sodium

White Bean Panzanella Salad

Fresh mozzarella, fragrant fennel, and white kidney beans transform this classic Italian salad into a fresh and flavorful meal. Grilling the bread adds a nice crunch and smoky flavor.

TOTAL TIME: 30 minutes

MAKES: 6 main-dish servings

12   ounces Italian bread, cut into ¾-inch-thick slices

6   tablespoons extra-virgin olive oil

2   tablespoons red wine vinegar

1   tablespoon drained and chopped capers

2   teaspoons Dijon mustard

¼   teaspoon dried oregano

⅜   teaspoon salt

⅜   teaspoon ground black pepper

3   pounds ripe tomatoes, chopped

12   ounces fresh mozzarella, cut in cubes

1   can (15 ounces) white kidney beans (cannellini), rinsed and drained

1   large fennel bulb (1 pound), cored and very thinly sliced, plus fronds for garnish

2   stalks celery, very thinly sliced

¼   cup fresh basil leaves, torn

1. Preheat outdoor grill for direct grilling over medium heat.

2. Brush bread slices with 2 tablespoons oil. Grill 5 to 6 minutes or until dark golden brown, turning over once. Cool slightly, then cut into ¾-inch cubes.

3. In large bowl, whisk vinegar, capers, mustard, oregano, and ¼ teaspoon each salt and pepper. Add remaining ¼ cup oil in slow, steady stream, whisking to blend.

4. To vinaigrette, add bread, tomatoes, mozzarella, beans, fennel, celery, basil, and remaining ⅛ teaspoon each salt and pepper, tossing. Garnish with fennel fronds.

EACH SERVING: About 540 calories, 20g protein, 50g carbohydrate, 29g total fat (10g saturated), 8g fiber, 45mg cholesterol, 760mg sodium ●

Prosciutto-Wrapped Grilled Fig Salad

Grilling adds a delicious charred flavor to prosciutto-wrapped fresh figs stuffed with tangy goat cheese. Serve them atop a bed of lightly dressed greens or on toothpicks as appetizers.

ACTIVE TIME: 15 minutes
TOTAL TIME: 20 minutes

MAKES: 4 first-course servings

½	teaspoon fresh thyme leaves
½	teaspoon fennel seeds
4	ounces soft goat cheese
¼	teaspoon plus pinch salt
½	teaspoon ground black pepper
10	fresh figs, each cut in half lengthwise
4	ounces very thinly sliced prosciutto, cut in half lengthwise
2	tablespoons sherry vinegar
1	tablespoon pure honey
1	tablespoon extra-virgin olive oil
5	ounces mixed baby greens

1. Prepare outdoor grill for direct grilling over medium heat.

2. Chop thyme and fennel seeds together; combine, in bowl, with cheese, pinch salt, and ¼ teaspoon pepper.

3. Scoop 1 level teaspoon goat cheese mixture onto cut side of 1 fig half. Repeat with remaining cheese and figs. Wrap 1 strip prosciutto around each fig half, enclosing cheese. If prosciutto doesn't stick to itself, secure with toothpicks.

4. Grill figs 2 to 3 minutes or until prosciutto is lightly charred and cheese is soft, turning once.

5. Meanwhile, in bowl, whisk vinegar, honey, oil, and remaining ¼ teaspoon each salt and pepper. Add greens; toss to coat.

6. Remove toothpicks, if used. Divide greens and figs among serving plates.

EACH SERVING: About 285 calories, 15g protein, 31g carbohydrate, 13g total fat (6g saturated), 4g fiber, 35mg cholesterol, 1,050mg sodium ✔ ☺

Sopressata and Roma Bean Salad

Slightly sweeter than green beans, look for Roma beans that are pale green and tender.

ACTIVE TIME: 10 minutes
TOTAL TIME: 25 minutes
MAKES: 4 main-dish servings

1¼   pounds Roma beans or green beans, trimmed
1   lemon
2   tablespoons extra-virgin olive oil
¼   teaspoon salt
⅛   teaspoon coarsely ground black pepper
4   ounces sopressata or Genoa salami, sliced into ½-inch strips
2   small bunches (4 ounces each) arugula, tough stems trimmed, or 2 bags (5 ounces each) arugula
2   ounces Pecorino-Romano cheese

1. If beans are very long, cut crosswise into 2½-inch pieces. In 12-inch skillet, heat *1 inch water* to boiling. Add beans; return to boiling. Reduce heat to low; simmer 6 to 8 minutes or until beans are tender-crisp. Drain and rinse with cold running water to stop cooking; drain again.

2. Meanwhile, from lemon, grate ½ teaspoon peel and squeeze 2 tablespoons juice. In large bowl, with wire whisk, mix lemon peel and juice with oil, salt, and pepper. Add beans, sopressata, and arugula to dressing in bowl; toss to coat.

3. To serve, spoon salad onto platter. With vegetable peeler, shave thin strips from wedge of Romano to top salad.

EACH SERVING: About 280 calories, 14g protein, 14g carbohydrate, 21g total fat (7g saturated), 5g fiber, 41mg cholesterol, 845mg sodium ◔ ☺

Italian Tuna and White Bean Salad

Packed with protein, this tuna-topped salad is appropriate for lunch or dinner. Serve it with a warm, flaky baguette to round out the meal.

TOTAL TIME: 20 minutes
MAKES: 4 main-dish servings

1   lemon
1   can (6 ounces) solid white tuna in water, drained
1   can (15 to 19 ounces) white kidney beans (cannellini), rinsed and drained
1   ripe tomato
½   fennel bulb, cored and chopped (1¼ cups)
2   tablespoons chopped red onion
2   tablespoons chopped Kalamata olives
2   teaspoons finely chopped fresh rosemary leaves
1   tablespoon olive oil
½   teaspoon salt
1   bag (5 ounces) mixed greens

1. From lemon, grate 1 teaspoon peel and squeeze 2 tablespoons juice; place in medium bowl.

2. With fork, flake tuna into bowl with lemon. Add beans, tomato, fennel, onion, olives, rosemary, oil, and salt. Toss to mix well. (Tuna salad can be made up to 6 hours ahead; cover and refrigerate.)

3. To serve, divide greens among plates; top each with tuna salad.

EACH SERVING: About 215 calories, 16g protein, 25g carbohydrate, 5g total fat (1g saturated), 8g fiber, 16mg cholesterol, 680mg sodium ◔ ☺ ▤

Lemony Mushroom and Arugula Salad

It's the lemony marinated mushrooms that make this salad perfect for a party or make-ahead dinner side dish. They taste even better when they're made in advance, won't get soggy, and stay all-day delicious.

ACTIVE TIME: 20 minutes
TOTAL TIME: 30 minutes plus marinating
MAKES: 12 side-dish servings

1 to 2 lemons
¼   cup olive oil
2   garlic cloves, each cut in half
½   teaspoon salt
¼   teaspoon ground black pepper
2   pounds white mushrooms, trimmed and cut into quarters
½   cup loosely packed fresh parsley leaves, chopped
3   tablespoons snipped chives, plus additional for garnish
1   bag (5 ounces) baby arugula
1   bag (5 ounces) mixed baby greens
Thinly shaved Pecorino-Romano cheese for garnish

1. From lemons, grate ½ teaspoon peel and squeeze ½ cup juice. In 4-quart saucepan, heat lemon peel and juice, 3 tablespoons oil, garlic, salt, and pepper to boiling on high. Reduce heat to medium and simmer 30 seconds.

2. Stir in mushrooms, parsley, and chives. Transfer to large resealable plastic bag. Seal bag, pressing out excess air. Place bag in bowl and refrigerate 6 hours or overnight.

3. Place sieve over large bowl; drain mushrooms over bowl. Set drained marinade and mushrooms aside separately; discard garlic clove. Add remaining 1 tablespoon oil to marinade in bowl; whisk until blended. Add arugula and mixed greens; toss to combine.

4. Serve mushrooms on greens. Garnish with additional snipped chives and Romano shavings.

EACH SERVING: About 65 calories, 3g protein, 5g carbohydrate, 5g total fat (1g saturated), 1g fiber, 0mg cholesterol, 105mg sodium ☺ ♥

Lentil Stew with Butternut Squash

Here's a hearty vegetarian meal that's packed with fiber and low in sodium. A slow cooker makes this stew a cinch to prepare. For photo, see page 6.

ACTIVE TIME: 20 minutes
SLOW-COOK TIME: 8 hours on Low

MAKES: 11½ cups or 8 main-dish servings

3	large stalks celery, cut into ¼-inch-thick slices
1	large onion (12 ounces), chopped
1	large butternut squash (2½ pounds), peeled, seeded, and cut into 1-inch chunks (see box, page 131)
1	bag (1 pound) brown lentils
4	cups water
1	can (14½ ounces) vegetable broth
½	teaspoon rosemary
¾	teaspoon salt
¼	teaspoon ground black pepper
1	ounce Parmesan or Pecorino-Romano cheese, shaved with vegetable peeler
¼	cup loosely packed fresh parsley leaves, chopped

1. In 4½- to 6-quart slow-cooker bowl, combine celery, onion, squash, lentils, water, broth, rosemary, salt, and pepper. Cover with lid and cook on Low 8 hours.

2. To serve, spoon lentil stew into bowls; top with Parmesan shavings and sprinkle with chopped parsley.

EACH SERVING: About 285 calories, 20g protein, 51g carbohydrate, 2g total fat (1g saturated), 20g fiber, 3mg cholesterol, 420mg sodium ☺ ❤ 🍲 🍲

Chicken and Escarole Soup

Try this Italian take on chicken noodle soup. This quick version pairs leftover cooked chicken with orzo pasta and escarole, a mild green that's beloved by Italians.

ACTIVE TIME: 15 minutes
TOTAL TIME: 35 minutes

MAKES: 10 cups or 5 main-dish servings

1	tablespoon olive oil
2	cups shredded or matchstick carrots
1	small onion, finely chopped
2	garlic cloves, minced
3	cans (14½ ounces each) chicken broth
2	cups water
2	heads escarole (1½ pounds), cut into 1-inch pieces
½	cup orzo pasta
2	cups chopped leftover cooked chicken (10 ounces)
⅛	teaspoon coarsely ground black pepper
½	cup freshly grated Parmesan cheese

1. In 6-quart Dutch oven, heat oil over medium-high. Add carrots, onion, and garlic; cook 4 minutes or until onion softens, stirring frequently. Stir in broth and water; heat to boiling. Stir in escarole and orzo; heat to boiling.

2. Reduce heat to medium-low; simmer, uncovered, 6 minutes or until escarole and orzo are tender. Stir in chicken and pepper. Reduce heat to low and simmer 3 minutes or until chicken is heated through. Serve with Parmesan.

EACH SERVING: About 285 calories, 28g protein, 25g carbohydrate, 9g total fat (3g saturated), 6g fiber, 49mg cholesterol, 890mg sodium ☺ 🍲

Mixed Vegetable Minestrone

Minestrone means "big soup" and our rustic version, brimming with hearty vegetables, cannellini beans, and tubetti pasta, lives up to the name. We added edamame for color and texture. You could also add frozen peas, or an additional can of beans.

ACTIVE TIME: 20 minutes
TOTAL TIME: 40 minutes

MAKES: 6 main-dish servings

2   tablespoons extra-virgin olive oil

1   onion, finely chopped

2   garlic cloves, crushed with garlic press

¾   teaspoon salt

¾   teaspoon ground black pepper

1   can (28 ounces) diced tomatoes

4   cups water

1   pound carrots, peeled and cut into ½-inch pieces

1   small bunch Swiss chard (12 ounces), stems removed and discarded, leaves thinly sliced (5½ cups)

8   ounces green beans, trimmed and cut into 1-inch pieces

1½ cups frozen shelled edamame (soybeans)

1   can (15 to 19 ounces) white kidney beans (cannellini), rinsed and drained

1   cup tubetti or other short pasta

½   cup plus 6 tablespoons freshly grated Parmesan cheese

1. In 5- to 6-quart saucepot, heat 1 tablespoon oil over medium. Stir in onion, garlic, and ½ teaspoon each salt and pepper. Cover and cook 4 to 5 minutes or until tender. Add tomatoes and water. Bring to boiling over medium-high heat. Add carrots; cover and cook 10 minutes, stirring occasionally. Add chard and green beans; cook 6 minutes or until beans are just tender, stirring occasionally. Add edamame and white beans; cook 5 minutes or until edamame are just cooked through. (Soup can be prepared to this point up to 2 days ahead; transfer to airtight container and refrigerate. Reheat before continuing with recipe.)

2. Meanwhile, cook pasta in *boiling salted water* as label directs. Drain well and stir into saucepot with soup. Stir in ½ cup Parmesan and remaining ¼ teaspoon each salt and pepper. Ladle into soup bowls. Sprinkle each portion with 1 tablespoon Parmesan and drizzle with ½ teaspoon olive oil.

EACH SERVING: About 575 calories, 38g protein, 63g carbohydrate, 21g total fat (3g saturated), 17g fiber, 7mg cholesterol, 775mg sodium

Chilled Tuscan-Style Tomato Soup

The lush flavors of summer shine in this refreshing, easy-to-make cold tomato soup. For photo, see page 38.

TOTAL TIME: 15 minutes plus chilling

MAKES: 6 cups or 4 first-course servings

1	teaspoon olive oil
1	garlic clove, minced
3	ounces country-style bread, cut into 1-inch cubes (2 cups)
3	pounds ripe tomatoes, each cut into quarters
¼	cup loosely packed fresh basil leaves, chopped, plus additional leaves for garnish
1	teaspoon sugar
½	teaspoon salt

1. In small skillet, heat oil over medium. Add garlic and cook 1 minute, stirring. Remove skillet from heat.

2. In food processor with knife blade attached, pulse bread until coarsely chopped. Add tomatoes and garlic; pulse until soup is almost pureed. Pour soup into bowl; stir in chopped basil, sugar, and salt. Cover and refrigerate until well chilled, at least 2 hours or overnight. Garnish soup with basil leaves to serve.

EACH SERVING: About 145 calories, 5g protein, 28g carbohydrate, 3g total fat (1g saturated), 4g fiber, 0mg cholesterol, 445mg sodium ☺ 🍲

Summery Vegetable Soup

Inspired by one of our favorite recipe testers, Sarah Reynolds, this sublime summer soup can be served warm or cold.

ACTIVE TIME: 20 minutes
TOTAL TIME: 35 minutes plus optional chilling

MAKES: 8 cups or 6 first-course servings

2	tablespoons olive oil
3	garlic cloves, crushed with garlic press
2	cups water
3	large ripe tomatoes (12 ounces each), coarsely chopped
3	medium zucchini and/or yellow summer squash (8 ounces each), coarsely chopped
1	red or yellow pepper, coarsely chopped

Pinch crushed red pepper

1½ teaspoons salt

1 large sprig fresh basil, plus basil leaves for garnish

1. In 5-quart saucepot, heat oil on medium. Add garlic; cook 1 minute, stirring. Add water, tomatoes, zucchini, red or yellow pepper, crushed red pepper, salt, and basil sprig; heat to boiling on high, stirring often. Reduce heat to medium; cook, uncovered, 10 minutes or until tender.

2. Discard basil sprig. Transfer 3 cups soup to blender; with center part of cover removed to allow steam to escape, blend until pureed. Return pureed soup to soup remaining in saucepot; heat through if serving warm, or cover and refrigerate at least 4 hours or overnight to serve cold. Garnish with basil leaves.

EACH SERVING: About 95 calories, 2g protein, 12g carbohydrate, 5g total fat (1g saturated), 4g fiber, 0mg cholesterol, 600mg sodium ☺ 🍲

Stracciatella with Escarole

This is the Italian version of egg drop soup. Stracciare means "to rip up" in Italian, and this soup is filled with the little shreds of egg that form when beaten egg is drizzled into hot broth.

ACTIVE TIME: 10 minutes
TOTAL TIME: 20 minutes

MAKES: 10 ½ cups or 4 main-dish servings

3	cans (14 ½ ounces) chicken broth
3	cups water
1	head escarole (12 ounces), trimmed and cut into 1-inch pieces
3	large eggs
⅓	cup freshly grated Pecorino-Romano cheese
½	teaspoon salt
¼	teaspoon coarsely ground black pepper

1. In 4-quart covered saucepan, heat broth and water to boiling on high. Stir in escarole; reduce heat to medium and simmer 5 minutes or until escarole is tender and wilted.

2. Meanwhile, in 2-cup measuring cup or small bowl, whisk together eggs, Romano, salt, and pepper until combined.

3. Drizzle egg mixture from measuring cup into simmering broth, gently stirring just until egg shreds are set. Ladle soup into warm bowls and serve immediately.

EACH SERVING: About 115 calories, 12g protein, 5g carbohydrate, 6g total fat (2g saturated), 2g fiber, 166mg cholesterol, 1,245mg sodium

LET'S TALK BROTH

Homemade broth is a wonderful ingredient to have on hand, but don't underestimate the convenience and quality of the canned variety. In addition to standard canned chicken, beef, and vegetable broths, supermarkets carry high-quality broths in vacuum-packed containers that rival homemade.

Many brands also offer reduced-sodium, no-salt-added, and fat-free broth options. Reduced-sodium and no-salt-added broths are recommended for recipes when regular canned broth would oversalt the finished dish. Another possibility: To tame the saltiness of regular canned chicken broth, you can dilute one 14 ½-ounce can of broth with ¾ cup water.

Fat-free broth is healthful, but it's just as easy to remove the fat from canned broth yourself. Freeze the unopened can of broth for one or two hours or chill it overnight; this will solidify a thin layer of surface fat. Open the can, lift off the fat, and discard.

Veal and Mushroom Stew

In this recipe, the veal is slowly simmered with a touch of sweet Marsala wine until tender. Peas contribute subtle sweetness and color.

ACTIVE TIME: 30 minutes
TOTAL TIME: 1 hour 30 minutes
MAKES: 6 main-dish servings

1½   pounds boneless veal shoulder, cut into 1½-inch chunks
¾   teaspoon salt
¼   teaspoon ground black pepper
3   tablespoons vegetable oil
1   pound white mushrooms, trimmed and cut in half
¼   pound shiitake mushrooms, stems removed
½   cup water
⅓   cup sweet Marsala wine (see box, page 166)
1   package (10 ounces) frozen peas, thawed

1. Preheat oven to 350°F. Pat veal dry with paper towels and sprinkle with salt and pepper. In non-reactive 5-quart Dutch oven, heat 2 tablespoons oil over medium-high until very hot. Add half of veal and cook until browned, using slotted spoon to transfer meat to bowl as it is browned. Repeat with remaining veal.

2. In Dutch oven, heat remaining 1 tablespoon oil over medium-high. Add white and shiitake mushrooms and cook, stirring occasionally, until lightly browned.

3. Return veal to Dutch oven; stir in water and Marsala, stirring until browned bits are loosened from bottom of pan. Heat to boiling.

4. Cover Dutch oven and bake, stirring occasionally, until veal is tender, 1 hour to 1 hour 15 minutes. Stir in peas and heat through.

EACH SERVING: About 250 calories, 26g protein, 12g carbohydrate, 11g total fat (2g saturated), 3g fiber, 94mg cholesterol, 448mg sodium ☺ ♥ ▤

Pasta e Fagioli with Sausage

This Italian pasta and bean soup becomes a meal in a pot with the addition of sweet sausage and fresh spinach. Using canned beans speeds up the cooking.

ACTIVE TIME: 15 minutes
TOTAL TIME: 1 hour 15 minutes

MAKES: 16 cups or 8 main-dish servings

1	pound sweet Italian-sausage links, casings removed
1	tablespoon olive oil
2	onions, chopped
2	garlic cloves, crushed with garlic press
1	can (28 ounces) plum tomatoes
2	cans (14 ½ ounces each) chicken broth
2	cups water
3	cans (15 to 19 ounces) Great Northern or white kidney beans (cannellini), rinsed and drained
6	ounces ditalini or tubetti pasta (1 rounded cup)
5	ounces spinach, washed and dried very well, tough stems trimmed and leaves cut into 1-inch-wide strips

Freshly grated Parmesan cheese (optional)

1. Heat nonreactive 5-quart Dutch oven over medium-high until very hot. Add sausage and cook until well browned, breaking up meat with side of spoon. Transfer to bowl.

2. Reduce heat to medium; add oil to Dutch oven. Add onions and cook until tender and golden, about 10 minutes. Add garlic; cook 1 minute. Add tomatoes with their juice, breaking them up with side of spoon.

3. Add broth and water; heat to boiling over high. Reduce heat; cover and simmer 15 minutes. Add beans and return to boiling; cover stew and simmer 15 minutes longer. Add sausage and heat through.

4. Meanwhile, in 4-quart saucepan, cook pasta as label directs, but do not add salt to water; drain pasta.

5. Just before serving, stir spinach and cooked pasta into soup. Serve with Parmesan, if you like.

EACH SERVING: About 560 calories, 28g protein, 65g carbohydrate, 22g total fat (7g saturated), 12g fiber, 43mg cholesterol, 1,432mg sodium

HOMEMADE BEANS BASICS

Want more bang for your buck? Dry beans cost less than one-third as much as canned. The range of cooking times varies widely depending on the bean, so follow package directions. (You can either presoak the beans overnight, or boil them for three minutes then quick-soak for one hour before cooking.) Once the beans have cooked and cooled, divide them into 1 ½ cup portions (the equivalent of a 14 ½-ounce can), pack in airtight containers, and freeze for up to six months.

Mediterranean Seafood Stew

Added in the final 30 minutes, the fresh cod, shrimp, and mussels in this satisfying slow-cooker stew retain their scrumptious flavor. We like to serve this with crusty rolls to soak up the succulent broth.

ACTIVE TIME: 20 minutes
SLOW-COOK TIME: 3 hours 30 minutes on High
MAKES: 6 main-dish servings

2	large leeks, white and pale green parts only
2	medium fennel bulbs (12 ounces each), trimmed and finely chopped
2¼	pounds ripe tomatoes, chopped
2	garlic cloves, chopped
1	teaspoon salt
½	teaspoon ground black pepper
4	sprigs fresh thyme
8	sprigs fresh flat-leaf parsley, stems and leaves separated
1	pound mussels, beards removed, scrubbed (see box, page 147)
1	pound shrimp (16 to 20 count), shelled and deveined (see box, page 162)
12	ounces skinless cod fillet, cut into 4-inch pieces
2	teaspoons extra-virgin olive oil

1. Cut root ends from leeks. Cut each leek lengthwise in half, then into ¼-inch-thick slices. Place in large bowl of cold water. With hands, swish leeks to remove grit. Repeat process, changing water several times. Drain.

2. Transfer leeks to 6-quart slow-cooker bowl along with fennel, tomatoes, garlic, salt, and pepper. With kitchen twine, tie thyme and parsley stems together, reserving the parsley leaves. Bury in vegetable mixture.

3. Cover with lid and cook on High 3 hours. Stir in mussels and shrimp, and lay fish on top. Immediately cover and cook 30 to 40 minutes longer, or until mussels open and shrimp and fish turn opaque throughout.

4. Divide mussels among serving dishes, discarding any that have not opened. Discard herb bundle. Ladle stew over mussels. Drizzle oil over all. Chop reserved parsley leaves and sprinkle over stew.

EACH SERVING: About 375 calories, 32g protein, 46g carbohydrate, 7g total fat (1g saturated), 6g fiber, 112mg cholesterol, 1,250mg sodium ☺ 📖 📖

Pizzas, Panini & Frittatas

Of the many things to thank Italy for, pizza is near the top of our list. Since Americans spend a staggering $39.8 billion on fresh and frozen pizza each year, we assume you share our enthusiasm! Start with store-bought dough and you'll have a delicious homemade pizza in the time it takes for one to be delivered. Or make your own dough using our easy recipe—complete with step-by-step instructions on how to roll and shape it. Get a jumpstart like many Italian pizzaioli's do and make dough balls the night before, then refrigerate them overnight. This not only reduces the work the next day, but gives the dough a more complex flavor.

Your family will enjoy eating their vegetables when they're the topping for a ricotta, yellow pepper, and asparagus pie. Or fill and fold the dough to create calzones—we included ricotta-spinach and spicy sausage options. If you're entertaining, we offer three irresistible takes on grilled pizza plus brunch-perfect Asparagus-Fontina Pizzettes.

How can you make a tasty sandwich even better? Put it on a grill or in a panini press and watch foccacia or country-style bread turn golden brown as the cheese melts and mingles with the other ingredients between the slices. Or, if you're serving a crowd, invite them to sink their teeth into a Muffuletta, a hearty Italian-American sub stuffed with deli meat, provolone, roasted red peppers, and pickled vegetables.

For brunch, try one of our frittatas, Italy's answer to the omelet, that's finished under a broiler and sliced into wedges for serving. Or whip up our Crustless Tomato Ricotta Pie—it's delectable.

Grilled Pizza with Zucchini plus variations (recipe page 66)

Ricotta, Yellow Pepper, and Asparagus Pizza

Fresh ricotta pairs with yellow and green vegetables for a pizza worthy of any Italian pizzeria. Choose part-skim ricotta to keep it skinny.

ACTIVE TIME: 20 minutes plus time to make dough
TOTAL TIME: 40 minutes

MAKES: 8 main-dish servings

1	recipe Homemade Pizza Dough (opposite, or see Tip)
1	pound thin asparagus, trimmed and cut into 2-inch pieces
1	teaspoon olive oil
¼	teaspoon salt
1	yellow pepper, cut into thin strips
1	cup part-skim ricotta cheese, store-bought or homemade (page 15)
2	tablespoons freshly grated Parmesan cheese
¼	teaspoon coarsely ground black pepper

1. Prepare Homemade Pizza Dough. Preheat oven to 450°F; position rack at bottom. If you're using a pizza stone, heat it in the oven an hour before baking.

2. In small bowl, toss asparagus with oil and salt. Top pizza dough with pepper strips and asparagus. Dollop with ricotta; sprinkle with Parmesan and black pepper.

3. Bake pizza until crust is golden and crisp, 20 to 25 minutes.

EACH SERVING: About 215 calories, 10g protein, 35g carbohydrate, 4g total fat (2g saturated), 4g fiber, 11mg cholesterol, 405mg sodium ☺ ♥

TIP: *If you're short on time, purchase ready-made pizza dough at your neighborhood pizza shop or supermarket. The dough is sold raw and raised, so all you have to do is roll it out and top it. Or use frozen dough; you'll need to thaw it in the refrigerator overnight and remove from the fridge 30 minutes before rolling.*

Homemade Pizza Dough

Use this basic recipe to make the pizza at left and the recipes that follow. Substitute whole-wheat flour for half of the all-purpose, if you like.

TOTAL TIME: 20 minutes

MAKES: about 1 pound dough (enough for one 15-inch pizza)

2½ cups all-purpose flour
1   package (¼ ounce) quick-rise yeast
1   teaspoon salt
1   cup very warm water (120°F to 130°F)
2   teaspoons cornmeal

1. In large bowl, combine 2 cups flour with yeast and salt. Stir in water until dough is blended and comes away from side of bowl.

2. Turn dough onto floured surface and knead until smooth and elastic, about 8 minutes, working in more flour (about ½ cup) while kneading. Shape dough into ball; cover with plastic wrap and let rest 10 minutes. If desired, dough can now be frozen: shape into disk, wrap tightly in plastic, then freeze in resealable plastic bag for up to 3 months. Thaw dough by placing in refrigerator overnight, then removing 30 minutes before rolling.

3. Grease 15-inch pizza pan; sprinkle with cornmeal. Pat dough onto bottom of pizza pan, shaping ½-inch-high rim at edge of pan. Dough is now ready to top as desired.

ROLLING AND SHAPING PIZZA DOUGH

Making pizza crusts from scratch is surprisingly easy. Just follow these steps.

1. For a perfect crust, place risen dough on floured surface.
2. Punch down with knuckles.
3. Flour dough, hands, and rolling pin. Roll dough in long, even strokes. Give it a quarter turn and repeat until dough is desired shape, size, and thickness (ranging from ⅛ inch for thin crust to ¼ inch for thick).
4. Transfer to cornmeal-sprinkled pizza pan or baking sheet. Spread with sauce and add toppings.

Broccoli and Mushroom Pizza

Here's another popular veggie topping for our homemade dough.

ACTIVE TIME: 20 minutes plus time to make dough
TOTAL TIME: 40 minutes

MAKES: 8 main-dish servings

1 recipe Homemade Pizza Dough (page 61)
2 teaspoons olive oil
1 package (16 ounces) mushrooms, sliced
1 large garlic clove, crushed with garlic press
1 package (16 ounces) broccoli flowerets
¼ teaspoon salt
½ cup marinara sauce, store-bought or homemade (page 93)
½ cup packed basil leaves, chopped
4 ounces part-skim mozzarella, shredded (1 cup)

1. Prepare Homemade Pizza Dough. Preheat oven to 450°F; position rack at bottom.

2. In nonstick 12-inch skillet, heat oil over medium. Add mushrooms and garlic; cook until mushrooms are golden. Meanwhile, in sauce-pot, heat *1 inch water* to boiling over high. Place steamer basket in pot; add broccoli. Reduce heat to medium; cover and steam until tender. Remove broccoli from water; transfer to skillet with mushrooms, add salt, and toss to combine.

3. Spread dough with sauce. Spoon broccoli mixture on top of sauce. Sprinkle with basil and cheese. Bake until crust is golden and crisp, 20 to 25 minutes.

EACH SERVING: About 230 calories, 12g protein, 38g carbohydrate, 4g total fat (2g saturated), 4g fiber, 10mg cholesterol, 570mg sodium ☺

Veggie Whole-Wheat Pizza

Pizza takes a healthy turn with whole-wheat crust topped with a heap of sautéed mixed vegetables.

ACTIVE TIME: 10 minutes
TOTAL TIME: 20 minutes

MAKES: 4 main-dish servings

1 pound assorted cut-up fresh vegetables (spinach, broccoli, zucchini, peppers, and/or onions)
2 garlic cloves, minced
Salt and ground black pepper to taste
1 cup marinara sauce, store-bought or homemade (page 93)
2 tablespoons olive salad
2 tablespoons chopped sun-dried tomatoes
1 thin, large (12-inch) ready-made whole-wheat pizza crust
2 ounces part-skim mozzarella cheese, finely shredded (½ cup)

1. Preheat oven to 425°F. Heat large nonstick skillet on medium-high; coat with olive oil cooking spray. Add vegetables and garlic; cook mixture 2 to 5 minutes or until veggies are tender-crisp. Season with salt and pepper.

2. In medium bowl, combine sauce, olive salad, and sun-dried tomatoes. Spread on crust; top with veggies and mozzarella. Place pizza directly on oven rack; bake 10 to 15 minutes or until crust is golden brown.

EACH SERVING: About 335 calories, 15g protein, 49g carbohydrate, 10g total fat (3g saturated), 10g fiber, 1mg cholesterol, 815mg sodium ☺ ☺

Cheese and Salad Pizza

Kids love this recipe for white pizza, which boasts creamy ricotta and mozzarella cheeses, plus a fun topping of tossed cherry tomatoes and fresh basil.

ACTIVE TIME: 10 minutes
TOTAL TIME: 30 minutes

MAKES: 4 main-dish servings

1	tablespoon olive oil
1	pound fresh or thawed frozen pizza dough, store-bought or homemade (page 61)
1	cup part-skim ricotta cheese, store-bought or homemade (page 15)
½	cup shredded part-skim mozzarella cheese
¼	cup freshly grated Pecorino-Romano cheese
¼	teaspoon salt
¼	teaspoon ground black pepper
1	pint cherry or grape tomatoes, cut in half
¼	cup loosely packed fresh basil leaves, thinly sliced

1. Position rack in lower third of oven; preheat oven to 450°F. Grease 15 ½″ by 10 ½″ jelly-roll pan with oil. With fingers, pat dough onto bottom and up sides of pan.

2. Spread ricotta on dough; sprinkle with mozzarella, Romano, salt, and pepper. Bake pizza 20 minutes or until topping is hot and bubbly and crust is browned. Sprinkle with tomatoes and basil to serve.

EACH SERVING: About 460 calories, 20g protein, 56g carbohydrate, 20g total fat (6g saturated), 3g fiber, 32mg cholesterol, 735mg sodium ◔

Asparagus-Fontina Pizzettes with Bacon

A pizza lover's dream brunch—or dinner.
Serve with Escarole Frisée Salad (page 41).

ACTIVE TIME: 35 minutes
TOTAL TIME: 50 minutes
MAKES: 6 main-dish servings

8	ounces asparagus, trimmed and sliced on diagonal into 2-inch pieces
6	ounces shiitake mushrooms, stems discarded, thinly sliced
¼	cup olive oil
2	garlic cloves, crushed with garlic press
¼	teaspoon salt, plus more to taste
1½	pounds fresh or thawed frozen pizza dough, store-bought or homemade (page 61; make 1½ recipes)
5	slices bacon
6	ounces Fontina cheese, shredded (1½ cups)
6	large eggs

Ground black pepper to taste

1. Arrange oven racks in top and bottom thirds of oven. Preheat oven to 475°F. Lightly grease two 18″ by 12″ jelly-roll pans.

2. Place asparagus in large bowl, along with mushrooms, oil, garlic, and ¼ teaspoon salt; toss until well coated.

3. Divide dough into 6 balls. On lightly floured surface, with floured rolling pin, roll and press each dough ball into 6-inch round and place on prepared pans.

4. Evenly divide asparagus mixture among rounds, creating well in center of each pizzette. Bake 10 minutes or until edges are golden brown, rotating pans between upper and lower oven racks halfway through.

5. Meanwhile, place bacon on paper-towel-lined plate. Cover with two additional sheets paper towel. Microwave on High 4 to 6 minutes or until beginning to crisp. Cool slightly; tear into small pieces.

6. Sprinkle pizzettes with bacon and Fontina. Bake 1 to 2 minutes or until cheese melts. Carefully crack eggs directly onto centers of pizzettes. Bake 6 to 8 minutes or until whites are opaque and set, switching pans halfway through. Sprinkle with salt and pepper to taste; serve warm.

EACH SERVING: About 585 calories, 27g protein, 57g carbohydrate, 28g total fat (9g saturated), 1g fiber, 226mg cholesterol, 1,130mg sodium

Grilled Pizza with Zucchini

Grilling adds delicious smoky flavor to pizza. This vegetarian pie, topped with grilled zucchini, fresh ricotta, nutty Gruyère, and savory Parmesan, comes together in minutes. Try our variations: Pizza with Sausage and Mushrooms and Pizza with Arugula and Prosciutto (all pictured on page 58).

ACTIVE TIME: 10 minutes
TOTAL TIME: 20 minutes

MAKES: 4 main-dish servings

2	large zucchini, cut into ⅓-inch-thick slices
1	garlic clove, crushed with garlic press
1	tablespoon extra-virgin olive oil
⅛	teaspoon dried oregano
⅛	teaspoon crushed red pepper
⅛	teaspoon salt
1	pound fresh pizza dough, store-bought or homemade (page 61)
½	cup ricotta cheese, store-bought or homemade (page 15)
2	ounces Gruyère cheese, shredded (½ cup)
¼	cup freshly grated Parmesan cheese
¼	cup packed fresh basil leaves, thinly sliced, plus leaves for garnish

1. Prepare outdoor grill for direct grilling on medium-high heat.

2. In large bowl, toss zucchini, garlic, oil, oregano, crushed red pepper, and salt. Grill zucchini 4 minutes or until just tender, turning over once. Transfer zucchini to plate to cool.

3. Adjust grill heat to medium-low.

4. Divide dough into 4 balls; cover loosely with plastic wrap. Transfer 1 ball to large cookie sheet, leaving other balls covered; gently pat and stretch dough to make ¼-inch-thick freeform shape. Repeat to shape all dough balls.

5. Carefully lift each dough piece and lay flat on grill. Cook 2 to 3 minutes or until dough is puffed and releases easily from grill. Carefully turn crusts over.

6. Divide ricotta and Gruyère among crusts, spreading evenly. Top with zucchini, then Parmesan and basil. Cook 3 to 5 minutes or until cheese melts and dough is cooked through. Garnish with basil leaves.

EACH SERVING: About 460 calories, 22g protein, 58g carbohydrate, 16g total fat (7g saturated), 2g fiber, 35mg cholesterol, 810mg sodium ●

PIZZA WITH SAUSAGE AND MUSHROOMS: Prepare grill for direct grilling on medium-low heat. In 12-inch skillet, cook *2 sweet Italian sausage links*, casings removed, on medium heat 5 to 6 minutes or until browned, stirring and breaking into small chunks. Add *1 cup thinly sliced shiitake mushroom caps* and *¼ teaspoon ground black pepper.* Cook 3 minutes or until shiitakes are tender and browned, stirring. Remove from heat; stir in *1 cup thinly sliced cremini mushrooms.* Proceed as directed in steps 4 through 6, opposite, but top crusts with *¼ cup crushed tomatoes*, then *¾ cup shredded Pecorino-Romano cheese, ½ cup sliced roasted red peppers*, and sausage mixture.

EACH SERVING: About 605 calories, 29g protein, 61g carbohydrate, 25g total fat (11g saturated), 2g fiber, 73mg cholesterol, 1,495mg sodium ⊙

PIZZA WITH ARUGULA AND PROSCIUTTO: Prepare grill for direct grilling on medium-low heat. In large bowl, toss *5 ounces baby arugula, 1 pint halved cherry tomatoes,* and *¼ cup fresh mint leaves* with *1 teaspoon extra-virgin olive oil, ⅛ teaspoon salt,* and *¼ teaspoon coarsely ground black pepper.* Add *2 tablespoons fresh lemon juice*; toss to coat. Proceed as directed in steps 4 through 6, opposite, but top crusts with thinly sliced *8-ounce ball fresh mozzarella cheese.* Remove from grill; top with arugula salad, then *4 ounces very thinly sliced prosciutto.*

EACH SERVING: About 530 calories, 30g protein, 60g carbohydrate, 19g total fat (9g saturated), 2g fiber, 67mg cholesterol, 1,465mg sodium ⊙

PIZZA-GRILLING POINTERS

Don't be timid when you prepare pizza over hot fire. Act boldly from start to finish—but keep some extra dough on hand just in case results aren't perfect the first time around.

◆ Arrange all your toppings near the grill, so you can work quickly when it's time to add them to your crust.

◆ When shaping the dough, be careful not to stretch it so thinly that holes appear. Do not a make a lip around the edge, but do take care to maintain even thickness.

◆ To transfer the dough to the grill, use your fingertips to gently lift it by the two corners closest to you, then drape it onto the grill. When you turn the dough over to grill on the other side, use tongs.

◆ Don't overcook the crust; it will become tough and dry. An ideal grilled pizza should be both chewy and crisp.

Chicago Deep-Dish-Style Veggie Pizza

Better than takeout: This make-at-home deep-dish pie is as flavorful and fast as pizzeria versions—at a fraction of the cost.

ACTIVE TIME: 10 minutes
TOTAL TIME: 45 minutes
MAKES: 4 main-dish servings

1⅓ pounds fresh or thawed frozen pizza dough, store-bought or homemade (page 61)

¼ cup water

1 tablespoon olive oil

8 ounces part-skim mozzarella cheese, shredded (2 cups)

1 cup frozen chopped broccoli, thawed

2 roasted red peppers, thinly sliced

¼ cup pitted Kalamata olives, each cut in half

1 can (14 to 14½ ounces) chopped tomatoes with garlic and basil, drained

¼ cup freshly grated Pecorino-Romano cheese

1. Preheat oven to 475°F.

2. Pat dough into 14-inch round; wrap loosely between two large sheets plastic wrap. Microwave water on High 1 minute, then remove water and let dough sit in closed microwave to rise 20 minutes.

3. Use oil to coat 12-inch cast-iron or other heavy ovenproof skillet. Unwrap one side of dough. Carefully transfer dough to skillet, unwrapped side down; peel off remaining plastic wrap and flip dough once, to coat both sides evenly with oil. Gently press dough into skillet, bringing it 1 to 2 inches up sides.

4. Sprinkle mozzarella evenly over dough; top with broccoli, red peppers, olives, tomatoes, and Pecorino. Bake pizza 20 to 25 minutes or until dough is puffed and golden brown.

EACH SERVING: About 565 calories, 27g protein, 75g carbohydrate, 21g total fat (7g saturated), 5g fiber, 38mg cholesterol, 1,255mg sodium

ROASTING BELL PEPPERS

Roasting brings out the natural sweetness of peppers and adds delicious smoky flavor to any dish. Red, yellow, and orange peppers are all good candidates. Preheat the broiler. Line a broiling pan (without rack) with foil. Cut each pepper lengthwise in half, and discard the stems and seeds. Place the pepper halves in the pan, cut side down, flattening each with your hand. Broil them 5 to 6 inches from the heat source until the skins are charred and blistered, 10 to 15 minutes. Wrap foil around the peppers and allow them to steam at room temperature for 15 minutes or until they are cool enough to handle. Peel off and discard the skins, then proceed with your recipe.

Ricotta-Spinach Calzone

No one can resist the cheesy goodness that is a calzone. This one is a delightfully devious way to make sure you eat your spinach.

ACTIVE TIME: 10 minutes
TOTAL TIME: 30 minutes
MAKES: 4 main-dish servings

- 1 package (10 ounces) frozen chopped spinach
- 1 cup part-skim ricotta cheese, store-bought or homemade (page 15)
- 4 ounces mozzarella cheese, shredded (1 cup)
- 1 tablespoon cornstarch
- ½ teaspoon dried oregano
- 1 tube (10 ounces) refrigerated pizza-crust dough
- ½ cup marinara sauce, store-bought or homemade (page 93)

1. Preheat oven to 400°F.

2. In small microwave-safe bowl, heat spinach in microwave on High 2 to 3 minutes, until spinach is mostly thawed but still cool enough to handle. Squeeze to remove excess water.

3. In small bowl, combine ricotta, mozzarella, cornstarch, and oregano; set aside.

4. Coat large cookie sheet with nonstick cooking spray. Unroll pizza dough on center of cookie sheet. With fingertips, press dough into 14" by 10" rectangle.

5. Sprinkle cheese mixture lengthwise over half of dough, leaving 1-inch border. Spoon marinara sauce over cheese mixture; top with spinach. Fold other half of dough over filling. Pinch edges together to seal.

6. Bake calzone until well browned on top, 20 to 25 minutes. Cut into 4 equal pieces to serve.

EACH SERVING: About 400 calories, 21g protein, 43g carbohydrate, 15g total fat (5g saturated), 4g fiber, 19mg cholesterol, 1,055mg sodium ☻ ☺

TIP: *These make a stellar lunch on the run; reheat a slice in the microwave, wrap it in foil, and you're good to go.*

Sausage Calzones

Golden and hot from the oven, this express-lane meal makes the most of refrigerated dough, bottled marinara sauce, and zesty sausage.

ACTIVE TIME: 10 minutes
TOTAL TIME: 35 minutes

MAKES: 4 main-dish servings

1	cup part-skim ricotta cheese, store-bought or homemade (page 15)
1	link fully cooked Italian chicken sausage (3 ounces), diced
¾	cup frozen peas
2	ounces part-skim mozzarella cheese, shredded (½ cup)
1	tube (13 to 14 ounces) refrigerated pizza dough
1	cup marinara sauce, store-bought or homemade (page 93), warmed

1. Preheat oven to 400°F. In medium bowl, stir together ricotta, sausage, peas, and mozzarella.

2. Spray large cookie sheet with nonstick cooking spray. Unroll pizza dough on center of cookie sheet. With fingertips, press dough into 14" by 10" rectangle. Cut dough lengthwise, then crosswise into quarters.

3. Divide ricotta filling equally among dough rectangles, mounding filling on one half of dough. Fold other half of dough over filling and pinch edges together to seal.

4. Bake calzones 25 minutes or until well browned on top. Serve with marinara sauce.

EACH SERVING: About 485 calories, 25g protein, 59g carbohydrate, 16g total fat (7g saturated), 4g fiber, 51mg cholesterol, 1,210mg sodium

Crustless Tomato Ricotta Pie

This cross between a frittata and a quiche makes a tasty vegetarian dinner or brunch.

ACTIVE TIME: 20 minutes
TOTAL TIME: 55 minutes plus standing

MAKES: 6 main-dish servings

1	container (15 ounces) part-skim ricotta cheese or 1 recipe Homemade Ricotta (page 15)
4	large eggs
¼	cup freshly grated Pecorino-Romano cheese
½	teaspoon salt
⅛	teaspoon coarsely ground black pepper
¼	cup low-fat milk (1%)
1	tablespoon cornstarch
½	cup loosely packed fresh basil leaves, chopped
½	cup loosely packed fresh mint leaves, chopped
1	pound ripe tomatoes, thinly sliced

1. Preheat oven to 375°F. In large bowl, whisk ricotta, eggs, Romano, salt, and pepper.

2. In measuring cup, stir milk and cornstarch until smooth; whisk into cheese mixture. Stir in basil and mint.

3. Pour mixture into nonstick 10-inch skillet with oven-safe handle. Arrange tomatoes on top, overlapping slices if necessary. Bake pie 35 to 40 minutes or until top is lightly browned, edges are set, and center is puffed. Let stand 5 minutes before serving.

EACH SERVING: About 190 calories, 15g protein, 10g carbohydrate, 10g total fat (5g saturated), 2g fiber, 165mg cholesterol, 380mg sodium ☺

Caramelized Onion and Goat Cheese Panini

No time to grill? You can make these sandwiches hot and crunchy in a panini press or waffle iron.

TOTAL TIME: 30 minutes

MAKES: 8 appetizer servings (4 panini)

2	tablespoons olive oil
2	jumbo sweet onions such as Vidalia or Maui (1 pound each), thinly sliced
½	teaspoon salt
¼	teaspoon ground black pepper
½	teaspoon chopped fresh thyme leaves
8	slices country-style bread, cut from center of loaf, each ½ inch thick
4	ounces soft fresh goat cheese

1. In nonstick 12-inch skillet, heat oil over medium 1 minute. Stir in onions, salt, and pepper; cover and cook 15 minutes or until very soft, stirring occasionally. Uncover and cook 15 to 25 minutes longer or until onions are golden brown, stirring frequently. Stir in thyme; remove pan from heat.

2. Prepare outdoor grill for direct grilling over medium heat.

3. Meanwhile, assemble panini. Place 4 slices bread on work surface. Spread one-fourth of goat cheese on each slice and top with one-fourth of onion mixture. Top with remaining bread slices.

4. Place 2 panini on hot grill grate. Place heavy skillet (preferably cast iron) on top of panini, press down, and cook 7 to 8 minutes or until bread is toasted and browned on both sides, turning over once. Repeat with remaining panini. Cut in halves or quarters to serve.

EACH SERVING: About 190 calories, 7g protein, 24g carbohydrate, 8g total fat (3g saturated), 3g fiber, 7mg cholesterol, 375mg sodium

MOZZARELLA, TOMATO, AND BASIL PANINI: Prepare panini as above, but omit step 1. To assemble panini, divide *2 cored and sliced ripe plum tomatoes, 6 ounces sliced fresh mozzarella, ½ cup loosely packed fresh basil leaves, ⅛ teaspoon salt,* and *¼ teaspoon ground black pepper* evenly among 4 bread slices. Top with remaining bread and continue as directed.

EACH SERVING: About 145 calories, 7g protein, 17g carbohydrate, 6g total fat (3g saturated), 1g fiber, 17mg cholesterol, 230mg sodium ☺

RED PEPPER AND PROVOLONE PANINI: Prepare panini as above, but omit step 1. While grill heats, combine *1 jar (7 ounces) drained, sliced roasted red peppers; ¼ cup white wine vinegar; 1 crushed garlic clove;* and *¼ teaspoon ground black pepper.* Set aside 10 minutes; drain. To assemble panini, divide *6 ounces sliced provolone, 4 ounces sliced Genoa salami,* and marinated red peppers evenly among 4 bread slices. Top with remaining bread and continue as directed.

EACH SERVING: About 215 calories, 11g protein, 17g carbohydrate, 11g total fat (5g saturated), 1g fiber, 28mg cholesterol, 675mg sodium

Veggie Focaccia

Try this fresh and flavorful sandwich as an appetizer or a light lunch.

TOTAL TIME: 20 minutes

MAKES: 4 main-dish servings

1	tablespoon red wine vinegar
1	tablespoon extra-virgin olive oil
1	small shallot, finely chopped
½	teaspoon chopped fresh thyme leaves
⅛	teaspoon salt
⅛	teaspoon ground black pepper
1	jar (9 to 10 ounces) artichoke hearts, rinsed, drained, and cut into quarters
1	jar (16 ounces) roasted red peppers, patted dry
3	ounces baby spinach leaves (5 cups)
4	pieces (5-inch square) focaccia bread
¼	cup prepared basil pesto (see Tip)
2	tablespoons mayonnaise
1	pound (1 large ball) fresh mozzarella cheese, thinly sliced

1. In small bowl, whisk together vinegar, oil, shallot, thyme, salt, and black pepper. Place artichokes in medium bowl, roasted red peppers in second bowl, and spinach in third bowl. Divide dressing among all three bowls. Toss all food in bowls until well coated.

2. With serrated knife, split each focaccia square horizontally in half. In another small bowl, stir together pesto and mayonnaise. Spread on all cut sides of focaccia.

3. On each bottom focaccia half, layer one-fourth each of spinach, peppers, mozzarella, and artichokes. Replace top halves of focaccia.

EACH SERVING: About 785 calories, 31g protein, 69g carbohydrate, 43g total fat (18g saturated), 4g fiber, 97mg cholesterol, 1,260mg sodium ◗

TIP: *Pesto sold in the refrigerated case tastes fresher than the jarred type you'll find in the condiment aisle. Or make your own with a food processor; see page 82 for our recipe.*

Muffulettas

Created by Italian immigrants to New Orleans and now a classic, this sandwich features a sturdy round Sicilian loaf stuffed with salami, ham, provolone, olives, and giardiniera, a pickled mix of vegetables that adds tons of flavor, fast.

TOTAL TIME: 20 minutes plus chilling

MAKES: 4 main-dish servings

1	cup giardiniera, store-bought or homemade (page 23), rinsed, drained, and roughly chopped
¼	cup pimiento-stuffed olives, rinsed, drained, and sliced
¼	cup peperoncini, rinsed, drained, and sliced
2	stalks celery, thinly sliced at an angle
¼	cup packed fresh flat-leaf parsley leaves
2	tablespoons extra-virgin olive oil
⅛	teaspoon ground black pepper
1	loaf (8-inch round) artisanal country bread
4	ounces thinly sliced Genoa salami
4	ounces thinly sliced reduced-sodium deli ham
4	ounces thinly sliced provolone cheese

1. In large bowl, combine giardiniera, olives, peperoncini, celery, parsley, 1 tablespoon oil, and pepper. Toss until well mixed.

2. Use serrated knife to cut bread in half horizontally. Pull out most of soft center, leaving 1 inch bread all around crust. Reserve center of bread for another use.

3. Drizzle remaining 1 tablespoon oil all over cut sides of loaf. Layer salami and ham on bottom half of bread. Top with giardiniera mixture, then cheese. Cover with top half of bread, pressing down. Use serrated knife to cut sandwich into quarters. Wrap sandwiches tightly and refrigerate for a few hours or up to 1 day to allow flavors to meld before serving.

EACH SERVING: About 385 calories, 20g protein, 16g carbohydrate, 26g total fat (9g saturated), 1g fiber, 61mg cholesterol, 1,600mg sodium ☺ 🗑

Tomato, Portobello, and Mozzarella Melts

Open-faced focaccia sandwiches are topped with peppery greens, grilled tomatoes and portobellos, and melted cheese. Yum!

ACTIVE TIME: 10 minutes
TOTAL TIME: 20 minutes
MAKES: 4 main-dish servings (2 sandwiches)

2   cups loosely packed arugula or watercress, trimmed

2   tablespoons balsamic vinegar

1   loaf (1 inch thick) focaccia or ciabatta bread

4   large portobello mushrooms (1 pound total), stems removed and each cut in half (see Tip)

2   ripe tomatoes, each cut into ¾-inch-thick slices

2   tablespoons extra-virgin olive oil

¼   teaspoon salt

¼   teaspoon coarsely ground black pepper

4   ounces fresh mozzarella cheese, thinly sliced

1. Prepare outdoor grill for direct grilling over medium-high heat.

2. In small bowl, toss arugula with vinegar until evenly coated. From loaf of focaccia, cut two 8″ by 2″ pieces, using serrated knife. Slice each piece horizontally in half to make four 8″ by 2″ pieces of focaccia.

3. Brush mushrooms and tomatoes on both sides with oil; sprinkle with salt and pepper. Place mushrooms, stem sides up, and tomato slices on hot grill rack and cook until tender and charred, 6 to 8 minutes, turning over once. Transfer tomatoes to plate. Arrange mozzarella on mushrooms; cover and cook until cheese melts, 1 to 2 minutes longer.

4. Place bread, cut sides up, on work surface; top with arugula mixture, grilled tomatoes, and cheese-topped mushrooms. Cut each sandwich in half and serve immediately.

EACH SERVING: About 355 calories, 14g protein, 43g carbohydrate, 15g total fat (5g saturated), 6g fiber, 22mg cholesterol, 595mg sodium ✔ ☺

TIP: *To clean portobello mushrooms, wipe the caps with a damp paper towel to remove any dirt—never soak them in water.*

Red Potato, Spinach, and Fontina Frittata

This veggie-packed frittata makes a satisfying brunch or lunch.

TOTAL TIME: 30 minutes

MAKES: 4 main-dish servings

1	pound red potatoes, cut into ½-inch chunks
2	teaspoons olive oil
1	red pepper, chopped
10	ounces baby spinach (5 cups)
2	garlic cloves, crushed with garlic press
6	large eggs
2	large egg whites
¼	teaspoon salt
1	yellow squash, shredded
1½	ounces Fontina cheese, shredded

1. Arrange oven rack 6 inches from heat source; preheat broiler.

2. Place potatoes in microwave-safe large bowl; cover with vented plastic wrap. Microwave on High 6 minutes or until potatoes are fork-tender.

3. In broiler-safe nonstick 12-inch skillet (see Tip), heat 1 teaspoon oil on medium 1 minute. Add red pepper; cook 5 minutes or until tender, stirring. Transfer to bowl with potatoes. Add spinach and garlic to skillet; cook 4 minutes or until moisture has evaporated, stirring. Transfer to same bowl.

4. In another large bowl, whisk eggs, egg whites, and salt until blended. Stir in squash and vegetable mixture until well mixed.

5. Wipe out skillet. Heat remaining 1 teaspoon oil on medium 1 minute; add egg mixture. Cover; cook 5 minutes or until edges are just set. Top frittata with Fontina and broil 4 minutes or until golden brown.

EACH SERVING: About 320 calories, 19g protein, 33g carbohydrate, 13g total fat (5g saturated), 6g fiber, 330mg cholesterol, 485mg sodium 🌀 ☺

TIP: *If your pan is not oven-safe, wrap the handle in heavy-duty foil before placing it in the broiler.*

Florentine Frittata

This vegetable-studded frittata would work well with Gorgonzola or Parmesan, too.

ACTIVE TIME: 10 minutes
TOTAL TIME: 20 minutes
MAKES: 4 main-dish servings

4   large eggs
4   large egg whites
1   package (10 ounces) frozen chopped spinach, thawed and squeezed dry
2   green onions, thinly sliced
¼   cup crumbled feta or goat cheese
3   ounces part-skim mozzarella cheese, shredded (¾ cup)
¼   teaspoon salt
1   tablespoon olive oil
1   cup grape or cherry tomatoes

1. Arrange oven rack 5 to 6 inches from heat source; preheat broiler.

2. In large bowl, with wire whisk or fork, beat whole eggs, egg whites, spinach, green onions, feta, ½ cup mozzarella, and salt until blended.

3. In broiler-safe nonstick 10-inch skillet, heat oil over medium (see Tip, page 78). Pour egg mixture into skillet; arrange tomatoes on top, pushing some down. Cover skillet and cook until egg mixture just sets around edge, 5 to 6 minutes.

4. Place skillet under broiler until frittata just sets in center, 4 to 5 minutes. Sprinkle with remaining ¼ cup mozzarella; return to broiler until cheese melts, about 1 minute longer. To serve, cut into wedges.

EACH SERVING: About 230 calories, 18g protein, 6g carbohydrate, 14g total fat (6g saturated), 2g fiber, 233mg cholesterol, 570mg sodium ✅ ☺

SIDE SALAD IN A SNAP

Complete the meal, Italian style. Toss any of these with our Classic Balsamic Vinaigrette (page 40), or simply drizzle with olive oil (make it extra-virgin) and a squeeze of fresh lemon juice and dinner is served. Each recipe makes 4 side-dish servings.

SPINACH AND ENDIVE WITH PEARS AND WALNUTS: Toss together one 6-ounce bag baby spinach, 2 heads sliced Belgian endive, 1 cored and thinly sliced Bosc pear, and ½ cup toasted walnut pieces.

BABY ROMAINE WITH FENNEL AND CITRUS: Toss together one 5-ounce bag baby romaine, 1 cup thinly sliced fennel, 1 cup jarred citrus segments, ½ cup rinsed and drained garbanzo beans, and 6 thinly sliced radishes.

APPLE COLESLAW WITH GOLDEN RAISINS AND PINE NUTS: Toss together one 16-ounce bag coleslaw mix; 1 Granny Smith apple, cored and cut into ½-inch chunks; ½ cup golden raisins; and ¼ cup toasted pine nuts.

MEDITERRANEAN SALAD WITH GOAT CHEESE AND OLIVES: Toss together one 5-ounce bag spring mix with herbs; 1 cup grape tomatoes; 1 seedless (English) cucumber, cut into ½-inch chunks; and ½ cup pitted Kalamata olives. Top with ¼ cup crumbled goat cheese.

Best-Loved Pastas

For a casual get-together or family meal, there's nothing more satisfying—or economical—than a bowl of pasta. Everyone can serve themselves as much as they want, and some crusty bread and a simple side salad are all that are needed to complete the meal.

If you haven't ventured much beyond spaghetti and meatballs, then we invite you to explore this collection of luscious pasta recipes, both traditional and inventive, featuring a wide array of noodle shapes and delectable sauces.

Hearty choices like Beef Ragu with Minted Penne and Chicken Carbonara, our twist on this creamy bacon-studded sauce, are sure to satisfy even the largest appetites. And pasta is the perfect playground for all sorts of seasonal vegetables: Try Ravioli with Fresh Tomatoes in the summer or Butternut Squash and Pesto Rotini come fall. Baked pastas and lasagnas are always a good choice when you're serving a crowd: Eggplant and Ricotta Baked Ziti or authentic Northern-Style Lasagna are sure to garner kudos from your guests.

Create your own pasta dishes with ingredients you have in your pantry and fridge or start with one of our simple sauces. We provide foolproof recipes for Homemade Marinara, Classic Italian Pesto, and two versions of Bolognese Sauce, one fast, one slow; make them ahead and freeze for up to three months, so you can quickly toss together dinner on busy nights. Tips on cooking pasta until it's al dente, swapping in whole-wheat pasta, and selecting lasagna noodles all help ensure pasta perfection every time!

Tomato-Ricotta Rigatoni (recipe page 101)

Pasta with Tuna Puttanesca

We've used tuna instead of anchovies in this tasty no-cook twist on a traditional spicy sauce. For the most authentic Italian flavor, use tuna packed in olive oil.

ACTIVE TIME: 15 minutes
TOTAL TIME: 40 minutes
MAKES: 6 main-dish servings

1   package (16 ounces) rotini or medium shells
3   tablespoons capers, drained and chopped
3   tablespoons finely chopped shallot
2   tablespoons red wine vinegar
1   tablespoon olive oil
½   teaspoon salt
¼   teaspoon coarsely ground black pepper
1   can (6 ounces) light tuna in olive oil
2   bunches watercress (4 to 6 ounces each), tough stems removed
½   cup loosely packed fresh basil leaves, chopped

1. In large saucepot, cook pasta in *boiling salted water* as label directs. Drain, reserving *½ cup cooking water.*

2. Meanwhile, in large bowl, with fork, mix capers, shallots, lemon peel, vinegar, oil, salt, and pepper until well combined. Add undrained tuna and watercress; toss to combine.

3. In saucepot, combine pasta, basil, tuna mixture, and reserved pasta cooking water; toss well.

EACH SERVING: About 375 calories, 18g protein, 59g carbohydrate, 7g total fat (1g saturated), 3g fiber, 11mg cholesterol, 630mg sodium ☺

Classic Italian Pesto

Pesto is the perfect use for all that fresh summer basil. To serve it with pasta, save ¼ cup pasta cooking water and stir it, along with the pesto, into 1 pound cooked pasta. To store the pesto, spoon it into half-pint containers and drizzle a few tablespoons of olive oil on top. Cover and refrigerate it for up to 2 days or freeze for up to 2 months.

TOTAL TIME: 10 minutes
MAKES: about ¾ cup sauce

2   cups firmly packed fresh basil leaves
1   garlic clove, crushed with garlic press
2   tablespoons pine nuts (*pignoli*) or walnuts
¼   cup olive oil
1   teaspoon salt
¼   teaspoon coarsely ground black pepper
½   cup freshly grated Parmesan cheese

In blender or food processor with knife blade attached, puree basil, garlic, pine nuts, oil, salt, and pepper until smooth. Add Parmesan and blend until combined.

EACH TABLESPOON: About 65 calories, 2g protein, 1g carbohydrate, 6g total fat (1g saturated), 0g fiber 3mg cholesterol, 256mg sodium ♥ ☺ ♥ ▥

Six-Herb Linguine

Celebrate your herb garden with this pasta—flecked with a mix of fresh green herbs and dusted with Parmesan cheese, it's simple and delicious.

ACTIVE TIME: 30 minutes
TOTAL TIME: 35 minutes
MAKES: 4 main-dish servings

12	ounces linguine
2	teaspoons extra-virgin olive oil
2	medium shallots, finely chopped
2	garlic cloves, finely chopped
8	fresh sage leaves, finely chopped
1	tablespoon fresh oregano leaves, finely chopped
1	teaspoon fresh rosemary, finely chopped
¼	teaspoon salt
¼	teaspoon ground black pepper
½	cup reduced-sodium chicken broth
½	cup dry white wine
½	cup packed fresh basil leaves
¼	cup loosely packed fresh flat-leaf parsley leaves, plus sprigs for garnish
¼	cup snipped fresh chives
½	cup freshly grated Parmesan cheese

1. Cook linguine in *boiling salted water* as package label directs.

2. Meanwhile, in 10-inch skillet, heat oil on medium. Add shallots; cook 2 minutes, stirring frequently. Add garlic, sage, oregano, rosemary, salt, and pepper. Cook 1 minute, stirring. Add broth and wine. Heat to boiling on high. Reduce heat to medium; cook 5 minutes or until reduced by half, stirring. Remove from heat.

3. Finely chop basil and parsley; set aside. When pasta is done, reserve *¼ cup pasta cooking water*; drain pasta and return to saucepot. Stir in wine mixture along with basil, parsley, chives, and reserved pasta water. Toss until well combined.

4. Divide pasta among serving plates; top with Parmesan. Garnish with parsley sprigs.

EACH SERVING: About 415 calories, 18g protein, 68g carbohydrate, 8g total fat (3g saturated), 3g fiber, 13mg cholesterol, 500mg sodium ☺

Spaghetti with Pesto Verde

Studded with zucchini and tomatoes, this pretty pasta makes great use of summer produce. Adding broccoli to traditional basil pesto contributes extra flavor and vitamins; whole-grain noodles amp up the fiber.

ACTIVE TIME: 20 minutes
TOTAL TIME: 30 minutes
MAKES: 4 main-dish servings

8	ounces whole-grain spaghetti
6	ounces baby spinach
10	ounces frozen broccoli flowerets
1	garlic clove, peeled
1	cup water
2	medium zucchini (8 ounces each), trimmed
2	ripe tomatoes, cored
1	cup fresh basil leaves
2	tablespoons fresh lemon juice
2	tablespoons pine nuts
½	teaspoon salt
¼	teaspoon ground black pepper
¼	cup extra-virgin olive oil
1	ounce freshly grated Parmesan cheese

1. Cook spaghetti in *boiling salted water* as package label directs.

2. Meanwhile, in microwave-safe bowl, combine spinach, broccoli, garlic, and water. Cover with vented plastic wrap and microwave on High 3 to 5 minutes or until broccoli is thawed and spinach is tender. Drain; let cool completely.

3. Meanwhile, with vegetable peeler, peel zucchini into wide ribbons. Chop tomatoes.

4. Place cooled broccoli mixture, basil, lemon juice, pine nuts, ¼ teaspoon salt, and pepper in food processor; pulse until smooth. With processor running, drizzle in oil. Add Parmesan; pulse until well combined.

5. Drain spaghetti well and return to pot; add pesto, zucchini, tomatoes, and remaining ¼ teaspoon salt; toss well. Serve immediately.

EACH SERVING: About 460 calories, 17g protein, 54g carbohydrate, 21g total fat (4g saturated), 15g fiber, 6mg cholesterol, 575mg sodium ●

LET'S TALK PINE NUTS

Called *pignoli* in Italian, this high-fat nut comes from several varieties of pine trees. Small, elongated, and ivory-colored, the nuts are found inside the pine cone, which generally must be heated to facilitate their removal. This labor-intensive process is what makes the nuts so expensive. Pine nuts from Italy and the Mediterranean have a light, delicate flavor that's featured in both sweet and savory dishes and are well known as a flavorful addition to pesto. Available packaged in many supermarkets, they can also be found in bulk at specialty food shops and health food stores. They turn rancid easily; store in the refrigerator for up to three months or freeze for up to nine months.

Fusilli with Herbed Ricotta and Grape Tomatoes

Add just a little bit of pasta cooking water to ricotta, and you've got an almost instant sauce for this fusilli!

ACTIVE TIME: 10 minutes
TOTAL TIME: 25 minutes
MAKES: 4 main-dish servings

12 ounces fusilli or corkscrew pasta
1 pint grape tomatoes
1 cup part-skim ricotta cheese, store-bought or homemade (page 15)
1 tablespoon fresh oregano leaves, chopped
¼ cup grated Pecorino-Romano cheese, plus additional for serving
¼ cup packed fresh basil leaves, chopped

1. Cook fusilli in *boiling salted water* as label directs, adding tomatoes to pot 3 minutes before pasta is done.

2. Meanwhile, in small bowl, combine ricotta, oregano, Romano, and half of basil.

3. When pasta and tomatoes are done, reserve *¼ cup pasta cooking water*. Drain mixture; return to pot.

4. Add reserved cooking water to ricotta mixture; stir into pasta and tomatoes. Toss with remaining basil. Serve with additional Romano for sprinkling.

EACH SERVING: About 440 calories, 20g protein, 71g carbohydrate, 8g total fat (4g saturated), 3g fiber, 24mg cholesterol, 295mg sodium ☻ ☺ ♥

Butternut Squash and Pesto Rotini

This tempting toss is loaded with autumn flavor. For photo, see page 2.

ACTIVE TIME: 20 minutes
TOTAL TIME: 25 minutes
MAKES: 4 main-dish servings

12 ounces multigrain rotini
1 package (20 ounces) peeled, diced butternut squash
½ cup roasted almonds
2 garlic cloves
2 cups fresh basil leaves
1 teaspoon freshly grated lemon peel
½ teaspoon salt
⅛ teaspoon ground black pepper
¼ cup extra-virgin olive oil
½ cup freshly grated Parmesan cheese

1. Heat large covered saucepot of *salted water* to boiling on high. Add rotini and squash and cook for as long as pasta label directs.

2. Meanwhile, in food processor, pulse almonds and garlic until finely chopped. Add basil, lemon peel, salt, and pepper. Pulse until finely chopped. Remove *⅔ cup cooking water* from boiling saucepot. With processor running, add oil and pasta water in slow, steady stream. Add Parmesan and pulse to incorporate.

3. Drain pasta and squash. Return to saucepot along with pesto. Toss until well coated. Garnish with additional Parmesan, if desired.

EACH SERVING: About 615 calories, 25g protein, 80g carbohydrate, 28g total fat (4g saturated), 17g fiber, 9mg cholesterol, 565mg sodium ☻

Cheese Ravioli
with Fresh Tomatoes

Who knew you could prepare pasta in a microwave? And the simple, from-scratch sauce doesn't require any cooking—just be sure to use perfectly ripe tomatoes. Whipped up fresh and fast and tossed with ricotta ravioli, this makes a flavorful meal in minutes.

TOTAL TIME: 25 minutes

MAKES: 4 main-dish servings

1½	pounds ripe tomatoes, chopped (4 cups)
½	cup packed fresh basil leaves, chopped
3	tablespoons olive oil
¼	teaspoon freshly grated lemon peel
¼	teaspoon salt
¼	teaspoon ground black pepper
1	bag (18 ounces) microwavable cheese ravioli (see Tip)
¼	cup freshly grated Parmesan cheese

TIP: *If you can't find microwavable ravioli, use one bag (13 to 16 ounces) frozen ravioli. Place ravioli in microwave-safe large bowl with 2 ½ cups water; cover with vented plastic wrap and microwave on High 10 minutes or until cooked through, stirring once.*

1. In large bowl, combine tomatoes, basil, olive oil, lemon peel, salt, and pepper. Let stand at room temperature at least 15 minutes or up to 30 minutes to blend flavors.

2. Meanwhile, cook ravioli in microwave as label directs.

3. Add hot pasta to tomato mixture and toss to coat. Sprinkle with Parmesan to serve.

EACH SERVING: About 375 calories, 14g protein, 45g carbohydrate, 16g total fat (4g saturated), 16g fiber, 19mg cholesterol, 535mg sodium 🟢 ☺

Farfalle with Baby Artichokes and Mushrooms

Baby artichokes have the sweet, rich flavor of their full-grown counterparts, without the need to remove the inedible center thistle. When cut, uncooked artichokes discolor quickly, so be sure to rub lemon on any exposed surfaces.

ACTIVE TIME: 30 minutes
TOTAL TIME: 1 hour
MAKES: 6 main-dish servings

1   lemon, cut in half
1   pound baby artichokes (about 14)
1   pound farfalle or orechiette pasta
2   tablespoons olive oil
1   package (10 ounces) sliced mushrooms
½   teaspoon salt
¼   teaspoon ground black pepper
2   garlic cloves, crushed with garlic press
1   cup chicken broth
½   cup dry white wine
1   tablespoon chopped fresh thyme leaves
2   tablespoons chopped fresh parsley leaves
Freshly grated Parmesan cheese for serving
    (optional)

1. Heat large covered saucepot of *salted water* to boiling over high heat. In covered nonstick 12-inch skillet, heat 1 inch water to boiling over high heat. Fill medium bowl with cold water and add juice of 1 lemon half.

2. Meanwhile, trim artichokes: Bend back outer green leaves and snap off at base until remaining leaves are green on top and yellow on bottom. Cut off top half of each artichoke and discard. Rub cut surfaces with remaining lemon half to prevent browning. With vegetable peeler, peel stems. Cut off stems level with bottom of artichoke and coarsely chop; add to bowl of lemon water. Cut each artichoke into quarters; add to lemon water.

3. Drain artichokes and stems and place in boiling water in skillet. Cook, covered, 8 to 10 minutes or until artichokes are tender when pierced with tip of knife. Drain well and set aside.

4. Add pasta to boiling water in saucepot and cook as label directs.

5. While pasta is cooking, dry skillet with paper towel. Add oil to skillet and heat over medium-high until hot. Add mushrooms, salt, and pepper, and cook about 3 minutes or until mushrooms begin to soften, stirring occasionally. Add artichoke quarters and stems and garlic, and cook about 5 minutes longer or until mushrooms are lightly browned and artichokes are very tender. Stir broth, wine, and thyme into skillet, and heat to boiling; boil 1 minute. Stir in parsley.

6. Reserve *¼ cup pasta cooking water.* Drain pasta; add to skillet. Cook 1 minute to blend flavors, tossing to combine. Stir in reserved cooking water if pasta is dry. Serve with grated Parmesan, if you like.

EACH SERVING: About 360 calories, 13g protein, 63g carbohydrate, 6g total fat (1g saturated), 4g fiber, 0mg cholesterol, 495mg sodium ☺

Pasta with Broccoli Rabe and Garbanzos

This classic Italian combination of bitter greens and sweet golden raisins tossed with pasta and beans makes for a quick and wholesome meal.

ACTIVE TIME: 20 minutes
TOTAL TIME: 40 minutes
MAKES: 6 main-dish servings

1   pound penne or ziti pasta
2   bunches broccoli rabe (12 ounces each), tough stems removed
2   tablespoons olive oil
3   garlic cloves, crushed with side of chef's knife
¼   teaspoon crushed red pepper
1   can (15 to 19 ounces) garbanzo beans, rinsed and drained (see Tip)
¼   cup golden raisins
1¼ teaspoons salt
Grated Parmesan cheese (optional)

1. Cook penne in *boiling salted water* as package label directs.

2. Meanwhile, fill another large saucepot with water and heat to boiling. Add broccoli rabe, and cook 3 to 5 minutes or until thickest parts of stems are tender. Drain broccoli rabe; cool slightly. Cut into 2-inch pieces.

3. Wipe saucepot dry. Add oil, and heat over medium-high. Add garlic and crushed red pepper and cook 1 minute, stirring. Add broccoli rabe, garbanzo beans, and raisins, and cook about 3 minutes to heat through, stirring often. Remove from heat.

4. When pasta has cooked to desired doneness, reserve ⅔ *cup pasta cooking water;* drain pasta. Add pasta, reserved cooking water, and salt to broccoli rabe mixture; toss well. Serve with Parmesan, if you like.

EACH SERVING: About 445 calories, 17g protein, 80g carbohydrate, 7g total fat (1g saturated), 8g fiber, 0mg cholesterol, 775mg sodium ☺

TIP: *Bean, lentils, and legumes, like the garbanzo beans in this pasta, load any meatless main with protein.*

Spaghetti Pie

This spaghetti casserole's sure-to-please ingredients like bacon and cheese just might make it your family's new favorite dinner.

ACTIVE TIME: 20 minutes
TOTAL TIME: 1 hour
MAKES: 6 main-dish servings

1	pound spaghetti
4	strips bacon, chopped
1	large red onion (12 ounces), finely chopped
1	container (15 ounces) part-skim ricotta cheese, or 1 recipe Homemade Ricotta (page 15)
4	large eggs
2	cups reduced-fat milk (2%)
1	teaspoon cayenne (ground red) pepper
1	cup freshly grated Parmesan cheese
¼	teaspoon salt
2	cups frozen peas

1. Preheat oven to 350°F.

2. Cook spaghetti in *boiling salted water* as package label directs.

3. Meanwhile, in 12-inch skillet, cook bacon over medium 6 to 8 minutes or until crisp, stirring occasionally. With slotted spoon, transfer bacon to paper towels to drain. To fat in pan, add onion. Cook 4 minutes or until tender, stirring occasionally.

4. While onion cooks, in very large bowl, whisk together ricotta, eggs, milk, cayenne, half of Parmesan, and salt.

5. Drain spaghetti well. Stir into ricotta mixture along with peas, bacon, and onion. Spread in even layer in 3-quart shallow baking dish. Sprinkle remaining Parmesan on top.

6. Bake 30 to 35 minutes or until set.

EACH SERVING: About 660 calories, 36g protein, 76g carbohydrate, 23g total fat (11g saturated), 6g fiber, 175mg cholesterol, 700mg sodium

Penne alla Vodka

Serve creamy tomato sauce spiked with vodka on penne for this sophisticated—and luscious!—Italian classic.

ACTIVE TIME: 20 minutes
TOTAL TIME: 40 minutes
MAKES: 6 main-dish servings

1	pound penne pasta
¾	cup half-and-half or light cream
1	teaspoon cornstarch
2	tablespoons olive oil
1	small onion, chopped
2	garlic cloves, crushed with garlic press
¼	teaspoon crushed red pepper
1	can (28 ounces) diced tomatoes
¼	teaspoon ground black pepper
¼	cup vodka
½	cup freshly grated Parmesan cheese, plus additional for garnish

Crusty Italian bread (optional)

IS IT DONE YET?

Forget about throwing spaghetti against the wall to see if it sticks; if it does, it's overcooked! The only way to tell if pasta is ready to eat is by tasting. Use tongs to fish a piece out of the pot and take a bite. Start testing the noodles early, about two-thirds of the way through the cooking time. Pasta should be al dente—tender but still firm and chewy, with no white core at the center.

---

1. Cook penne in *boiling salted water* as package label directs.

2. Meanwhile, in 1-cup measure, combine half-and-half and cornstarch.

3. In 12-inch skillet, heat oil over medium. Add onion and cook 6 to 8 minutes or until lightly browned and tender, stirring frequently. Add garlic and red pepper and cook 1 to 2 minutes longer, stirring.

4. Add tomatoes with their juice and black pepper and heat to simmering; cook 4 to 5 minutes or until some liquid evaporates. Add vodka and continue to simmer 7 to 8 minutes or until sauce is slightly thickened.

5. When pasta is done, drain and return to pot.

6. To half-and-half mixture in cup, add ¼ cup tomato mixture and stir to combine; pour into skillet. Heat sauce to boiling over medium-high. Cook 2 minutes longer, stirring occasionally.

7. Remove vodka sauce from heat; stir in Parmesan. Add sauce to pasta in pot; stir to combine.

8. Spoon pasta into shallow bowls; sprinkle with additional Parmesan. Serve with crusty bread, if you like.

EACH SERVING: About 430 calories, 15g protein, 65g carbohydrate, 11g total fat (4g saturated), 3g fiber, 16mg cholesterol, 663mg sodium ☺

Homemade Marinara Sauce

Half an hour: That's all it takes to have stovetop instead of store-bought sauce. This versatile tomato sauce may be used in recipes throughout the book wherever jarred marinara is called for.

TOTAL TIME: 30 minutes

MAKES: about 3½ cups (enough for 1 pound pasta, cooked)

2   tablespoons olive oil
1   small onion, chopped
1   garlic clove, finely chopped
1   can (28 ounces) plum tomatoes
2   tablespoons tomato paste
2   tablespoons chopped fresh basil or parsley (optional)
½   teaspoon salt

In nonreactive 3-quart saucepan, heat oil over medium heat; add onion and garlic and cook, stirring, until onion is tender, about 5 minutes. Stir in tomatoes with their juice, tomato paste, basil, if using, and salt. Heat to boiling, breaking up tomatoes with side of spoon. Reduce heat; partially cover and simmer, stirring occasionally, until sauce has thickened slightly, about 20 minutes.

EACH ½-CUP SERVING: About 65 calories, 1g protein, 7g carbohydrate, 4g total fat (1g saturated), 1g fiber, 0mg cholesterol, 388mg sodium ⊘ ☺ 📇

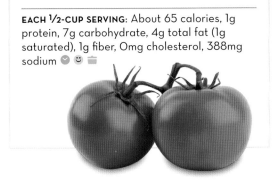

Sausage and Mushroom Penne

Multigrain pasta adds nutty flavor to this hearty dish.

ACTIVE TIME: 20 minutes
TOTAL TIME: 30 minutes

MAKES: 6 main-dish servings

1   pound multigrain pasta
12   ounces sweet Italian sausage, casings removed
1   onion, finely chopped
2   packages (10 ounces each) sliced mushrooms
1   package (5 ounces) baby kale or baby arugula
Salt and ground black pepper to taste
⅓   cup freshly grated Parmesan cheese

1. Cook pasta in *boiling salted water* as package label directs.

2. Meanwhile, heat 12-inch skillet over medium-high. Add sausage; cook 5 minutes or until browned, stirring and breaking up meat. Add onion; cook 4 minutes or until browned, stirring. (If pan becomes too dry, add a few tablespoons of water.) Stir in mushrooms; cook 8 minutes or until softened, stirring often.

3. When pasta is done, reserve *¼ cup pasta cooking water*, then drain; return pasta to pot. Add kale, sausage mixture, reserved pasta water, salt, and pepper. Toss over medium-low until well mixed. Top with Parmesan.

EACH SERVING: About 505 calories, 27g protein, 61g carbohydrate, 22g total fat (7g saturated), 13g fiber, 37mg cholesterol, 690mg sodium ⊘

Whole-Wheat Penne Genovese

An onion-flecked white bean sauté adds heft to this fresh and healthy pesto pasta dish. If they're in season, buy a mixed-color package of grape tomatoes—the red, yellow, and orange hues look especially beautiful on the plate.

ACTIVE TIME: 20 minutes
TOTAL TIME: 30 minutes
MAKES: 6 main-dish servings

12   ounces whole-wheat penne or rotini
1½   cups packed fresh basil leaves
1   garlic clove
3   tablespoons water
3   tablespoons extra-virgin olive oil
¼   teaspoon salt
¼   teaspoon ground black pepper
½   cup freshly grated Parmesan cheese
1   small onion, chopped
1   can (15 to 19 ounces) white kidney beans (cannellini), rinsed and drained
1   pint grape tomatoes in assorted colors, cut into quarters

1. Cook penne in *boiling salted water* as package label directs.

2. Meanwhile, make pesto: In food processor with knife blade attached, blend basil, garlic, water, 2 tablespoons oil, salt, and pepper until pureed, stopping processor occasionally and scraping bowl with rubber spatula. Add Parmesan; pulse to combine. Set aside.

3. In 12-inch skillet, heat remaining 1 tablespoon oil over medium; add onion and cook 5 to 7 minutes or until beginning to soften. Stir in white beans, and cook 5 minutes longer, stirring occasionally.

4. Reserve *¼ cup pasta cooking water*. Drain pasta and return to saucepot; stir in white bean mixture, pesto, tomatoes, and reserved cooking water. Toss to coat.

EACH SERVING: About 375 calories, 15g protein, 59g carbohydrate, 10g total fat (2g saturated), 9g fiber, 5mg cholesterol, 435mg sodium ✓ ☺ ♥

Linguine with Frisée, Bacon, and Egg

Enjoy breakfast standbys in a bowl of pasta with this creative take on Pasta alla Carbonara.

ACTIVE TIME: 20 minutes
TOTAL TIME: 30 minutes
MAKES: 4 main-dish servings

4	slices bacon, chopped
3	garlic cloves, very finely chopped
¼	teaspoon crushed red pepper
½	cup frozen peas
⅜	teaspoon salt
12	ounces linguine or spaghetti
4	large eggs
⅛	teaspoon freshly ground black pepper
1	medium bunch frisée, cut into 1-inch pieces
2	green onions, light and dark green parts only, thinly sliced on diagonal

1. Heat large covered saucepot of *salted water* to boiling on high. In nonstick 12-inch skillet on medium heat, cook bacon 8 to 9 minutes or until browned and crisp, stirring occasionally. With slotted spoon, transfer bacon to paper-towel-lined plate to drain; set bacon aside.

2. Discard all but 2 tablespoons bacon fat from skillet. To same skillet on medium, add garlic and red pepper. Cook 30 seconds or until garlic is golden, stirring frequently. Remove from heat and add peas, stirring to coat and warm through. Transfer mixture to large bowl. Season with ¼ teaspoon salt and stir well to blend. Set aside.

3. Cook pasta in boiling water as label directs. Meanwhile, wipe out same skillet with paper towel and heat on medium-low. Without breaking yolks, carefully add eggs to hot skillet and cook 5 to 6 mintes or until whites are set but yolks are still runny. Sprinkle eggs with ⅛ teaspoon each salt and pepper.

4. Reserve *¼ cup cooking water*. Drain pasta and add to bowl with pea mixture, along with frisée, reserved bacon, and pasta cooking water. Toss to combine. Divide among 4 shallow serving bowls. Top each with 1 egg and garnish with green onions.

EACH SERVING: About 545 calories, 23g protein 76g carbohydrate, 16g total fat (6g saturated), 10g fiber, 224mg cholesterol, 630mg sodium ☑

Ratatouille Rigatoni

Traditional vegetables for caponata (eggplant, yellow summer squash, peppers, and onions) are roasted and turned into a healthy vegetarian sauce for rigatoni pasta.

ACTIVE TIME: 15 minutes
TOTAL TIME: 1 hour
MAKES: 6 main-dish servings

1	small eggplant (1 pound), trimmed and cut into ½-inch cubes
1	small onion, cut into ½-inch pieces
3	tablespoons extra-virgin olive oil
½	teaspoon salt
½	teaspoon ground black pepper
1	pound rigatoni pasta
2	yellow summer squash, cut into ½-inch pieces
1	red pepper, cut into ½-inch pieces
1	can (14½ ounces) crushed tomatoes
1	garlic clove, crushed with garlic press
½	cup fresh basil leaves, very thinly sliced
½	cup freshly grated Parmesan cheese

1. Preheat oven to 450°F. In 18" by 12" jelly-roll pan, combine eggplant, onion, 2 tablespoons oil, and ¼ teaspoon each salt and black pepper until well mixed. Spread in even layer. Roast vegetables 15 minutes.

2. Meanwhile, begin cooking rigatoni in *boiling salted water* as label directs.

3. To pan with eggplant, add squash, red pepper, remaining 1 tablespoon oil and remaining ¼ teaspoon each salt and black pepper. Stir gently until well mixed, then spread vegetables in even layer. Roast 25 to 30 minutes longer or until vegetables are very tender.

4. When pasta is done, drain and set aside. In same saucepot, heat tomatoes with their juice and garlic to boiling over medium-high; cook 4 minutes or until slightly thickened. Remove saucepot from heat; add pasta, roasted vegetables, and basil; stir until well combined.

5. Divide pasta and vegetable mixture among warm serving bowls. Sprinkle with grated Parmesan to serve.

EACH SERVING: About 445 calories, 16g protein, 72g carbohydrate, 11g total fat (3g saturated), 7g fiber, 7mg cholesterol, 670mg sodium ☺

PASTA SWAP-OUTS

Long gone are the days when spaghetti and elbow macaroni were the only readily available noodle—and thank goodness for that! The next time you're at the supermarket, instead of tossing the usual pasta into your cart, take a closer look at the delightful array of pasta options, then choose a similar-but-different substitution based on our chart below. We've recommended replacement noodles with a size and shape that's similar to the original noodle's.

IF YOU LIKE . . .	. . . THEN TRY	BEST FOR . . .
Penne Rigate	**Rigatoni** or **Tortiglioni** 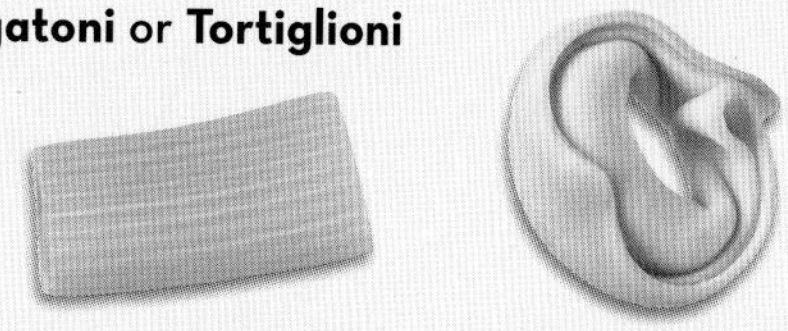	. . . Tomato sauces with veggies or meat—they nestle inside the tubes.
Rotini	**Cavatappi** or **Fusilli** 	. . . Olive oil or chunky tomato sauces, which cling to the corkscrews.
Elbows	**Cavatelli** or **Gemelli** 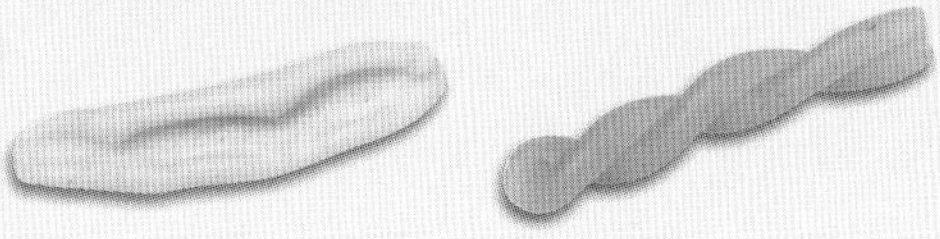	. . . Creamy or oil-based sauces, which are captured by all the crevices.
Shells	**Campanelle** or **Oreccchiette** 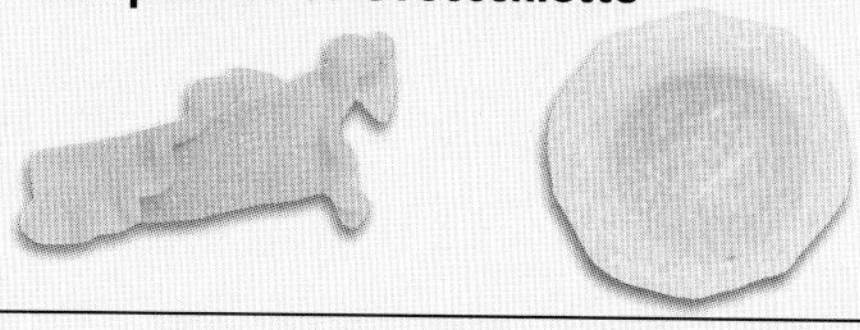	. . . Sauces with veggies or meat chopped to a similar size as the pasta.
Spaghetti	**Fettuccine** or **Perciatelli** 	. . . Thicker tomato or cream-based sauces that are sturdy, not delicate.

Spaghetti and Meatballs

Ultimate Italian-American comfort food! We tweaked the meatballs using a mix of lean ground beef and turkey. Serve with a side of garlic bread (page 219).

ACTIVE TIME: 1 hour
TOTAL TIME: 1 hour 30 minutes
MAKES: 12 main-dish servings

MEATBALLS

4	slices firm white bread, coarsely grated
1/3	cup water
1	pound lean ground beef
1	pound lean ground turkey or lean ground pork
2	large egg whites
1/4	cup freshly grated Pecorino-Romano or Parmesan cheese
1	garlic clove, crushed with garlic press
1	teaspoon salt
1/4	teaspoon coarsely ground black pepper

TOMATO SAUCE

2	tablespoons olive oil
3	carrots, peeled and finely chopped
2	onions, cut into 1/4-inch dice
3	garlic cloves, crushed with garlic press
3	cans (28 ounces each) Italian-style plum tomatoes in puree
3/4	teaspoon salt
1/4	teaspoon ground black pepper
1 1/2	pounds spaghetti

1. Prepare meatballs: Preheat oven to 450°F. In large bowl, with hands, mix grated bread and water until bread is evenly moistened. Add beef and turkey, egg whites, Romano, garlic, salt, and pepper; mix just until evenly combined. With wet hands, shape mixture into 2-inch meatballs. (You will have about 24 meatballs.) Place in 15 1/2" by 10 1/2" jelly-roll pan and bake 18 to 20 minutes, until meatballs are cooked through and lightly browned.

2. Meanwhile, prepare sauce: In 6-quart Dutch oven over medium, heat oil. Add carrots and onions; cook until tender and golden, about 15 minutes. Add garlic, and cook 1 minute, stirring.

3. Place tomatoes with puree in large bowl. With hands, slotted spoon, or kitchen shears, break up tomatoes until well crushed.

4. Add crushed tomatoes with puree, salt, and pepper to Dutch oven; heat to boiling over high heat, stirring occasionally. Reduce heat to medium; cover and cook 10 minutes. Uncover, add meatballs, and cook 15 minutes longer, stirring occasionally.

5. Meanwhile, cook spaghetti in *boiling salted water* as label directs, then drain and return to pot. Toss spaghetti with sauce and meatballs. Serve each diner 1 cup cooked spaghetti, 1/4 cup sauce, and two meatballs.

EACH SERVING: About 385 calories, 26g protein, 50g carbohydrate, 10g total fat (2g saturated), 3g fiber, 44mg cholesterol, 560mg sodium ☺ 🍽

Beef Ragu with Minted Penne

Our version of this Mediterranean pasta dish is healthier than most because we used lean beef instead of lamb and substituted whole-grain penne for regular pasta.

ACTIVE TIME: 15 minutes
TOTAL TIME: 30 minutes

MAKES: 6 main-dish servings

1	package (13¼ ounces) whole-grain penne
1	teaspoon extra-virgin olive oil
1	pound lean ground beef (93%)
½	teaspoon salt
½	teaspoon ground black pepper
1	large carrot, peeled and finely chopped
1	large stalk celery, finely chopped
1	small onion, finely chopped
¼	teaspoon ground cumin
¼	teaspoon ground coriander
1	pinch crushed red pepper
1	can (28 ounces) no-salt-added fire-roasted diced tomatoes
1	cup packed fresh mint leaves, finely chopped

1. Prepare penne in *boiling salted water* as label directs, but cook it 1 minute less than recommended minimum time.

2. Meanwhile, in 12-inch skillet, heat oil on high. Add beef in even layer. Sprinkle with ¼ teaspoon each salt and black pepper. Cook 2 minutes or until browned; stir, breaking beef into pieces.

3. Add carrot, celery, and onion. Cook 5 minutes or until tender and golden, stirring occasionally. Add cumin, coriander, and crushed red pepper. Cook 30 seconds, stirring. Stir in tomatoes; heat to boiling. Reduce heat to maintain steady simmer. Simmer 10 minutes.

4. When pasta is ready, drain and return to saucepot. Stir in tomato sauce; cook over medium 2 minutes or until pasta is al dente and well coated, stirring. Stir in mint and remaining ¼ teaspoon each salt and black pepper.

EACH SERVING: About 385 calories, 27g protein, 58g carbohydrate, 6g total fat (2g saturated), 8g fiber, 47mg cholesterol, 385mg sodium ♥ ☺ ♥

Tomato-Ricotta Rigatoni

Like a savored favorite from a classic red-checkered tablecloth restaurant, this satisfying pasta melds time-honored tastes to create the kind of meal you will want to make (and enjoy) over and over again. For photo, see page 81.

ACTIVE TIME: 15 minutes
TOTAL TIME: 30 minutes

MAKES: 6 main-dish servings

2	cans (28 ounces each) whole, peeled San Marzano tomatoes
2	tablespoons extra-virgin olive oil
2	garlic cloves, very thinly sliced
½	cup fresh bread crumbs
⅛	teaspoon crushed red pepper
2	sprigs fresh basil
2	tablespoons finely chopped basil leaves
½	teaspoon salt
1	pound rigatoni
1	sprig fresh oregano
½	teaspoon freshly ground black pepper
1	cup part-skim ricotta, store-bought or homemade (page 15)

1. Set large medium-mesh sieve over large bowl. With hands, crush tomatoes over sieve and place crushed tomatoes in sieve (see Tip); let strain. Set aside crushed tomatoes and juices in bowl for later use. Discard remaining juices in can.

2. In 12-inch skillet, combine 1 tablespoon oil and half of garlic. Cook on medium 1 minute or until golden. Add bread crumbs and cook 3 to 4 minutes or until golden brown, stirring. Transfer to large plate.

3. In same skillet, combine red pepper, basil sprigs, remaining 1 tablespoon oil, and remaining garlic. Cook on medium 30 seconds or until fragrant. Add tomatoes and ¼ teaspoon salt. Cook on medium-low 15 minutes or until thickened, stirring.

4. Prepare rigatoni in *boiling salted water* as label directs, but cook it 2 minutes less than recommended minimum time.

5. While tomatoes and pasta cook, on paper towel, microwave oregano on High 1 minute or until leaves are dry and brittle. Into small bowl, crumble leaves with fingers; discard stem. Stir in ricotta and ¼ teaspoon pepper.

6. Drain pasta and return to pot. Add tomato mixture, reserved tomato juice, and remaining ¼ teaspoon each salt pepper. Cook on medium 2 minutes or until pasta is well-coated and al dente, tossing and stirring.

7. Divide pasta mixture among bowls; top with dollop of ricotta mixture. Stir chopped basil into crumbs; sprinkle over pasta.

EACH SERVING: About 415 calories, 17g protein, 67g carbohydrate, 9g total fat (3g saturated), 3g fiber, 13mg cholesterol, 700mg sodium 🟢 ☺

TIP: *In true Italian tradition, we recommend crushing the tomatoes with your hands. (It's quick, surprisingly unmessy, and makes a juicier sauce.) If you prefer, you can snip them into small bits with scissors instead.*

Sausage Lover's Pasta

Cold-weather vegetables, like the butternut squash used in this recipe, stand up well to the flavors of hearty multigrain pasta and sweet Italian sausage.

ACTIVE TIME: 25 minutes
TOTAL TIME: 35 minutes

MAKES: 6 main-dish servings

1	box (14½ ounces) multigrain penne
11	to 12 ounces sweet Italian sausage, casings removed
1	large onion (12 ounces), finely chopped
1	butternut squash (2¾ pounds), peeled, seeded, and cut into ½-inch chunks (see box, page 131)
¼	cup freshly grated Parmesan cheese
8	fresh sage leaves, very thinly sliced
¼	teaspoon salt
1	teaspoon ground black pepper

1. Cook pasta in *boiling salted water* 2 minutes less than label directs..

2. Meanwhile, in 12-inch skillet, cook sausage over medium heat 5 to 6 minutes or until browned, stirring occasionally and breaking up meat. With slotted spoon, transfer to plate.

3. In same skillet, cook onion over medium-high heat 3 to 4 minutes or until golden, stirring occasionally and scraping up any browned bits. Add squash and *1 cup pasta cooking water* taken from boiling saucepot. Cover skillet and cook 15 minutes or until tender, stirring occasionally.

4. When pasta is done, reserve *1 cup pasta cooking water*. Drain pasta and return to pot.

5. Add half of Parmesan, half of sage, squash mixture, reserved sausage, salt, and pepper to pot. Cook on medium 2 minutes or until pasta is al dente and well coated, tossing. If mixture is dry, toss with some of reserved cooking water. To serve, top with remaining Parmesan and sage.

EACH SERVING: About 555 calories, 23g protein, 71g carbohydrate, 22g total fat (7g saturated), 14g fiber, 44mg cholesterol, 710mg sodium

Spaghetti Carbonara

Beaten eggs and plenty of Romano cheese form a lightly creamy sauce in this popular bacon-studded pasta dish.

TOTAL TIME: 35 minutes

MAKES: 4 main-dish servings

1	pound spaghetti
1	tablespoon olive oil
3	slices thick-cut bacon or 4 ounces pancetta, cut into ¼-inch pieces
1	small onion, chopped
5	large eggs
½	cup freshly grated Pecorino-Romano cheese, plus additional for serving
¼	teaspoon coarsely ground black pepper, plus additional to taste
¼	cup loosely packed fresh parsley leaves, chopped

1. Cook spaghetti in *boiling salted water* as package label directs.

2. Meanwhile, in 12-inch nonstick skillet, heat oil over medium 1 minute until hot. Add bacon and cook until browned. With slotted spoon, transfer bacon to paper towels. Pour off all but 2 tablespoons fat from skillet; add onion and cook 6 minutes or until tender. Remove skillet from heat.

3. When spaghetti is done, reserve *¼ cup pasta cooking water*. Drain spaghetti and add to skillet with reserved water and bacon. Cook over medium, stirring, until water is absorbed. In bowl, whisk eggs with Romano and pepper.

4. Remove skillet from heat; stir in egg mixture. Add parsley and toss until pasta is well coated. Spoon into warm pasta bowl; serve with additional Romano and coarsely ground black pepper to taste.

EACH SERVING: About 695 calories, 29g protein, 88g carbohydrate, 24g total fat (8g saturated), 3g fiber, 290mg cholesterol, 590mg sodium

LET'S TALK PANCETTA

Pancetta is an Italian bacon that's cured with salt and spiced but not smoked. It comes in a sausage-like roll and is sliced to order. Slightly salty and very flavorful, it's used in Italian cooking to flavor sauces, pastas, meats, vegetables, and more. It's available at Italian delicatessens, specialty food stores, and some supermarkets. Substitute regular smoked bacon if necessary. Pancetta can be tightly wrapped and refrigerated for up to 3 weeks or frozen for up to 6 months.

Orecchiette Shells with Veal Bolognese

Delicately flavored ground veal is more tender than ground beef, giving this pasta bolognese a different character from the classic.

ACTIVE TIME: 20 minutes
TOTAL TIME: 30 minutes
MAKES: 6 main-dish servings

1	pound orecchiette
2	cups frozen peas
1	can (28 ounces) whole tomatoes in puree
1	tablespoon olive oil
1	pound ground veal
1½	teaspoons packed fresh thyme leaves, chopped
¾	teaspoon salt
¾	teaspoon ground black pepper
½	cup light cream

1. Prepare orecchiette in *boiling salted water* as label directs, but cook 2 minutes less than recommended time. One minute before taking pasta off heat, add peas to pot.

2. Meanwhile, drain tomatoes in sieve set over large bowl; reserve 1 cup puree.

3. In 12-inch skillet, heat oil over medium-high. Add veal, half of thyme, and ¼ teaspoon each salt and pepper. Cook 2 minutes or until veal is browned, stirring and breaking up with wooden spoon. Add tomatoes; crush with back of spoon. Stir in ¾ cup reserved puree; heat to boiling. Reduce heat to maintain steady simmer; cook 10 minutes or until thickened. Stir in cream; simmer 5 minutes longer.

4. When pasta and peas are ready, reserve ½ *cup pasta cooking water*. Drain mixture; return to pot.

5. Add tomato sauce, ¼ cup reserved puree, remaining ½ teaspoon each salt and pepper, and remaining thyme to pot. Cook over medium 2 minutes or until pasta is al dente and well coated, tossing. If mixture is dry, toss with some reserved cooking water.

EACH SERVING: About 525 calories, 30g protein, 70g carbohydrate, 15g total fat (5g saturated), 5g fiber, 75mg cholesterol, 670mg sodium ⊘

Classic Bolognese Sauce

Freeze leftovers of this long-simmering meat sauce in small batches.

ACTIVE TIME: 10 minutes
TOTAL TIME: 1 hour 35 minutes
MAKES: 5 cups (enough for 2 pounds pasta)

2	tablespoons olive oil
1	medium onion, chopped
1	carrot, peeled and finely chopped
1	celery stalk, finely chopped
1½	pounds ground meat for meat loaf (beef, pork, and/or veal)
½	cup dry red wine
1	can (28 ounces) plum tomatoes, chopped
2	teaspoons salt
¼	teaspoon ground black pepper
⅛	teaspoon ground nutmeg
¼	cup heavy or whipping cream

1. In 5-quart Dutch oven, heat oil over medium. Add onion, carrot, and celery and cook, stirring occasionally, until vegetables are tender, about 10 minutes.

2. Add ground meat and cook, breaking up meat with side of spoon, until no longer pink. Stir in wine and heat to boiling. Stir in tomatoes with their juice, salt, pepper, and nutmeg. Heat to boiling over high. Reduce heat and simmer, stirring occasionally, 1 hour. Stir in cream and heat through.

EACH ½-CUP SERVING: About 210 calories, 13g protein, 6g carbohydrate, 15g total fat (6g saturated), 1g fiber, 58mg cholesterol, 696mg sodium

Quick Bolognese

Serve this rich meat sauce with grated Parmesan cheese.

TOTAL TIME: 35 minutes
MAKES: 7 cups (enough for 2 pounds pasta)

1½	pounds ground turkey or meat for meatloaf (beef, pork, and veal)
1	medium onion, chopped
1	celery stalk, chopped
1	carrot, peeled and shredded
¼	cup tomato paste
½	cup dry red wine
1	can (28 ounces) tomatoes in puree
1½	teaspoons salt
¼	teaspoon freshly ground black pepper
½	cup whole milk

1. Heat 6-quart Dutch oven over high. Add ground meat, onion, celery, and carrot; cook 10 minutes or until meat is no longer pink, breaking it up with side of spoon. Drain off fat. Stir in tomato paste; cook 2 minutes.

2. Add wine and cook 1 minute. Stir in tomatoes, salt, and pepper; heat to boiling, breaking up tomatoes with side of spoon. Reduce heat to medium-low; cover and simmer 15 minutes, stirring occasionally.

3. Stir milk into sauce; cover and simmer 5 minutes, stirring occasionally. Use half of sauce to toss with 1 pound cooked pasta. Freeze remaining sauce up to 3 months.

EACH ½-CUP SERVING: About 120 calories, 12g protein, 6g carbohdyrate, 6g total fat (2g saturated), 1g fiber, 36mg cholesterol, 435mg sodium

Spiced Lamb Ragu Shells

Mint adds a refreshing twist to this warm, spice-infused pasta dish with lamb. Heat things up by adding more red pepper if you like.

ACTIVE TIME: 15 minutes
TOTAL TIME: 30 minutes

MAKES: 6 main-dish servings

1	pound whole-wheat pasta shells
2	teaspoons olive oil
1	large onion (12 ounces), finely chopped
4	garlic cloves, chopped
5/8	teaspoon salt
1	pound ground lamb
2	teaspoons ground cumin
1	teaspoon ground coriander
1	teaspoon ground cinnamon
1/4	teaspoon crushed red pepper
1	can (28 ounces) crushed tomatoes
5	sprigs mint, plus leaves for garnish
1/2	cup freshly grated Pecorino-Romano cheese

1. Cook shells in *boiling salted water* as package label directs.

2. Meanwhile, in 12-inch skillet, heat oil over medium-high. Add onion, garlic, and 1/8 teaspoon salt. Cook 5 minutes or until tender, stirring. Stir in lamb, cumin, coriander, cinnamon, crushed red pepper, and remaining 1/2 teaspoon salt. Cook 3 minutes or until browned, stirring. Drain fat.

3. Stir in tomatoes and their juice along with mint sprigs; simmer 5 minutes or until ready to drain shells.

4. Drain shells; return to pot. Stir in lamb sauce. Discard mint sprigs. Top with Romano; garnish with mint leaves.

EACH SERVING: About 540 calories, 31g protein, 72g carbohydrate, 17g total fat (7g saturated), 10g fiber, 63mg cholesterol, 740mg sodium

Spaghetti All'Amatriciana

A spicy pairing of pancetta and red chiles gives this classic pasta its distinctive taste. It's named for the town of Amatrice, near Rome.

ACTIVE TIME: 10 minutes
TOTAL TIME: 40 minutes

MAKES: 4 main-dish servings

1	tablespoon olive oil
4	ounces sliced pancetta, chopped
1	small onion (4 to 6 ounces), chopped
1	garlic clove, finely chopped
¼	teaspoon crushed red pepper
1	can (28 ounces) plum tomatoes
½	teaspoon salt
1	package (16 ounces) spaghetti or bucatini
¼	cup chopped fresh parsley

1. In 5-quart Dutch oven, heat oil over medium. Add pancetta and cook, stirring, until lightly browned, about 5 minutes. Stir in onion and cook until tender, about 3 minutes. Stir in garlic and crushed red pepper; cook 15 seconds. Add tomatoes with their juice and salt; heat to boiling, breaking up tomatoes with side of spoon. Reduce heat and simmer, stirring occasionally, 30 minutes.

2. Meanwhile, cook pasta in *boiling salted water* as label directs. Drain. In warm serving bowl, toss pasta with sauce and parsley.

EACH SERVING: About 635 calories, 20g protein, 96g carbohydrate, 17g total fat (5g satured), 7g fiber, 63mg cholesterol, 826mg sodium

Farfalle with Gorgonzola and Peas

Farfalle, which means "butterflies" in Italian, are tossed with a creamy blue-cheese sauce and finished with a sprinkling of toasted walnuts.

ACTIVE TIME: 10 minutes
TOTAL TIME: 35 minutes

MAKES: 6 main-dish servings

1	package (16 ounces) farfalle or bow-tie pasta
1	cup half-and-half or light cream
¾	cup chicken broth
4	ounces Gorgonzola or blue cheese, crumbled
¼	teaspoon coarsely ground black pepper
1	cup frozen peas, thawed
½	cup chopped walnuts, toasted

1. Cook pasta in *boiling salted water* as package label directs. Drain.

2. Meanwhile, in 2-quart saucepan, heat half-and-half and broth just to boiling over medium-high. Reduce heat to medium; cook 5 minutes. Add Gorgonzola and pepper, stirring constantly until cheese has melted and sauce is smooth. Stir in peas.

3. In warm serving bowl, toss pasta with sauce; sprinkle with walnuts.

EACH SERVING: About 485 calories, 18g protein, 63g carbohydrate, 18g total fat (8g saturated), 2g fiber, 31mg cholesterol, 499mg sodium

Chicken Pasta Primavera

Thanks to this addictively rich sauce thickened with cream and Parmesan cheese, your family will clamor for seconds, while you'll appreciate the abundant veggies they're getting.

ACTIVE TIME: 25 minutes
TOTAL TIME: 30 minutes

MAKES: 6 main-dish servings

12	ounces cavatappi or fusilli pasta
2	green onions
4	teaspoons olive oil
1½	pounds boneless, skinless chicken-breast halves, cut into 1-inch chunks
½	teaspoon salt
¼	teaspoon ground black pepper
1	garlic clove, crushed with garlic press
1	pound asparagus, trimmed and cut into 1-inch pieces
1	red pepper, thinly sliced
½	cup heavy cream
¼	teaspoon crushed red pepper
½	cup freshly grated Parmesan cheese
¼	cup loosely packed fresh basil leaves, thinly sliced

1. Cook cavatappi in *boiling salted water* as label directs. Drain pasta, reserving *½ cup pasta cooking water*. Return pasta and reserved cooking water to pot.

2. Meanwhile, slice green onions; reserve 2 tablespoons sliced dark green tops for garnish. In 12-inch skillet, heat 2 teaspoons oil over medium-high. Sprinkle chicken with ¼ teaspoon salt and black pepper. Add chicken to skillet and cook 7 minutes or until chicken is browned and no longer pink throughout, stirring occasionally. Transfer chicken to medium bowl; set aside.

3. To same skillet, add remaining 2 teaspoons oil; reduce heat to medium. Add green onions and garlic and cook 1 minute, stirring. Add asparagus and red pepper; cook 6 to 7 minutes or until vegetables are tender-crisp, stirring frequently. Stir in cream, crushed red pepper, and remaining ¼ teaspoon salt. Heat mixture to boiling over medium high. Stir in reserved chicken pieces and remove from heat.

4. To saucepot with pasta and reserved cooking water, add Parmesan, chicken mixture, and basil; stir to combine. To serve, spoon into bowls and garnish with reserved dark green onion.

EACH SERVING: About 485 calories, 38g protein, 46g carbohydrate, 15g total fat (7g saturated), 3g fiber, 98mg cholesterol, 470mg sodium ◗

Campanelle with Chicken and Pea-Mint Pesto

Pureed peas add body and flavor to this verdant spring pesto. Shredded rotisserie chicken makes it a breeze to prepare.

ACTIVE TIME: 20 minutes
TOTAL TIME: 30 minutes

MAKES: 6 main-dish servings

1   package (16 ounces) campanelle or corkscrew pasta

1½ cups packed fresh mint leaves

1   package (10 ounces) frozen peas, thawed

½   cup freshly grated Parmesan cheese

¼   teaspoon salt

2   tablespoons olive oil

2   tablespoons water

3   cups coarsely shredded skinless rotisserie chicken meat (15 ounces)

Toasted pine nuts (optional)

1. Cook pasta in *boiling salted water* as package label directs.

2. Meanwhile, in food processor with knife blade attached, combine mint, peas, Parmesan, and salt; pulse until finely chopped. With processor running, pour in oil and water in a slow, steady stream until mixture is pureed and pesto is thick.

3. Drain pasta, reserving *½ cup pasta cooking water*. Return pasta to saucepot; add pesto and chicken to pasta in saucepot. Pour reserved cooking water into food processor and swirl to loosen any remaining pesto; add to pasta mixture and toss to combine. Transfer pasta mixture to serving bowl. Sprinkle with toasted pine nuts, if you like.

EACH SERVING: About 535 calories, 36g protein, 65g carbohydrate, 13g total fat (4g saturated), 6g fiber, 68mg cholesterol, 350mg sodium ♥ ♥

Ricotta Gnocchi with Brown Butter and Fresh Herbs

Lighter than the potato version, these gnocchi are a snap to make. A simple butter and herb sauce is the only dressing-up they need.

ACTIVE TIME: 1 hour
TOTAL TIME: 1 hour 20 minutes
MAKES: 4 main-dish servings

1	container (15 ounces) ricotta cheese or 1 recipe Homemade Ricotta (page 15)
6	tablespoons freshly grated Parmesan cheese
¾	cup chopped fresh parsley
¾	teaspoon salt
¾	cup all-purpose flour or as needed
3	tablespoons butter
1	teaspoon chopped fresh sage
¼	teaspoon ground black pepper

1. In medium bowl, combine ricotta, Parmesan, parsley, and ½ teaspoon salt. Sprinkle flour over ricotta mixture and, with hands, work into soft, smooth dough. If dough is sticky, add some flour. Work dough just until flour is incorporated into cheese; do not overwork.

2. Break off piece of dough; on lightly floured surface, roll into ¾-inch-thick rope. (If rope doesn't hold together, return to bowl with remaining dough and work in more flour.) Cut dough rope into ¾-inch lengths. Place 1 piece dough on inside curve of fork tines, gently pressing with thumb while rolling dough along tines. Allow dough to drop off fork, slightly curling in on itself and forming oval. One side will have ridges, and opposite side will be indented. Repeat rolling, cutting, and shaping with remaining dough. (Gnocchi can be made to this point up to 4 hours ahead. Arrange in floured jelly-roll pan; cover and refrigerate.)

3. Fill 5-quart saucepot with *water* and bring to boiling over high heat.

4. Meanwhile, make butter sauce: In 2-quart saucepan, melt butter over medium heat. Continue to cook, stirring, until butter turns golden brown. (If butter gets too dark, it will be bitter.) Remove from heat and add sage, remaining ¼ teaspoon salt, and pepper; set aside.

5. When water boils, add half of gnocchi and cook until gnocchi float to surface, 2 to 3 minutes. With slotted spoon, transfer to warm shallow serving bowl. Repeat with remaining gnocchi. To serve, toss gnocchi with sage butter.

EACH SERVING: About 390 calories, 18g protein, 22g carbohydrate, 26g total fat (16g saturated), 2g fiber, 84mg cholesterol, 788mg sodium ☺

Italian Wedding Pasta

Though rich and flavorful enough to celebrate a special occasion, our baked wedding pasta remains light on calories by employing reduced-fat milk and lean ground turkey.

ACTIVE TIME: 30 minutes
TOTAL TIME: 50 minutes

MAKES: 8 main-dish servings

1	pound ground turkey
¼	cup plain dried bread crumbs
¼	cup loosely packed fresh parsley leaves, chopped
3	garlic cloves, 1 clove crushed with garlic press and 2 thinly sliced
1	large egg
1	cup freshly grated Pecorino-Romano cheese
1	package (16 ounces) farfalle or bow-tie pasta
1	tablespoon cornstarch
1½	cups reduced-fat milk (2%)
1	can (14½ ounces) reduced-sodium chicken broth
1	bag (9 ounces) baby spinach
¼	teaspoon ground black pepper

1. Preheat oven to 400°F. Line 15 ½" by 10 ½" jelly-roll pan with parchment paper or foil.

2. In medium bowl, mix turkey, bread crumbs, parsley, crushed and sliced garlic, egg, and ¼ cup Romano cheese just until blended; do not overmix. Shape turkey mixture into 1-inch meatballs (you will have about 36); place in prepared pan. Bake 20 minutes.

3. Meanwhile, cook farfalle in *boiling salted water* as label directs, but drain 2 minutes before indicated cooking time; return to saucepot.

4. In 2-cup liquid measuring cup, whisk cornstarch into milk. Add milk mixture and broth to pasta in saucepot; heat to boiling over medium-high, stirring frequently. Boil 1 minute to thicken sauce slightly. Remove from heat; stir in spinach, ½ cup grated Romano, and pepper. Add meatballs and gently toss to combine. Transfer pasta mixture to 3-quart glass or ceramic baking dish; sprinkle with remaining ¼ cup grated Romano. Bake 20 minutes or until hot in center and golden brown on top.

EACH SERVING: About 390 calories, 25g protein, 49g carbohydrate, 10g total fat (4g saturated), 4g fiber, 85mg cholesterol, 380mg sodium ☺ ♥ ▭

Northern-Style Lasagna

Northern Italy is known for hearty, meaty fare like this classic lasagna, which incorporates ground beef, pork, and veal. Dairy is used in abundance, as in the luscious béchamel sauce that's layered between the noodles and meat sauce. Preparing this traditional regional dish takes time and effort, but the payoff is delicious.

ACTIVE TIME: 1 hour 15 minutes
TOTAL TIME: 2 hours 5 minutes plus standing
MAKES: 10 main-dish servings

MEAT SAUCE

½   cup water
½   ounce (about ½ cup) dried porcini mushrooms
2   tablespoons extra-virgin olive oil
3   large garlic cloves, finely chopped
2   large carrots, peeled and finely chopped
1   large onion (12 ounces), chopped
½   pound lean ground beef (90%)
½   pound ground pork
½   pound ground veal
½   cup dry red wine
1   can (28 ounces) diced tomatoes
½   teaspoon salt

BÉCHAMEL SAUCE

4   tablespoons butter or margarine
⅓   cup all-purpose flour
½   teaspoon ground black pepper
½   teaspoon salt
¼   teaspoon ground nutmeg
2½ cups whole milk

ASSEMBLY

8   ounces Fontina cheese, shredded (2 cups)
½   cup freshly grated Parmesan cheese
1   package (9 ounces) oven-ready lasagna noodles

1. Prepare meat sauce: In microwave-safe 1-cup liquid measuring cup, heat water in microwave oven on High 1 minute. Stir in porcini mushrooms; let stand 15 minutes.

2. Meanwhile, in 12-inch skillet, heat oil over medium. Add garlic, carrots, and onion; cook 15 minutes or until vegetables are tender, stirring occasionally. Increase heat to high. Add beef, pork, and veal; cook 10 minutes or until meat is browned, breaking up meat with side of spoon.

3. While meat is browning, with slotted spoon, remove porcini mushrooms from soaking liquid, reserving liquid. Rinse mushrooms to remove any grit, then coarsely chop. Strain *soaking liquid* through sieve lined with paper towel.

4. Add wine to meat in skillet and heat to boiling; boil 2 to 3 minutes or until most liquid evaporates. Stir in tomatoes with their juice, salt, mushrooms, and reserved soaking liquid; heat to boiling. Reduce heat to medium-low; simmer, uncovered, 20 minutes or until sauce thickens slightly, stirring occasionally.

5. Preheat oven to 375°F.

6. Prepare béchamel sauce: In 2-quart saucepan, melt butter over medium heat. With wire whisk, stir in flour, pepper, salt, and nutmeg, and cook 1 minute. Gradually add milk and heat to boiling, stirring frequently with whisk to prevent lumps. Remove pan from heat; set aside.

7. Assemble lasagna: In small bowl, stir Fontina and Parmesan until well combined. Spoon 1 cup meat sauce evenly in bottom of 13″ by 9″ glass baking dish. Arrange 4 noodles over sauce, overlapping slightly and making sure noodles do not touch sides of dish. (If your package has only 12 noodles, use 3 per layer and do not overlap.) Spoon about 1½ cups meat sauce over noodles. Spread about ⅔ cup béchamel sauce over meat; sprinkle with about ½ cup cheese filling. Repeat layering three more times, beginning with noodles, then meat sauce, béchamel, and cheese.

8. Cover lasagna with foil, preferably nonstick, and bake 30 minutes. Remove foil and bake 20 minutes longer or until heated through and cheese is lightly browned. Let stand 10 minutes for easier serving.

EACH SERVING: About 465 calories, 30g protein, 38g carbohydrate, 21g total fat (9g saturated), 2g fiber, 80mg cholesterol, 1,020mg sodium 🍴

LASAGNA NOODLE BASICS

Classic lasagna noodles must be boiled before you assemble and bake your lasagna. No-boil noodles are convenient because they have been precooked, then dried before packaging. For best results, use the type of lasagna noodle specified in the recipe. But if you are short on time and want to substitute no-boil noodles for classic, stir 1 cup additional water or tomato juice into the sauce.

Baked Cavatelli with Sausage and Broccoli Rabe

Served in individual-sized ramekins, this pasta dish goes from hearty homestyle to party perfect. Place each oven-baked portion on a pretty, napkin-lined plate for service.

ACTIVE TIME: 30 minutes
TOTAL TIME: 45 minutes

MAKES: 8 main-dish servings

1	bunch broccoli rabe (1 pound)
1	package (16 ounces) cavatelli or orecchiette pasta
3/4	pound hot Italian-sausage links, casings removed
2	teaspoons olive oil
2	garlic cloves, thinly sliced
1/8	teaspoon crushed red pepper
1	pint grape or cherry tomatoes
2	tablespoons cornstarch
1 1/2	cups reduced-fat (2%) milk
1	can (8 ounces) tomato sauce or 1 cup tomato-basil sauce
4	ounces Fontina cheese, cut into 1/4-inch cubes
3/4	cup freshly grated Pecorino-Romano cheese

1. Preheat oven to 400°F. Heat large covered saucepot of *salted water* to boiling over high heat. Meanwhile, trim tough stems from broccoli rabe and discard. Coarsely chop remaining broccoli rabe; set aside.

2. Add pasta to boiling water and cook 2 minutes less than label directs. Drain pasta; return to saucepot.

3. While pasta cooks, in nonstick 12-inch skillet, cook sausage over medium-high heat 5 minutes or until browned, breaking up sausage with side of spoon. Discard fat in skillet. Add olive oil, garlic, and crushed red pepper to sausage in skillet. Reduce heat to medium, and cook 2 minutes or until garlic is golden.

4. Stir in broccoli rabe; cover and cook 2 minutes or until broccoli rabe begins to wilt, stirring occasionally. Add tomatoes and cook 5 minutes or until tomatoes split.

5. In 2-cup liquid measuring cup, whisk cornstarch into milk. Stir milk mixture into sausage mixture; heat to boiling over medium-high, stirring frequently. Boil 1 minute to thicken slightly.

6. Add sausage mixture, tomato sauce, Fontina cubes, and 1/2 cup Romano cheese to pasta in saucepot; toss to combine. Transfer pasta mixture to eight 1 1/2-cup ramekins; sprinkle with remaining 1/4 cup Romano. Place ramekins on large cookie sheet or jelly-roll pan for ease of handling. Bake 15 minutes or until hot in the center and golden on top.

EACH SERVING: About 490 calories, 23g protein, 54g carbohydrate, 19g total fat (9g saturated), 3g fiber, 56mg cholesterol, 650mg sodium

Sausage and Pepper Baked Ziti

Cheesy, zesty, and studded with savory Italian sausage, our baked ziti feeds a crowd and then some—without trapping you in the kitchen. This recipe makes two casseroles; freeze one so you can give your family a cozy meal on even the busiest weeknight.

ACTIVE TIME: 40 minutes
TOTAL TIME: 1 hour 5 minutes plus standing
MAKES: 2 casseroles (or 8 main-dish servings)

1	pound sweet and/or hot Italian sausage links, casings removed
4	garlic cloves, crushed with garlic press
2	large red, green, and/or yellow peppers, cut into ¼-inch slices
1	jumbo onion (1 pound), cut in half, then cut crosswise into ¼-inch slices
1	pound sliced white mushrooms
1	can (28 ounces) whole tomatoes in puree
1	can (15 ounces) tomato puree
1	teaspoon salt
1	pound ziti or penne pasta
1	package (8 ounces) shredded part-skim mozzarella cheese
½	cup freshly grated Pecorino-Romano cheese

1. In deep 12-inch nonstick skillet, cook sausage on medium 10 minutes or until browned, stirring and breaking up meat with side of spoon. With slotted spoon, transfer to medium bowl.

2. Leaving drippings in skillet, add garlic, peppers, onion, and mushrooms and cook, covered, 10 minutes. Uncover and cook 8 minutes longer or until vegetables are tender and most of liquid has evaporated. Stir in tomatoes, tomato puree, and salt; heat to boiling over medium-high, stirring and breaking up tomatoes with side of spoon. Reduce heat to medium-low; cover and cook sauce 10 minutes, stirring occasionally.

3. Meanwhile, prepare ziti in *boiling salted water* as label directs, but cook 2 minutes less than recommended time.

4. Preheat oven to 400°F. Reserve *½ cup pasta cooking water*. Drain pasta. Return pasta and reserved cooking water to pot; stir in tomato sauce to coat pasta. Add mozzarella and reserved sausage; toss to combine. Divide mixture evenly between two shallow ungreased 2½-quart ceramic baking dishes. Sprinkle with Romano.

5. Bake one casserole 20 to 25 minutes or until top browns and sauce is bubbling. Let stand 10 minutes. Meanwhile, prepare second casserole for freezing (see box, page 13).

EACH SERVING: About 575 calories, 28g protein, 63g carbohydrate, 24g total fat (10g saturated), 6g fiber, 62mg cholesterol, 1,410mg sodium

Pasta e Fagioli Bake

We turned the much-loved Italian pasta-and-bean soup into a casserole by adding a little extra pasta and Romano cheese and topping it with bread crumbs.

ACTIVE TIME: 35 minutes
TOTAL TIME: 50 minutes
MAKES: 6 main-dish servings

8	ounces ditalini pasta (1¾ cups)
2	slices bacon, cut into ½-inch pieces
1	medium onion (6 to 8 ounces), diced
2	teaspoons plus 1 tablespoon olive oil
3	garlic cloves, minced
2	cans (15½ to 19 ounces each) white kidney beans (cannellini), rinsed and drained
1	can (16 ounces) plum tomatoes
¾	cup chicken broth
¼	teaspoon coarsely ground black pepper
¼	cup plus 2 tablespoons grated Pecorino-Romano cheese
2	slices firm white bread, torn into ¼-inch pieces
1	tablespoon chopped fresh parsley leaves

1. Preheat oven to 400°F. In large saucepot, cook pasta in *boiling salted water* as label directs. Drain well, reserving *½ cup pasta cooking water*. Return the pasta to saucepot.

2. Meanwhile, in 4-quart saucepan, cook bacon over medium heat until browned, stirring occasionally. Transfer bacon to paper towels to drain.

3. Pour off all but 1 teaspoon bacon fat from saucepan. Reduce heat to medium-low. Add onion and 2 teaspoons olive oil, and cook 5 minutes or until onion is tender, stirring occasionally. Stir in 1 teaspoon minced garlic, and cook 1 minute, stirring. Stir in beans, tomatoes with their juice, chicken broth, pepper, and cooked bacon, breaking up tomatoes with side of spoon; heat to boiling over high heat. Reduce heat to medium and simmer mixture, uncovered, 5 minutes, stirring occasionally.

4. To pasta in saucepot, add bean mixture, ¼ cup Romano, and reserved cooking water; toss well. Transfer mixture to 3-quart casserole.

5. In small bowl, toss bread pieces with parsley, remaining olive oil, remaining minced garlic, and remaining 2 tablespoons Romano until evenly coated. Sprinkle bread mixture over pasta. Bake pasta 15 minutes, uncovered, until hot and bubbly and top is golden.

EACH SERVING: About 405 calories, 19g protein, 63g carbohydrate, 9g total fat (3g saturated), 9g fiber, 9mg cholesterol, 815mg sodium ☺ 🍴

Penne with Three Cheeses and Porcini Mushrooms

This rustic baked pasta dish showcases a creamy cheese sauce and earthy porcini mushrooms.

1   package (16 ounces) penne rigate or ziti pasta
1   cup water
1   ounce dried porcini mushrooms (1 cup)
2   tablespoons butter or margarine
1   medium onion, finely chopped
1   teaspoon fresh thyme leaves, chopped
3   tablespoons all-purpose flour
2½ cups reduced-fat (2%) milk
⅛   teaspoon ground nutmeg
1   teaspoon salt
¼   teaspoon ground black pepper
4   ounces Fontina cheese, cubed
1   cup part-skim ricotta cheese, store-bought or homemade (page 15)
1   cup freshly grated Parmesan cheese

1. Prepare penne in *boiling salted water* as label directs, but cook it 2 minutes less than recommended minimum time. Drain pasta and return to pot.

2. Meanwhile, preheat oven to 375°F. In microwave-safe 4-cup liquid measuring cup or medium bowl, heat water in microwave oven on High 1½ to 2 minutes or until boiling. Stir in porcini mushrooms; let stand 15 minutes. With slotted spoon, remove porcini from soaking liquid; rinse to remove any grit. Finely chop and set aside. Strain *soaking liquid* through sieve lined with paper towel and set aside.

3. In 4-quart saucepan, melt butter over medium heat. Add onion and cook 8 to 9 minutes or until tender and lightly browned, stirring occasionally. Stir in porcini and thyme.

4. Sprinkle flour over onion mixture in saucepan; cook 1 minute, stirring. Whisk in milk, mushroom-soaking liquid, nutmeg, salt, and pepper. Heat to boiling over medium-high; cook 2 to 3 minutes or until mixture thickens slightly, stirring frequently.

5. Add porcini sauce to pasta in saucepot. Stir in Fontina, ricotta, and ½ cup Parmesan until well combined. Spoon pasta into 3-quart ceramic baking dish; sprinkle with remaining 1 cup Parmesan. Bake 30 minutes or until center is hot and top is golden.

EACH SERVING: About 465 calories, 24g protein, 55g carbohydrate, 16g total fat (8g saturated), 2g fiber, 42mg cholesterol, 765mg sodium ▭

Summer Vegetable Garden Lasagna

This lasagna is meat-free and loaded with veggies. It tastes great as a leftover, so make it ahead of time and serve it later in the week.

ACTIVE TIME: 25 minutes
TOTAL TIME: 1 hour 15 minutes
MAKES: 4 main-dish servings

2	medium zucchini or yellow summer squash, thinly sliced
1	tablespoon olive oil
¼	teaspoon salt
1	bunch Swiss chard, tough stems discarded, thinly sliced
1	small onion, finely chopped
2	garlic cloves, crushed with garlic press
1	teaspoon fresh thyme leaves, chopped
1	pound plum tomatoes, cored and thinly sliced
4	no-boil lasagna noodles, rinsed with cold water
2	carrots, peeled and shredded
1	cup part-skim ricotta cheese, store-bought or homemade (page 15)
2	ounces provolone cheese, finely shredded (½ cup)

1. Arrange one oven rack 4 inches from broiler heat source and place second rack in center of oven. Preheat broiler.

2. In large bowl, toss zucchini with 1 teaspoon oil and ⅛ teaspoon salt. Arrange on 18″ by 12″ jelly-roll pan in single layer. Broil 6 minutes or until golden brown, turning over once. Set aside. Reset oven control to 425°F.

3. Rinse Swiss chard in cold water; drain, leaving some water clinging to leaves.

4. In 12-inch skillet, heat remaining 2 teaspoons oil over medium. Add onion; cook 3 minutes or until soft, stirring often. Add chard, garlic, thyme, and remaining ⅛ teaspoon salt. Cook 6 to 7 minutes or until chard is very soft, stirring often. Remove from heat and set aside.

5. In 8-inch square baking dish, layer half of tomatoes, noodles, chard, carrots, zucchini, and ricotta. Repeat layering once. Top with provolone. Cover with foil. (Lasagna can be prepared to this point and refrigerated up to overnight.) Bake 30 minutes, covered (if refrigerated, bake 40 minutes). Uncover and bake 20 minutes longer or until golden brown and bubbling.

EACH SERVING: About 310 calories, 17g protein, 33g carbohydrate, 13g total fat (6g saturated), 6g fiber, 29mg cholesterol, 520mg sodium ☺

Eggplant and Ricotta Baked Ziti

If you want to prepare this dish ahead, roast the eggplant and make the sauce, and refrigerate them separately. When you're ready to bake, cook the pasta and assemble the dish. You'll need to add about 10 minutes to the baking time to compensate for the chilled ingredients.

ACTIVE TIME: 40 minutes
TOTAL TIME: 1 hour

MAKES: 6 main-dish servings

1	medium eggplant (1½ to 2 pounds), cut into 1-inch pieces
3	tablespoons olive oil
¾	teaspoon salt
1	small onion, finely chopped
2	garlic cloves, minced
1	can (28 ounces) plum tomatoes
2	tablespoons tomato paste
¼	teaspoon ground black pepper
3	tablespoons chopped fresh basil
1	pound ziti or penne pasta
¼	cup freshly grated Parmesan cheese
1	cup ricotta cheese, store-bought or homemade (page 15)

1. Preheat oven to 450°F. In large bowl, toss eggplant, 2 tablespoons oil, and ¼ teaspoon salt until evenly coated. Arrange eggplant in single layer in two 15½" by 10½" jelly-roll pans. Roast eggplant until tender and golden, about 30 minutes, rotating pans between upper and lower racks halfway through cooking and stirring twice. Remove pans from oven; set aside. Turn oven control to 400°F.

2. Meanwhile, in 3-quart saucepan, heat remaining 1 tablespoon oil over medium heat until hot. Add onion and cook until tender, about 5 minutes, stirring occasionally. Add garlic and cook 1 minute longer, stirring frequently. Stir in tomatoes with their juice, tomato paste, pepper, and remaining ½ teaspoon salt; heat to boiling over high heat. Reduce heat to low and simmer until sauce thickens slightly, about 10 minutes, stirring occasionally and breaking up tomatoes with side of spoon. Stir in 2 tablespoons basil.

3. Cook ziti in *boiling salted water* as label directs. Drain and return pasta to saucepot.

4. To pasta in pot, add roasted eggplant, tomato sauce, and Parmesan; toss until evenly mixed. Spoon mixture into six 2-cup gratin dishes or shallow casseroles; top with dollops of ricotta. Cover casseroles with foil and bake until hot and bubbly, about 20 minutes.

5. To serve, sprinkle tops with remaining 1 tablespoon basil.

EACH SERVING: About 500 calories, 19g protein, 73g carbohydrate, 15g total fat (5g saturated), 2g fiber, 24mg cholesterol, 695mg sodium

Risotto, Polenta & Other Grains

The Italians take rice and grains to a truly delectable level with creamy risottos, hearty polentas, and soups and salads featuring ancient grains like barley and farro.

Readily available short-grain rice like Arborio, Carnaroli, and Vialone Nano are the basis of classic Italian risotto. Made the traditional way, risotto is a time-consuming dish that requires constant stirring as you add hot broth to the rice, one ladle at a time. We've simplified the process by employing the microwave to make four luscious risottos—classic Milanese, lemony shrimp, and two veggie-filled versions—so you can enjoy great Italian flavor for a fraction of the work. Or use your slow cooker to make Butternut Squash Barley Risotto with equal ease.

Italy's answer to Southern-style grits, polenta can be boiled or microwaved to serve soft, or placed in a pan to set up for slicing and baking. We share basic recipes for all of these methods, then move on to main dishes that pair polenta with spinach and cheese, chicken or sausage, and baked eggs for brunch. On a cold winter night, Chicken, Peppers, and Onions on Polenta or Spicy Sausage and Polenta Casserole are always welcome.

Or, for something out of the ordinary, try Barley Minestrone with Pesto or Warm Farro Salad with Roasted Vegetables. You'll discover that these whole grains are not only good for you, but boast a nutty flavor and toothesome texture that's sure to win you over.

Butternut Squash Barley Risotto (recipe page 131)

Risotto Milanese

The traditional preparation of this saffron-scented rice dish always pleases a crowd but rarely pleases the chef. Made the old-fashioned way, risotto requires laboring over a steamy stove without pause as you stir hot broth into the rice, ladleful by ladleful, and wait for the liquid to be absorbed. Our much simpler strategy puts the microwave to work, shaving your active time to just ten minutes and reducing the stirring to a few little strokes.

ACTIVE TIME: 10 minutes
TOTAL TIME: 35 minutes

MAKES: 6 first-course or 4 main-dish servings

1   carton (32 ounces) chicken broth

1¼   cups water

½   cup dry white wine

¼   teaspoon crushed saffron threads (see Tip)

1   tablespoon butter or margarine

1   tablespoon olive oil

1   small onion, minced

2   cups Arborio or Carnaroli rice (Italian short-grain rice)

⅓   cup freshly grated Parmesan cheese, plus additional for serving

½   teaspoon salt

½   teaspoon ground black pepper

1. In covered saucepan, heat broth, water, wine, and saffron to boiling.

2. Meanwhile, in microwave-safe 4-quart bowl, combine butter, oil, and onion. Cook, uncovered, in microwave on High 2 minutes or until onion softens. Add rice and stir to coat; cook, uncovered, on High 1 minute.

3. Stir hot broth mixture into rice mixture. Cover bowl with vented plastic wrap, and cook in microwave on Medium (50% power) 16 to 18 minutes or until most liquid is absorbed and rice is tender but still firm, stirring halfway through cooking. Do not overcook; risotto mixture will look loose but will soon thicken to proper creamy consistency.

4. Stir in ⅓ cup Parmesan, salt, and pepper. Serve with additional Parmesan.

EACH FIRST-COURSE SERVING: About 355 calories, 9g protein, 62g carbohydrate, 6g total fat (2g saturated), 2g fiber, 4mg cholesterol, 620mg sodium

MUSHROOM RISOTTO: Follow instructions for Risotto Milanese, but in step 1, use only *1 cup water* and omit saffron. In step 2, omit oil. In step 3, while rice cooks, in 12-inch skillet, heat *1 tablespoon oil* on medium. Add *8 ounces sliced cremini mushrooms* and cook 8 minutes or until tender, stirring occasionally. After rice has cooked 8 minutes, stir in mushrooms; cook 8 minutes longer. In step 4, add *½ teaspoon chopped fresh thyme* along with Parmesan.

EACH FIRST-COURSE SERVING: About 365 calories, 11g protein, 64g carbohydrate, 6g total fat (2g saturated), 2g fiber, 4mg cholesterol, 635mg sodium

---

TIP: *The yellow-orange stigmas from a small purple crocus, saffron is hand-picked and then dried—an extremely labor-intensive process. Look for it in your market's spice section. It's pricey, but you only need a smidgeon to add great flavor and a beautiful yellow color to this classic Italian dish.*

Easy Pea Risotto

This pretty no-fuss rice dish is made in the microwave in 30 minutes.

ACTIVE TIME: 15 minutes
TOTAL TIME: 30 minutes
MAKES: 4 main-dish servings

1	can (14½ ounces) chicken broth (1¾ cups)
2¼	cups plus 2 tablespoons water
1	pound frozen peas
1	tablespoon olive oil
2	cups Arborio or Carnaroli rice (Italian short-grain rice)
½	cup freshly grated Parmesan cheese, plus shaved Parmesan for garnish
¼	teaspoon salt
¼	teaspoon ground black pepper

1. In 2-quart covered saucepan, heat broth and 2¼ cups water to boiling on high.

2. Meanwhile, in microwave-safe large bowl, place peas and remaining 2 tablespoons water; cover with vented plastic wrap and microwave on High 4 minutes. In blender, combine 1½ cups peas and ¼ cup hot broth mixture. Remove center part of blender top; cover blender and blend peas and broth mixture until pureed. Set remaining peas aside.

3. In microwave-safe 3½- to 4-quart bowl, combine olive oil and rice. Cook, uncovered, in microwave on High 1 minute. Stir in remaining hot broth mixture; cover bowl with vented plastic wrap and cook in microwave on Medium (50% power) 10 minutes, stirring once halfway through cooking.

4. Stir in pea puree; cover with vented plastic wrap and cook on Medium 8 minutes longer or until most of liquid is absorbed. Stir in Parmesan, salt, pepper, and remaining peas.

5. To serve, spoon risotto into shallow serving bowls and garnish with shaved Parmesan.

EACH SERVING: About 590 calories, 20g protein, 106g carbohydrate, 7g total fat (2g saturated), 7g fiber, 8mg cholesterol, 735mg sodium ☺

Spring Vegetable Risotto with Shrimp

The addition of asparagus, peas, and plenty of lemon juice make this classic dish fresh and flavorful.

ACTIVE TIME: 10 minutes
TOTAL TIME: 35 minutes
MAKES: 6 main-dish servings

1	carton (32 ounces) chicken broth
1¼	cups water
½	cup dry white wine
8	ounces asparagus, cut into 1-inch pieces
1	tablespoon olive oil
1	small onion (4 to 6 ounces), finely chopped
1	carrot, peeled and finely chopped
2	cups Arborio or Carnaroli rice (Italian short-grain rice)
1	pound large shrimp, shelled and deveined
1	cup frozen peas
2	tablespoons fresh lemon juice
1	tablespoons chopped fresh parsley or basil leaves
¼	teaspoon salt
¼	teaspoon ground black pepper

1. In 2-quart saucepan, heat broth, water, and wine to boiling on high. When boiling, add asparagus and cook 2 minutes. With slotted spoon, remove asparagus to small bowl; set aside.

2. Meanwhile, in microwave-safe 4-quart bowl or casserole, combine oil, onion, and carrot. Cook, uncovered, in microwave on High 3 minutes or until vegetables begin to soften. Add rice and stir to coat with oil; cook, uncovered, on High 1 minute.

3. Stir hot broth mixture into rice mixture. Cover bowl with vented plastic wrap, and cook in microwave on Medium (50% power) 15 minutes or until most of liquid is absorbed and rice is tender but still firm, stirring halfway through.

4. Add shrimp, frozen peas, and cooked asparagus; cover and cook in microwave on High 3 to 4 minutes longer or just until shrimp lose their pink color throughout. Do not overcook; mixture will look loose and soupy but will soon thicken to the proper creamy consistency.

5. Stir in lemon juice, parsley, salt, and pepper.

EACH SERVING: About 425 calories, 24g protein, 67g carbohydrate, 4g total fat (1g saturated), 3g fiber, 115mg cholesterol, 545mg ☺

Fresh Tomato, Corn, and Basil Risotto

Colorful vegetables and basil contribute garden-fresh flavor and color to this summery risotto.

ACTIVE TIME: 30 minutes
TOTAL TIME: 40 minutes
MAKES: 6 main-dish servings

1	bag (12 ounces) microwave-in-bag green beans
1	can (14 1/2 ounces) chicken broth
2	cups water
2	tablespoons butter (no substitutions)
1	small onion, chopped
2	cups Arborio or Carnaroli rice (Italian short-grain rice)
2	pounds ripe tomatoes
2	cups fresh corn kernels
2	ounces freshly grated Parmesan cheese
2	tablespoons chopped fresh basil
1/2	teaspoon salt
1/4	teaspoon ground black pepper

1. Cook green beans as label directs. Cool slightly; cut into 1-inch pieces.

2. In 2-quart covered saucepan, heat broth and water to boiling.

3. While broth mixture heats, in 4-quart microwave-safe bowl, microwave butter and onion, uncovered, on High 3 minutes or until softened. Stir in rice. Cook 1 minute longer.

4. Stir broth mixture into rice mixture. Cover with vented plastic wrap; microwave on Medium (50% power) 10 minutes.

5. Meanwhile, in food processor, puree half of tomatoes; strain juice through sieve into measuring cup, pressing on solids. Discard solids. Chop remaining tomatoes.

6. Stir 1 1/2 cups tomato juice into rice mixture. Cover with vented plastic wrap and microwave on Medium 5 minutes or until most of liquid is absorbed.

7. Stir corn into rice mixture, cover with vented plastic wrap; microwave on Medium 3 minutes or until corn is heated through.

8. Stir Parmesan, green beans, tomatoes, half of basil, salt, and pepper into risotto. Garnish with remaining basil.

EACH SERVING: About 390 calories, 12g protein, 70g carbohydrate, 8g total fat (5g saturated), 6g fiber, 8mg cholesterol, 485mg sodium ☺ ♥

Butternut Squash Barley Risotto

Creamy, comforting barley-based risotto is not only delicious, it is healthy, too, full of fiber and essential nutrients. A slow cooker makes it blissfully convenient to prepare. For photo, see page 124.

ACTIVE TIME: 15 minutes
SLOW-COOK TIME: 3 hours 45 minutes on High

MAKES: 8 main-dish servings

2	tablespoons butter or margarine
2	shallots, thinly sliced
2	sprigs fresh thyme
2	cups pearl barley
1	carton (32 ounces) vegetable broth
2	cups water
1	large butternut squash (2½ pounds), peeled and seeded, cut into ½-inch cubes
1½	teaspoons salt
⅔	cup freshly grated Parmesan cheese
¼	teaspoon ground black pepper
2	tablespoons chopped flat-leaf parsley leaves

1. In 12-inch skillet, melt 1 tablespoon butter over medium-high. Add shallots and cook 2 minutes or until golden, stirring often. Add thyme; cook 30 seconds. Add barley and cook 2 minutes or until toasted and golden, stirring often.

2. Transfer to 6-quart slow-cooker bowl with broth, water, squash, and ½ teaspoon salt. Cover and cook on High 3 hours 30 minutes to 4 hours or until liquid is absorbed and squash is tender.

3. Discard thyme, then add Parmesan, remaining 1 tablespoon butter, 1 teaspoon salt, and pepper. Gently stir until butter and Parmesan melt. Transfer risotto to serving plates and garnish with parsley. Risotto can be stored, covered, in refrigerator up to 3 days.

EACH SERVING: About 235 calories, 7g protein, 45g carbohydrate, 4g total fat (1g saturated), 10g fiber, 3mg cholesterol, 670mg sodium ☺ ▣ ▣

PREPARING BUTTERNUT SQUASH

The best way to peel this large vegetable is to cut it into smaller pieces first. Holding it firmly on its side and using a sharp knife, cut it crosswise into 2-inch-thick rounds. Place each round flat side down and cut away the peel. Then scoop out the seeds and cut as desired. To save time and effort, you can substitute a package of peeled, precut butternut squash (available in the produce section of many supermarkets).

Barley Minestrone

A wholesome take on minestrone features barley in place of pasta. Top with a dollop of our homemade pesto, which you can make in a mini food processor. In a real hurry? Store-bought refrigerated pesto makes an excellent stand-in— although it's not as light as our version.

ACTIVE TIME: 50 minutes
TOTAL TIME: 1 hour 15 minutes

MAKES: 6 main-dish servings

MINESTRONE

1	cup pearl barley
1	tablespoon olive oil
2	cups thinly sliced green cabbage
2	large carrots, each peeled and cut lengthwise in half, then crosswise into ½-inch-thick slices
2	large stalks celery, cut into ½-inch dice
1	onion, cut into ½-inch dice
1	garlic clove, finely chopped
3	cups water
2	cans (14½ ounces each) vegetable broth
1	can (14½ ounces) diced tomatoes
¼	teaspoon salt
1	medium zucchini (8 ounces), cut into ½-inch dice
4	ounces green beans, trimmed and cut into ½-inch pieces (1 cup)

LIGHT PESTO

1	cup firmly packed fresh basil leaves
2	tablespoons olive oil
2	tablespoons water
¼	teaspoon salt
¼	cup freshly grated Pecorino-Romano cheese
1	garlic clove, finely chopped

1. Prepare minestrone: Heat 5- to 6-quart Dutch oven over medium-high. Add barley and toast until fragrant, 3 to 4 minutes, stirring constantly. Transfer to small bowl; set aside.

2. In same Dutch oven, heat oil over medium-high. Add cabbage, carrots, celery, and onion; cook until vegetables have softened and lightly browned, 8 to 10 minutes, stirring occasionally. Add garlic and cook until fragrant, 30 seconds. Stir in barley, water, broth, tomatoes with their juice, and salt. Cover and heat to boiling. Reduce heat to low and simmer 25 minutes.

3. Stir zucchini and green beans into barley mixture; increase heat to medium, cover, and cook until all vegetables are barely tender, 10 to 15 minutes longer.

4. Meanwhile, prepare pesto: In blender container with narrow base or in mini food processor, combine basil, oil, water, and salt; cover and blend until mixture is pureed. Transfer pesto to small bowl; stir in Romano and garlic. Makes about ½ cup.

5. Ladle minestrone into large soup bowls. Top each serving with a dollop of pesto.

EACH SERVING SOUP: About 215 calories, 7g protein, 42g carbohydrate, 4g total fat (0g saturated), 9g fiber, 0mg cholesterol, 690mg sodium ☺ ▣

EACH 1 TEASPOON PESTO: About 15 calories, 0g protein, 0g carbohydrate, 1g total fat (0g saturated), 0g fiber, 1mg cholesterol, 35mg sodium ♥ ☺ ♥ ▣

Warm Farro Salad with Roasted Vegetables

If you've never tried farro, this hearty main-dish salad provides the perfect introduction.

ACTIVE TIME: 25 minutes
TOTAL TIME: 1 hour 5 minutes
MAKES: 4 main-dish servings

1 to 2 lemons

2 large carrots, peeled and cut into ½-inch pieces

2 small fennel bulbs (8 ounces each), trimmed and cut into 1-inch pieces

1 red onion, halved and thinly sliced through root end

3 tablespoons olive oil

1 teaspoon salt

1⅛ teaspoons ground black pepper

1 bunch radishes, cut into ½-inch pieces

1 tablespoon red wine vinegar

2½ cups water

1 cup farro

1 cup lightly packed fresh basil leaves, chopped

1. Preheat oven to 400°F. From lemons, grate 2 teaspoons peel and squeeze 3 tablespoons juice; set aside.

2. In large bowl, combine carrots, fennel, onion, 1 tablespoon oil, ½ teaspoon salt, and 1 teaspoon pepper; toss. Turn onto 15½" by 10½" jelly-roll pan and spread evenly. Roast 20 minutes, stirring once. Stir in radishes and roast until vegetables are tender, about 10 minutes. Stir in vinegar.

3. Meanwhile, in medium saucepan, bring water, farro, and ¼ teaspoon salt to boiling over high heat. Reduce heat to medium-low; cover and simmer until farro is tender and water is absorbed, 25 to 30 minutes.

4. In large bowl, whisk together reserved lemon juice and peel, along with remaining 2 tablespoons oil, ¼ teaspoon salt, and ⅛ teaspoon pepper. Add farro, roasted vegetables, and basil; toss to combine. Serve warm.

EACH SERVING: About 320 calories, 9g protein, 51g carbohydrate, 10g total fat (2g saturated), 9g fiber, 0mg cholesterol, 708mg sodium ☺ 🍽

LET'S TALK FARRO

This ancient grain (pronounced FAHR-oh) is enjoying a resurgence of popularity thanks to Italian dishes that feature it. Farro is related to wheat (and also known as emmer wheat). It contains starch that is similar to the starch found in short-grain rices; try it instead of Arborio rice the next time you make risotto. High in fiber, vitamin B, and protein, farro has a nutty wheat flavor and chewy texture.

Farro and Mushroom Sauté

Farro's earthy, nutty flavor pairs deliciously with toasted walnuts and meaty cremini mushrooms.

ACTIVE TIME: 30 minutes
TOTAL TIME: 35 minutes

MAKES: 6 side-dish servings

2½ cups water

¾ teaspoon salt

1 cup farro

1 tablespoon butter

1 tablespoon olive oil

2 stalks celery, diced

1 onion, chopped

2 packages (8 ounces each) sliced cremini mushrooms

⅓ cup walnuts, toasted and chopped

3 tablespoons chopped fresh flat-leaf parsley

⅛ teaspoon ground black pepper

1. In medium saucepan, bring water and ¼ teaspoon salt to boiling over high heat. Stir in farro and return to boiling. Reduce heat to medium-low; cover and simmer until water is absorbed and farro is tender, 25 to 30 minutes.

2. Meanwhile, in large skillet, heat butter and oil over medium-high. Add celery and onion; cook until golden brown, about 5 minutes, stirring. Stir in mushrooms and remaining ½ teaspoon salt. Cook until moisture evaporates and mushrooms brown, about 8 minutes, stirring frequently. Add farro and stir until hot.

3. Remove skillet from heat and stir in walnuts, parsley, and pepper.

EACH SERVING: About 210 calories, 8g protein, 28g carbohydrate, 8g total fat (2g saturated), 3g fiber, 5mg cholesterol, 340mg sodium ♥ ▢

Orzo Salad with Grape Tomatoes and Mint

Classic Mediterranean flavors give a tangy personality to this delicious pasta salad.

ACTIVE TIME: 15 minutes
TOTAL TIME: 25 minutes
MAKES: 6 side-dish servings

2	cups orzo pasta (see Tip)
1	lemon
1	tablespoon olive oil
1	pint grape tomatoes
1	cup crumbled goat cheese
1/3	cup pitted Kalamata olives, sliced
1/3	cup loosely packed fresh mint leaves, chopped
1/4	teaspoon coarsely ground black pepper

1. Cook orzo in *boiling salted water* as package label directs.

2. Meanwhile, from lemon, grate 1 teaspoon peel and squeeze 1 tablespoon juice; set aside. In 12-inch skillet, heat oil on medium. Add tomatoes; cook 5 to 6 minutes or until skins split, shaking pan occasionally. Transfer tomatoes to serving bowl.

3. Before draining cooked orzo, reserve *¼ cup cooking water.* Add orzo and cooking water to tomatoes in bowl; stir in lemon peel and juice, goat cheese, olives, mint, and pepper.

EACH SERVING: About 305 calories, 11g protein, 47g carbohydrate, 8g total fat (4g saturated), 3g fiber, 17mg cholesterol, 385mg sodium ✓ ▤

TIP: *In Italian, orzo means "barley," but it's actually a tiny grain-shaped pasta that's slightly smaller than a pine nut.*

Creamy Polenta

This classic method ensures lump-free results.

ACTIVE TIME: 5 minutes
TOTAL TIME: 30 minutes
MAKES: 8 side-dish servings

6½ cups cold water
1   teaspoon salt
1½ cups yellow cornmeal
½   cup freshly grated Parmesan cheese
4   tablespoons butter, cut into pieces

Bring 4½ cups water to a boil. In 5-quart Dutch oven, combine remaining 2 cups cold water and salt. With wire whisk, gradually beat cornmeal into salted water until smooth. Whisk in boiling water. Return to boiling over high heat. Reduce heat to medium-low and cook, stirring frequently, until mixture is very thick, 20 to 25 minutes. Stir Parmesan and butter into polenta until butter has melted. Serve immediately.

EACH SERVING: About 175 calories, 5g protein, 20g carbohydrate, 8g total fat (5g saturated), 0g fiber, 20mg cholesterol, 464mg sodium

Microwave Polenta

In 4-quart microwave-safe bowl, combine *2 cups low-fat milk (1%), 1 ½ cups cornmeal,* and *1 teaspoon salt.* Stir in *4 ½ cups boiling water.* Cook in microwave oven on High 12 to 15 minutes. After first 5 minutes, whisk vigorously until smooth (mixture will be lumpy at first). Stir twice more during cooking. When thick and creamy, stir in *4 tablespoons butter,* cut into pieces, and *½ cup freshly grated Parmesan cheese.* Serves 8.

EACH SERVING: About 205 calories, 6g protein, 27g carbohydrate, 8g total fat (5g saturated), 1g fiber, 22mg cholesterol, 447mg sodium

Broiled Rosemary Polenta Wedges

Line 13″ by 9″ baking pan with foil, extending foil over rim. Prepare Creamy Polenta as directed but use only *3 ½ cups boiling water* and cook until mixture is very thick and indentation remains when spoon is dragged through polenta, 30 to 35 minutes. Stir in Parmesan and butter as directed. Spoon mixture into prepared pan, smoothing top. Refrigerate until very firm, at least 1 hour. Position oven rack 5 to 7 inches from heat source and preheat broiler. Lift foil with polenta from baking pan; place on cookie sheet. Cut polenta into 16 triangles and separate triangles slightly. Melt *1 tablespoon butter* and combine with *½ teaspoon chopped fresh rosemary or ¼ teaspoon dried rosemary*; brush onto polenta wedges. Broil until lightly browned and heated through, about 10 minutes. Serves 16.

EACH TRIANGLE: About 100 calories, 3g protein, 12g carbohydrate, 5g total fat (3g saturated), 1g fiber, 12mg cholesterol, 216mg sodium

Polenta and Spinach Gratin

A creamy spinach topping is layered over slices of ready-made polenta for a satisfying side dish. You can assemble this casserole up to one day ahead and refrigerate. Just increase the baking time to 40 minutes.

ACTIVE TIME: 20 minutes
TOTAL TIME: 55 minutes

MAKES: 16 side-dish servings

2   logs (24 ounces each) precooked plain polenta

2   tablespoons olive oil

1   large onion (12 ounces), chopped

2   garlic cloves, minced

¼   teaspoon crushed red pepper

3   packages (10 ounces each) frozen chopped spinach, thawed and squeezed dry

3½ cups milk

2   tablespoons cornstarch

1   teaspoon salt

1   cup freshly grated Parmesan cheese

1. Cut each polenta log crosswise in half, then cut each half lengthwise into 6 slices. In 13" by 9" ceramic or glass baking dish, place half of polenta slices, overlapping slightly.

2. Preheat oven to 425°F.

3. In 4-quart saucepan, heat oil over medium. Add onion and cook until tender and golden, 10 to 12 minutes, stirring occasionally. Add garlic and crushed red pepper and cook 1 minute, stirring. Add spinach and cook 3 minutes to heat through, stirring frequently and separating with fork.

4. In medium bowl, with wire whisk, mix milk and cornstarch. Stir in salt and all but 2 tablespoons Parmesan. Add milk mixture to spinach mixture in saucepan; heat to boiling over medium-high. Reduce heat to low; cook 2 minutes, stirring occasionally. Remove saucepan from heat.

5. Spoon half of spinach mixture over polenta slices in baking dish. Repeat layering with remaining polenta slices and spinach mixture. Sprinkle with reserved Parmesan. Bake until hot and bubbly, about 20 minutes.

EACH SERVING: About 155 calories, 8g protein, 19g carbohydrate, 5g total fat (3g saturated), 2g fiber, 12mg cholesterol, 625mg sodium ☺ 🍲

Baked Eggs and Polenta with Chunky Vegetable Sauce

Polenta makes a tasty—and unexpected—base for this saucy baked-egg casserole, just the thing for an Italian-inspired brunch.

ACTIVE TIME: 30 minutes
TOTAL TIME: 50 minutes
MAKES: 4 main-dish servings

1	cup boiling water
1	cup low-fat milk (1%)
½	cup yellow cornmeal
½	teaspoon salt
½	cup freshly grated Parmesan cheese
1	tablespoon olive oil
1	carrot, peeled and chopped
1	small onion, chopped
1	small zucchini (6 ounces), chopped
1	can (14½ ounces) tomatoes in juice, chopped
1	can (8 ounces) tomato sauce
¼	teaspoon coarsely ground black pepper
4	large eggs

1. Preheat oven to 400°F.

2. In deep 2½-quart microwave-safe bowl or casserole, stir boiling water, milk, cornmeal, and salt. Cook, uncovered, in microwave on High 3 minutes. Remove bowl from microwave and whisk cornmeal mixture vigorously until smooth (mixture may be lumpy at first). Microwave 2 to 3 minutes longer or until thickened; whisk once after cooking is done. Stir in Parmesan. Spread polenta in greased 8-inch square glass baking dish.

3. Meanwhile, in 12-inch skillet, heat oil over medium. Add carrot and onion, and cook until tender and beginning to brown, about 10 minutes. Stir in zucchini and cook just until zucchini is tender, about 5 minutes. Add tomatoes with their juice, tomato sauce, and pepper; heat to boiling over medium-high heat. Reduce heat to medium and cook 5 minutes, stirring occasionally. Spread tomato mixture over polenta in baking dish.

4. With large spoon, make four indentations in tomato mixture. Crack 1 egg into custard cup and slip into indentation; repeat with remaining eggs. Bake until eggs are set, 12 to 14 minutes.

EACH SERVING: About 290 calories, 16g protein, 29g carbohydrate, 13g total fat (4g saturated), 4g fiber, 223mg cholesterol, 1,325mg sodium ☺

CHOPPING CANNED TOMATOES

Chopping canned tomatoes can be messy, with juice running all over your cutting board and onto the counter. An easy way to avoid that is to "chop" the tomatoes right in the can using kitchen shears. Or, do as the Italians do and squeeze them in your fist to break them up before adding to the pan.

Chicken, Peppers, and Onions on Polenta

Here's a hassle-free supper that delivers maximum flavor with minimal effort.
A precooked polenta log and boneless, skinless chicken-breast halves ensure that the meal is on the table in just 30 minutes.

ACTIVE TIME: 15 minutes
TOTAL TIME: 30 minutes

MAKES: 4 main-dish servings

1	log (16 ounces) precooked plain polenta, cut into 8 slices
2	tablespoons olive oil
½	teaspoon salt
¾	teaspoon ground black pepper
1½	pounds boneless, skinless chicken-breast halves, cut into ½-inch-wide strips
2	red, orange, and/or yellow peppers (4 to 6 ounces each), thinly sliced
1	onion, thinly sliced
½	cup dry vermouth or dry white wine
1	tablespoon capers, drained and chopped

1. Arrange oven rack 6 inches from heat source and preheat broiler. Place polenta slices on cookie sheet and brush slices with 1 teaspoon oil on both sides; sprinkle with ¼ teaspoon salt and ½ teaspoon black pepper to season both sides. Broil polenta 18 to 20 minutes or until golden. Set aside.

2. Meanwhile, in 12-inch skillet, heat 2 teaspoons oil over medium. Sprinkle chicken with remaining ¼ teaspoon each salt and black pepper. Add chicken to skillet and cook 5 to 6 minutes or until chicken is golden and no longer pink throughout, stirring occasionally. Transfer chicken to bowl.

3. To same skillet, add remaining 1 tablespoon oil; reduce heat to medium. Add peppers and onion; cook 8 minutes or until vegetables are tender, stirring occasionally. Stir in vermouth and capers; increase heat to medium-high and cook 2 minutes. Return chicken to skillet; cook 1 minute or until heated through, stirring. Serve chicken and vegetables over polenta slices.

EACH SERVING: About 365 calories, 43g protein, 43g carbohydrate, 9g total fat (2g saturated), 3g fiber, 99mg cholesterol, 820mg sodium ♥ ☺

Spicy Sausage and Polenta Casserole

This casserole delivers comfort Italian style: creamy polenta and a tasty ragu studded with spicy sausage and eggplant.

ACTIVE TIME: 40 minutes
TOTAL TIME: 1 hour 20 minutes plus standing
MAKES: 8 main-dish servings

12	ounces hot Italian turkey sausage, casings removed
12	ounces meat loaf mix (veal, pork, and beef) or ground beef chuck
1	jumbo onion (1 pound), chopped
2	garlic cloves, finely chopped
1	can (28 ounces) whole tomatoes in puree
1	small eggplant (1 to 1¼ pounds), cut into ½-inch pieces
4	cups water
1	can (14½ ounces) chicken broth
1½	cups cornmeal
½	teaspoon salt
¾	cup freshly grated Pecorino-Romano

1. In 5- to 6-quart Dutch oven, cook sausage and meat loaf mix over medium-high heat 5 to 6 minutes or until browned, stirring and breaking up meat with side of spoon. With slotted spoon, transfer mixture to medium bowl.

2. To same Dutch oven, add onion; cook over medium heat 8 to 10 minutes or until tender. Stir in garlic; cook 30 seconds. Add tomatoes with their puree; heat to boiling over high, breaking up tomatoes with side of spoon. Reduce heat to medium-low and simmer, uncovered, 10 minutes. Add eggplant and meat; cover and cook 5 minutes over medium heat. Uncover and cook 10 minutes longer or until eggplant is tender, stirring occasionally.

3. Meanwhile, preheat oven to 400°F. In microwave-safe 4-quart bowl, with wire whisk, combine water, broth, cornmeal, and salt. Microwave on High 15 to 20 minutes or until cornmeal mixture is very thick. After first 5 minutes of cooking, whisk vigorously until smooth (mixture will be lumpy at first); whisk twice more during remaining cooking time. Remove from microwave, whisk in Romano.

4. Spoon 4 cups hot polenta into 3-quart shallow casserole. Spread polenta over bottom and up sides of casserole. Spoon filling over polenta. Spread remaining polenta around casserole rim to form a border.

5. Bake casserole 40 minutes or until hot. Let stand 10 minutes for easier serving.

EACH SERVING: About 385 calories, 22g protein, 34g carbohydrate, 18g total fat (7g saturated), 6g fiber, 65mg cholesterol, 1,045mg sodium ☺ 🍱

Brussels Sprouts with Sausage and Grapes on Creamy Polenta

Hearty Italian sausage and polenta are guaranteed to satisfy even the mightiest appetite. They're balanced with a generous serving of roasted Brussels sprouts and the sweet taste of red grapes.

ACTIVE TIME: 20 minutes
TOTAL TIME: 35 minutes

MAKES: 4 main-dish servings

2	packages (9 to 10 ounces each) Brussels sprouts, trimmed, each cut in half if large
2	garlic cloves, smashed
2	teaspoons olive oil
3/8	teaspoon salt
3/8	teaspoon ground black pepper
1	cup red seedless grapes
4	links (1 pound) sweet Italian sausage, each cut into thirds
2¼ cups milk	
2	cups water
1	cup yellow cornmeal
1	tablespoon butter or margarine

1. Preheat oven to 450°F.

2. In 18" by 12" jelly-roll pan, combine sprouts, garlic, 1 teaspoon oil, and ⅛ teaspoon each salt and pepper; toss until well mixed. Arrange, cut sides down if halved, in single layer on one side of pan. Place grapes in center of pan; drizzle with remaining 1 teaspoon oil; stir grapes to coat. On other side of pan, arrange sausages in single layer. Roast 15 to 20 minutes or until sprouts are browned and sausages are no longer pink inside.

3. Meanwhile, prepare polenta: In 3-quart saucepan, heat milk and water to boiling on medium-high. Reduce heat to low. With wire whisk, stir in cornmeal. Cook 8 to 10 minutes or until very thick and creamy, whisking frequently. Whisk in butter and remaining, ¼ teaspoon each salt and pepper until well blended. Divide polenta among serving plates and top with Brussels sprouts, grapes, and sausages.

EACH SERVING: About 655 calories, 28g protein, 51g carbohydrate, 36g total fat (14g saturated), 7g fiber, 95mg cholesterol, 980mg sodium

Fish & Shellfish

Italy is a peninsula, surrounded by the sea on three sides (and the four regions not near the coast boast abundant lakes and rivers), so fish and shellfish have long played an important role in its cuisine. If you order fish at restaurants, but rarely prepare it at home, let these simple, flavorful recipes be your guide to home-cooked fish. After all, there are many reasons why seafood should make regular appearances on your dinner plate. It's quick cooking, low in fat, and a rich source of protein, vitamins, and minerals. And oily fish, such as salmon and tuna, is high in heart-healthy omega-3 fatty acids, which can help lower your blood cholesterol levels.

Dinners like our Sicilian Tuna with Puttanesca Sauce and Seared Scallops with Olive and Tomato Compote can be quickly prepared in a pan, while Salmon and Squash in Parchment is wrapped and slow-baked in the oven to seal in the juices. Roasted Halibut with Fennel and Potatoes is roasted on a bed of vegetables to create a hearty meal, while Bass with Tomato Pesto is served with a side of polenta—and spinach, if you choose.

Keep frozen shrimp in the freezer and you can cook up Shrimp and Fennel Spaghetti or Trattoria-Style Shrimp Fettuccine with ease. Or try one of our other easy seafood pastas, including the ever-popular Linguine with Red Clam Sauce. If you enjoy fried calamari or mussels in white wine sauce when you go out to eat, why not try preparing them at home? Our recipes are simple to follow and sure to impress your friends and family.

Shrimp and Fennel Spaghetti (recipe page 162)

Fried Calamari
Fra Diavolo

Crispy golden-fried squid teams up with a tomato dipping sauce that can be as spicy as Fra Diavolo ("Brother Devil")! Or simply serve with lemon wedges, if you prefer.

ACTIVE TIME: 10 minutes
TOTAL TIME: 35 minutes

MAKES: 4 first-course servings

1	tablespoon olive oil
2	garlic cloves, crushed with side of chef's knife
⅛ to ¼	teaspoon crushed red pepper
1	can (14 to 16 ounces) tomatoes
¾	teaspoon salt
1	pound cleaned squid
⅔	cup all-purpose flour
1	cup water

Vegetable oil for frying

1. In nonreactive 1-quart saucepan, heat oil over medium. Add garlic and crushed red pepper; cook until garlic is golden, about 30 seconds. Add tomatoes with their juice and ½ teaspoon salt, breaking up tomatoes with side of spoon; heat to boiling. Reduce heat; cover and simmer 10 minutes. Keep warm.

2. Rinse squid with cold running water and gently pat dry with paper towels. Slice squid bodies crosswise into ¾-inch rings. Cut tentacles into pieces if large.

3. To make batter, in small bowl, with fork, mix flour and water until smooth. In 10-inch skillet, heat ½-inch oil over medium until a small piece of bread dropped into oil first sinks, then rises to top and begins bubbling. In small batches, drop squid into batter. Allowing excess batter to drip off, add squid to hot oil. Fry, turning to brown on all sides, until golden, about 2 minutes. With slotted spoon, transfer squid to paper towels to drain; sprinkle with remaining ¼ teaspoon salt. Serve with tomato sauce for dipping.

EACH SERVING: About 325 calories, 21g protein, 25g carbohydrate, 16g total fat (2g saturated), 2g fiber, 264mg cholesterol, 660mg sodium

Mussels with Tomatoes and White Wine

Serve this saucy dish with plenty of good crusty bread for dipping.

ACTIVE TIME: 20 minutes
TOTAL TIME: 45 minutes

MAKES: 8 first-course or 4 main-dish servings

1	tablespoon olive or vegetable oil
1	small onion, chopped
2	garlic cloves, finely chopped
¼	teaspoon crushed red pepper
1	can (14 to 16 ounces) whole tomatoes in juice
¾	cup dry white wine
4	pounds large mussels, scrubbed and debearded
2	tablespoons chopped fresh parsley

1. In nonreactive 5-quart Dutch oven, heat oil over medium. Add onion and cook until tender and golden, 6 to 8 minutes. Add garlic and crushed red pepper and cook 30 seconds longer. Stir in tomatoes with their juice and wine, breaking up tomatoes with side of spoon. Heat to boiling; boil 3 minutes.

2. Add mussels; return to boiling. Reduce heat; cover and simmer until mussels open, about 5 minutes. As mussels open, transfer to large bowl. Discard any that have not opened after 5 minutes. Pour tomato sauce over mussels and sprinkle with parsley.

EACH FIRST-COURSE SERVING: About 105 calories, 9g protein, 6g carbohydrate, 3g total fat (1g saturated), 1g fiber, 18mg cholesterol, 277mg sodium ☺ ♥

SCRUBBING AND DEBEARDING MUSSELS

Scrub mussels well under cold running water. To debeard them, grasp the hairlike beard firmly with your thumb and forefinger and pull it away, or scrape it off with a knife. (Cultivated mussels usually do not have beards.)

Baked Snapper with Peppers and Mushrooms

This fast fish recipe is ultra low fat and low cal but bursting with flavor. Sweet peppers and mushrooms are sautéed in white wine and fresh thyme, then baked with the fillets. A squeeze of lemon juice further brightens the flavors.

ACTIVE TIME: 20 minutes
TOTAL TIME: 35 minutes

MAKES: 6 main-dish servings

1	tablespoon olive oil
2	orange and/or yellow peppers, thinly sliced
1	onion, chopped
1	package (10 ounces) sliced mushrooms
½	cup dry white wine
1	teaspoon fresh thyme leaves, chopped, plus additional thyme leaves for garnish
6	skinless, boneless snapper, sole, or flounder fillets (4 ounces each)
2	tablespoons fresh lemon juice
¼	teaspoon salt
¼	teaspoon ground black pepper

1. Preheat oven to 450°F. In 12-inch skillet, heat oil over medium. Add peppers and onion, and cook 10 minutes or until tender, stirring often. Add mushrooms, wine, and thyme; increase heat to medium-high and cook 3 minutes, stirring frequently.

2. Meanwhile, spray 13" by 9" glass or ceramic baking dish with cooking spray. Arrange fillets in baking dish, folding narrow ends under. Sprinkle with lemon juice, salt, and pepper.

3. Spoon hot vegetable mixture on top of fish. Bake 15 to 18 minutes or until opaque throughout. (An instant-read thermometer inserted horizontally into center of fish should register 145°F.) Garnish with additional thyme leaves.

EACH SERVING: About 175 calories, 26g protein, 9g carbohydrate, 4g total fat (1g saturated), 2g fiber, 42mg cholesterol, 175mg sodium ☺ ♥

Seared Scallops with Olive and Tomato Compote

Microwaving the polenta makes this rustic meal weeknight simple, but it's elegant enough to serve at a dinner party, if you like.

ACTIVE TIME: 10 minutes
TOTAL TIME: 30 minutes

MAKES: 4 main-dish servings

2 tablespoons olive oil
1 small onion, chopped
1 garlic clove, crushed with garlic press
1 can (28 ounces) whole tomatoes in juice
1 tablespoon red wine vinegar
¼ teaspoon coarsely ground pepper
¼ teaspoon salt
⅓ cup Kalamata olives, pitted and chopped
Microwave Polenta (page 137; optional)
1¼ pounds sea scallops, rinsed

SEA SCALLOP PREP

Even though scallops look ready to cook when you buy them, make sure to rinse them under running water to remove any residual sand from the crevices. The little crescent-shaped muscle on the side of each scallop is edible but tough, so it's best to remove them before cooking; you can easily pull them off with your fingers.

---

1. In 12-inch skillet, heat 1 tablespoon oil on medium. Add onion and cook 6 to 8 minutes or until soft and golden, stirring occasionally. Stir in garlic; cook 1 minute. Add tomatoes with their juice, vinegar, and ⅛ teaspoon pepper. Heat to boiling over medium-high. Cook 8 to 10 minutes or until thickened, stirring occasionally. Stir in olives and transfer tomato compote to bowl; cover to keep warm. Makes about 2 cups.

2. Meanwhile, prepare Microwave Polenta, if you like.

3. Remove and discard tough crescent-shaped muscle from each scallop. Pat dry with paper towels. Evenly season scallops, on both sides, with salt and remaining ⅛ teaspoon pepper.

4. In clean 12-inch skillet, heat remaining 1 tablespoon oil over medium-high. Add scallops and cook 5 minutes or just until opaque throughout and lightly browned. Serve scallops with tomato compote over polenta, if using.

EACH SERVING WITHOUT POLENTA: About 270 calories, 25g protein, 15g carbohydrate, 13g total fat (1g saturated), 3g fiber, 45mg cholesterol, 1,140mg sodium ✓ ☺

Cod Livornese

The Tuscan seaport town of Livorno is famous for this simple preparation of white fish featuring Mediterranean favorites: tomatoes, olives, and capers. The dish is classically made with snapper, but we used cod; you can also substitute flounder or tilapia.

ACTIVE TIME: 15 minutes
TOTAL TIME: 30 minutes

MAKES: 4 main-dish servings

1	tablespoon chopped fresh oregano leaves
2	teaspoons grated fresh lemon peel
2	teaspoons plus 2 tablespoons olive oil
¼	teaspoon salt
4	pieces cod fillet (6 ounces each)
1	pint cherry tomatoes
¼	cup Kalamata olives, pitted and coarsely chopped
2	tablespoons drained capers
⅛	teaspoon crushed red pepper flakes
2	garlic cloves, minced
¼	cup loosely packed fresh parsley leaves, chopped

REMOVING PIN BONES

Fish fillets, especially thick ones like cod or salmon, may have a few bones. Before cooking, run your fingers over the flesh, and if you find any strays, use tweezers to remove them.

1. In cup, combine oregano, lemon peel, 2 teaspoons oil, and salt. Rub mixture over both sides of cod fillets.

2. In 12-inch nonstick skillet, heat 1 tablespoon oil over medium. Add cod and cook 8 to 10 minutes or just until fish turns opaque throughout, turning over once. (An instant-read thermometer inserted horizontally into center of fish should register 145°F.) Transfer fillets to plates.

3. In same skillet, heat remaining 1 tablespoon oil over medium. Stir in tomatoes, olives, capers, crushed red pepper, and garlic; cook 6 to 8 minutes or just until tomatoes are heated through and skins split. Stir in chopped parsley; serve with cod.

EACH SERVING: About 250 calories, 31g protein, 6g carbohydrate, 11g total fat (2g saturated), 2g fiber, 73mg cholesterol, 450mg sodium

Farfalle Livornese with Tuna

Classic tangy and spicy Livornese flavors come alive in this easy-to-prepare pasta recipe.

ACTIVE TIME: 20 minutes
TOTAL TIME: 30 minutes
MAKES: 6 main-dish servings

12   ounces farfalle or rotini
8   ounces green beans, trimmed and cut into 1-inch pieces
1   pound tuna steak (1¼ inches thick)
1   tablespoon olive oil
¼   teaspoon salt
1   onion, chopped
1   garlic clove, crushed with garlic press
1   can (14½ ounces) diced tomatoes
2   tablespoons capers, drained and chopped
2   teaspoons grated fresh lemon peel
¼   teaspoon crushed red pepper
¼   cup loosely packed fresh parsley leaves, chopped
Caper berries for garnish (optional)

1. Cook pasta in *boiling salted water* as label directs, adding green beans to saucepot 2 minutes before pasta is done.

2. Meanwhile, sprinkle tuna with salt to season both sides. In 12-inch skillet, heat 2 teaspoons oil on medium-high until hot. Add tuna and cook 2 minutes on each side. Reduce heat to medium; cover skillet and cook 5 to 8 minutes longer or until tuna is almost opaque throughout, turning over once halfway through cooking. (An instant-read thermometer inserted horizontally into center of fish should register 145°F.) Transfer tuna to plate.

3. To same skillet, add remaining 1 teaspoon oil. Reduce heat to medium; add onion and garlic, and cook 6 to 8 minutes or until lightly browned and tender, stirring occasionally. Stir in tomatoes, capers, lemon peel, and crushed red pepper; heat to boiling on medium-high. Boil 1 minute. While vegetables are cooking, with two forks, flake tuna into bite-size pieces.

4. When pasta and beans are done, reserve ¼ *cup pasta cooking water*. Drain pasta and green beans, and return to saucepot; stir in vegetable mixture from skillet, flaked tuna, chopped parsley, and reserved pasta cooking water, and toss to coat. Transfer to warm bowls, and garnish each serving with whole caper berries, if you like.

EACH SERVING: About 335 calories, 28g protein, 50g carbohydrate, 4g total fat (1g saturated), 7g fiber, 34mg cholesterol, 585mg sodium ♥ ☺

Salt-Baked Fish

Baking a whole fish in a crust of kosher salt seals in the juices and guarantees exquisitely moist—and surprisingly unsalty—fish.

ACTIVE TIME: 5 minutes
TOTAL TIME: 30 minutes
MAKES: 2 main-dish servings

4	cups kosher salt
1	whole red snapper, striped bass, or porgy (1½ to 2 pounds), cleaned and scaled
1	lemon
3	sprigs rosemary or thyme

1. Preheat oven to 450°F. Line 13" by 9" baking pan with foil; spread 2 cups salt in bottom of pan.

2. Rinse snapper inside and out with cold running water; pat dry with paper towels. From lemon, cut 3 slices. Cut remaining lemon into wedges and set aside.

3. Place lemon slices and rosemary in cavity of fish. Place fish on bed of salt; cover with remaining 2 cups salt. Bake until fish is just opaque throughout when knife is inserted at backbone, about 30 minutes. (An instant-read thermometer inserted horizontally into center of fish should register 145°F.)

4. To serve, tap salt crust to release from top of fish; discard salt. Slide cake server under front section of top fillet and lift off fillet; transfer to platter. Slide server under backbone and lift it away from bottom fillet; discard. Slide server between bottom fillet and skin and transfer fillet to platter. Garnish with reserved lemon wedges.

EACH SERVING: About 190 calories, 37g protein, 6g carbohydrate, 3g total fat (1g saturated), 0g fiber, 66mg cholesterol, 800mg sodium ✓ ☺

LET'S TALK WHOLE FISH

If you've never cooked a whole fish, don't be intimidated: It's not difficult if you follow these instructions. The reward is crisp skin and delicate moist fish.

+ **Plan on ½ to ¾ pound per person.** Choose a fish with bright, shiny eyes and scales that cling tightly to the skin. Save yourself some trouble and ask your fishmonger to clean and scale it for you.

+ **Use fresh fish right away,** or at the very latest, the next day. To keep the fish overnight, remove from packaging and pat dry. Cover fish loosely with plastic wrap and layer with ice in a colander, placed over a bowl to catch drips.

+ **Broiling and roasting are good choices** for whole fish, as are braising and steaming if you have a cooking vessel that's large enough to hold the fish.

+ **To cook a whole fish,** begin by measuring the fish with a ruler at its thickest part. Cook about 10 minutes per inch of thickness, turning over halfway through cooking time. If you're cooking the fish in foil or parchment, or in a sauce, add 5 minutes to total cooking time.

+ **Fish is done** when an instant-read thermometer inserted horizontally into thickest part registers 145°F. The flesh will be just opaque in the center. Make a small incision with a thin-bladed knife in the thickest part and pry flesh apart to check that it is cooked through, down to the bone.

Roasted Halibut with Fennel and Potatoes

Sambuca is a popular Italian liqueur, but you can use any anise-flavored liqueur, including Pernod. A jigger of these spirits subtly enhances the natural licorice flavor in the fennel.

ACTIVE TIME: 15 minutes
TOTAL TIME: 1 hour

MAKES: 4 main-dish servings

1	large leek
1	pound Yukon Gold potatoes, peels left on, thinly sliced
2	medium fennel bulbs (12 ounces each), cored and thinly sliced, some fronds from bulb reserved for garnish
4	teaspoons extra-virgin olive oil
¾	teaspoon salt
⅜	teaspoon ground black pepper
4	pieces skinless halibut fillet (6 ounces each)
2	tablespoons Sambuca or other anise-flavored liqueur or white wine
1	teaspoon fennel seeds
1	lemon, thinly sliced

1. Cut off roots and trim dark-green top from leek. Discard any tough outer leaves. Thinly slice leek. Rinse leek slices thoroughly in bowl of cold water, swishing to remove sand. With hands, transfer leek slices to colander, leaving sand in bottom of bowl. Drain well.

2. Preheat oven to 425°F. Spray 13″ by 9″ glass baking dish with nonstick cooking spray. To baking dish, add leek, potatoes, fennel, 1 table-spoon oil, ½ teaspoon salt, and ¼ teaspoon pepper; toss to coat, then spread evenly. Roast vegetables 35 minutes or until tender, stirring once halfway through roasting.

3. Place halibut on vegetables; drizzle with liqueur and remaining oil. Sprinkle with fennel seeds and remaining ¼ teaspoon salt and ⅛ teaspoon pepper. Place lemon slices on halibut; return dish to oven and continue roasting 10 to 12 minutes or just until halibut turns opaque in center. (An instant-read thermometer inserted horizontally into center of fish should register 145°F.) To serve, sprinkle with roughly chopped fennel fronds.

EACH SERVING: About 365 calories, 39g protein, 33g carbohydrate, 9g total fat (1g saturated), 6g fiber, 54mg cholesterol, 570mg sodium ☻

Bass with Tomato Pesto

Use your food processor to easily create a homemade pesto of sun-dried tomatoes and almonds to top roasted sea bass. Quick-cooking polenta rounds out the meal.

TOTAL TIME: 20 minutes

MAKES: 4 main-dish servings

⅓ cup sun-dried tomatoes packed in oil, drained

¼ cup roasted almonds

2 tablespoons plus 1 teaspoon olive oil

⅜ teaspoon ground black pepper

1 cup quick-cooking polenta

2 cups low-fat milk (1%)

⅝ teaspoon salt

3 cups water

4 fillets black sea bass (6 ounces each)

1 package (9 ounces) microwave-in-bag spinach

2 tablespoons finely chopped fresh basil

1. Preheat oven to 450°F. In food processor with knife blade attachment, pulse tomatoes, almonds, 2 tablespoons oil, and ¼ teaspoon pepper until coarsely ground.

2. In large glass bowl, whisk polenta, milk, ½ teaspoon salt, and water. Microwave on High 4 minutes. Whisk; cook 7 minutes or until mixture is very thick.

3. Meanwhile, in jelly-roll pan, rub fish with remaining 1 teaspoon oil. Sprinkle with remaining ⅛ teaspoon each salt and pepper. Roast 8 to 10 minutes or until just opaque throughout. (An instant-read thermometer inserted horizontally into center of fish should register 145°F.) Cook spinach as label directs.

4. Stir basil and fish juices into pesto. Whisk polenta; place on plates with spinach and fish. Top with pesto.

EACH SERVING: About 475 calories, 42g protein, 35g carbohydrate, 19g total fat (3g saturated), 8g fiber, 74mg cholesterol, 710mg sodium

Roast Salmon with Capers and Parsley

A whole salmon fillet with a crusty crumb-and-herb topping looks festive and tastes fabulous.

ACTIVE TIME: 10 minutes
TOTAL TIME: 40 minutes
MAKES: 6 main-dish servings

3	tablespoons butter or margarine
1/3	cup plain dried bread crumbs
1/4	cup loosely packed fresh parsley leaves, minced
3	tablespoons drained capers, minced
1	teaspoon dried tarragon, crumbled
2	teaspoons grated fresh lemon peel
1/4	teaspoon salt
1/4	teaspoon coarsely ground black pepper
1	whole salmon fillet (2 pounds)

Lemon wedges

1. Preheat oven to 450°F. In 1-quart saucepan, melt butter over low heat. Remove saucepan from heat; stir in bread crumbs, parsley, capers, tarragon, lemon peel, salt, and pepper.

2. Line 15 1/2" by 10 1/2" jelly-roll pan with foil; grease foil. Place salmon, skin side down, in pan and pat crumb mixture on top. Roast until salmon turns opaque throughout and topping is lightly browned, about 30 minutes. (An instant-read thermometer inserted horizontally into center of fish should register 145°F.)

3. With two large spatulas, carefully transfer salmon to platter, allowing skin to remain attached to foil. Serve with lemon wedges.

EACH SERVING: About 325 calories, 28g protein, 5g carbohydrate, 21g total fat (7g saturated), 0g fiber, 94mg cholesterol, 407mg sodium ☺

Linguine with Red Clam Sauce

Scrub clams with a stiff-bristled brush under cold running water to remove sand. If you can't get fresh clams, substitute two 10-ounce cans of whole baby clams.

ACTIVE TIME: 20 minutes
TOTAL TIME: 1 hour
MAKES: 6 main-dish servings

1/2	cup dry white wine
2	dozen littleneck clams, scrubbed
12	ounces linguine
3 1/2	cups marinara sauce, store-bought or homemade (page 93)
1	tablespoon butter or margarine, cut into pieces (optional)
1/4	cup chopped fresh parsley

1. In 12-inch skillet, heat wine to boiling over high. Add clams; cover and cook until clams open, 5 to 10 minutes, transferring clams to bowl as they open. Discard any that have not opened after 10 minutes. Strain broth from skillet through sieve lined with paper towels; reserve *1/4 cup broth.* When cool enough to handle, remove and discard clam shells; coarsely chop clams.

2. Meanwhile, in large saucepot, cook pasta in *boiling salted water* as label directs. Drain.

3. In same clean 12-inch skillet, combine marinara, reserved clam broth, and clams; cook over low heat until heated through. In warm serving bowl, toss pasta with sauce and butter, if using. Sprinkle with parsley and serve.

EACH SERVING: About 395 calories, 20g protein, 65g carbohydrate, 6g total fat (1g saturated), 3g fiber, 28mg cholesterol, 661mg sodium ☺

Salmon and Summer Squash in Parchment

This party-perfect salmon and squash dish is baked in parchment paper, which seals in the juices and makes cleanup easy. Fresh lemon, oregano, and olive oil contribute a Mediterranean flavor profile.

ACTIVE TIME: 20 minutes
TOTAL TIME: 35 minutes

MAKES: 6 main-dish servings

1	lemon
2	yellow summer squash (8 ounces each), cut into half-moons
1	small shallot, minced
1	tablespoon chopped fresh oregano leaves
1	tablespoon extra-virgin olive oil
1	teaspoon salt
¼	teaspoon coarsely ground black pepper
2	zucchini (8 ounces each), thinly sliced lengthwise
6	pieces skinless salmon fillet (6 ounces each; see Tip)

1. Preheat oven to 400°F. From lemon, grate 1 teaspoon peel and squeeze 2 tablespoons juice.

2. In medium bowl, combine lemon juice, yellow squash, shallot, oregano, oil, ½ teaspoon salt, and pepper.

3. Cut six pieces parchment, 15" by 12" each, and spread out on work surface. On half of each parchment rectangle, starting 2 inches from a short edge, arrange one-sixth of zucchini slices lengthwise, overlapping slightly. Place salmon on zucchini; sprinkle with lemon peel and remaining ½ teaspoon salt, then top with yellow-squash mixture. Fold other half of parchment over ingredients. To seal packets, begin at a corner and tightly fold edges of paper over about ½ inch all around, overlapping folds.

4. Place packets on large cookie sheet. Bake 17 minutes or until salmon turns opaque throughout; when checking a packet for doneness, take care when opening, to avoid escaping steam. (An instant-read thermometer inserted horizontally into center of fish should register 145°F.) To serve, carefully cut each packet open, and with spatula, gently transfer salmon and vegetables to dinner plates. Spoon any liquid remaining in parchment over salmon and vegetables.

EACH SERVING: About 270 calories, 35g protein, 6g carbohydrate, 13g total fat (2g saturated), 2g fiber, 93mg cholesterol, 465mg sodium ☺ ♥

TIP: *Baking fish wrapped in grease- and moisture-resistant parchment paper allows it to steam in its own juices, locking in aroma and flavor. For even cooking, choose fillets of uniform thickness.*

Sicilian Tuna with Puttanesca Sauce

A robust sauce of tomatoes, Kalamata olives, capers, and chopped fresh basil complements the flavor of marinated tuna steaks. A high-acid wine like Chianti Classico or Barbera would pair well with this bold tomato sauce.

ACTIVE TIME: 25 minutes
TOTAL TIME: 30 minutes plus marinating
MAKES: 8 main-dish servings

6	tablespoons olive oil
5	tablespoons fresh lemon juice
4	anchovy fillets, chopped
1	garlic clove, finely chopped
¼	teaspoon dried thyme
⅛	teaspoon ground black pepper
8	tuna steaks, ¾ inch thick (5 ounces each)
1	large stalk celery, chopped
3	ripe plum tomatoes, chopped
2	green onions, sliced
¼	cup pitted Kalamata or Niçoise olives, coarsely chopped
2	tablespoons capers, drained
¼	cup chopped fresh basil

1. In 13" by 9" baking dish, combine 3 tablespoons oil, 3 tablespoons lemon juice, anchovies, garlic, thyme, and pepper. Add tuna, turning to coat. Cover and marinate at least 45 minutes or up to 2 hours, turning over once.

2. In 2-quart saucepan, heat remaining 3 tablespoons oil over medium. Add celery and cook 5 minutes. Stir in tomatoes, green onions, olives, and capers; cook until mixture has thickened slightly, about 5 minutes. Stir in basil and remaining 2 tablespoons lemon juice; keep sauce warm.

3. Place rack in position closest to heat source and preheat broiler. Place tuna on rack in broiling pan. Broil until pale pink in center (medium), about 3 minutes per side, or until desired doneness. (An instant-read thermometer inserted horizontally into center of fish should register 145°F.) Serve tuna with sauce.

EACH SERVING: About 240 calories, 24g protein, 3g carbohydrate, 14g total fat (2g saturated), 1g fiber, 39mg cholesterol, 291mg sodium ☺ ♥

Sicilian Citrus Salsa

If you crossed an orange and a raspberry and added a splash of red wine, you'd come close to the irresistible flavor of blood oranges. This scarlet-tinged fruit is not only delightful for pan sauces, sorbets, and creative cocktails, but wonderful on grilled tuna or salmon.

TOTAL TIME: 15 minutes
MAKES: 4 cups

Peel and dice *3 blood oranges.* Mix with *1½ cups finely chopped fennel, 3 tablespoons chopped green olives, 1 tablespoon extra-virgin olive oil,* and *¼ teaspoon each salt and freshly ground black pepper.*

EACH 2-TABLESPOON SERVING: About 15 calories, 0g protein, 2g carbohydrate, 1g total fat (0g saturated), 0g fiber, 0mg cholesterol, 31mg sodium ◔ ☺ ♥

Trattoria-Style Shrimp Fettuccine

Classic and quite simple to prepare, this shrimp and pasta dish is a complete one-dish meal, thanks to the bag of fresh spinach that gets incorporated at the last minute.

ACTIVE TIME: 20 minutes
TOTAL TIME: 30 minutes

MAKES: 6 main-dish servings

12   ounces fettuccine or spaghetti
2   tablespoons olive oil
1   onion, chopped
2   garlic cloves, thinly sliced
½   cup dry white wine
1   bottle (8 ounces) clam juice
½   teaspoon salt
1   pound shelled and deveined large shrimp, tail shells left on if you like
1   bag (5 to 6 ounces) baby spinach
⅓   cup loosely packed fresh parsley leaves, chopped

1. Cook pasta in *boiling salted water* as package label directs.

2. Meanwhile, in 12-inch skillet, heat oil over medium. Add onion and garlic, and cook 10 minutes or until golden and tender, stirring often. Add wine; increase heat to medium-high and cook 1 minute. Stir in clam juice and salt; heat to boiling. Stir in shrimp, and cook 2 to 3 minutes or until shrimp turn opaque throughout.

3. Drain pasta and add to skillet with spinach and parsley; toss to coat.

EACH SERVING: About 350 calories, 24g protein, 46g carbohydrate, 7g total fat (1g saturated), 4g fiber, 115mg cholesterol, 515mg sodium ☺ ☺

Shrimp Gemelli

Caramelizing the onions contributes to this dish's subtle sweetness. Finish with a sprinkling of golden-brown bread crumbs.

ACTIVE TIME: 10 minutes
TOTAL TIME: 30 minutes
MAKES: 6 main-dish servings

1	pound gemelli or corkscrew pasta (see Tip)
1	pound peeled and deveined medium (26- to 30-count) shrimp, tail shells left on if you like
1	pound small broccoli flowerets
3	tablespoons butter or margarine
½	cup fresh bread crumbs
¾	teaspoon plus pinch salt
½	teaspoon ground black pepper
2	large onions (12 ounces each), thinly sliced

1. Prepare gemelli in *boiling salted water* as package directs, cooking 1 minute less than recommended time. Three minutes before taking pasta off heat, add shrimp and broccoli to pot.

2. Meanwhile, in 12-inch skillet, melt ½ tablespoon butter over medium-high. Add bread crumbs and cook 2 to 3 minutes or until golden brown, stirring frequently. Stir in pinch salt, along with pepper. Transfer to plate.

3. In same skillet, melt 2 tablespoons butter over medium heat. Stir in onions and ¼ teaspoon salt. Cover and cook 20 minutes or until golden and very tender, stirring occasionally.

4. When pasta, shrimp, and broccoli are done, reserve *1 cup pasta cooking water*. Drain mixture and return to pot.

5. Add onion mixture, reserved cooking water, pepper, and remaining ½ teaspoon salt and ½ tablespoon butter. Cook on medium heat 2 minutes, tossing to coat. To serve, top with reserved toasted bread crumbs.

EACH SERVING: About 455 calories, 26g protein, 72g carbohydrate, 8g total fat (2g saturated), 7g fiber, 112mg cholesterol, 660mg sodium ♥

TIP: *Gemelli is made from two strands of pasta twisted together. If you can't find it in your local supermarket, substitute corkscrew pasta.*

Shrimp and Fennel Spaghetti

In this quick pasta dish, thinly sliced fennel and garlic mingle in a peppery tomato sauce enriched by the delicate brininess of shrimp. For photo, see page 144.

ACTIVE TIME: 15 minutes
TOTAL TIME: 25 minutes
MAKES: 6 main-dish servings

1	pound spaghetti
1	pound peeled and deveined medium (26- to 30-count) shrimp
2	medium fennel bulbs (12 ounces each)
3	garlic cloves
2	tablespoons olive oil
1	teaspoon sugar
1	teaspoon crushed red pepper
½	teaspoon salt
1	can (28 ounces) no-salt-added diced tomatoes
2	cups thawed frozen peas

1. Cook pasta in *boiling salted water* as label directs, adding shrimp to saucepot 2 minutes before pasta is done.

2. Meanwhile, core and thinly slice fennel; reserve fronds for garnish. Thinly slice garlic.

3. In 12-inch skillet, heat oil on medium-high. Add fennel, garlic, sugar, crushed red pepper, and ¼ teaspoon salt. Stir well, cover, and cook 5 minutes or until tender and brown, stirring occasionally. Stir in tomatoes and their juices; cook 5 minutes.

5. When pasta and shrimp are done, drain and return to pot. Add tomato mixture, peas, and remaining ¼ teaspoon salt. Toss over medium-low heat 2 minutes or until well mixed. Garnish with fennel fronds.

EACH SERVING: About 480 calories, 26g protein, 77g carbohydrate, 7g total fat (1g saturated), 9g fiber, 95mg cholesterol, 775mg sodium 🕑

SHELLING AND DEVEINING SHRIMP

You can use already peeled and deveined frozen shrimp in any of our shrimp recipes, but fresh shrimp is more succulent than frozen if you have the time to prep it. Here's how. Note: Be sure to use fresh shrimp within two days of purchase.

1. With kitchen shears or a small knife, cut the shrimp shell along the outer curve, just deep enough into the flesh to expose the dark vein.

2. Peel back the shell from the cut and gently separate the shell from shrimp. Discard the shell (or use it to make fish stock).

3. Remove the vein with the tip of a small knife and discard. Rinse the shrimp under cold running water.

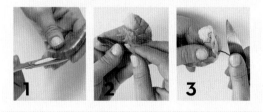

Grilled Squid and Peppers with Arugula

Squid can turn chewy if it's not cooked properly. To ensure a tender result, remove each piece from the grill just as it becomes opaque.

ACTIVE TIME: 15 minutes
TOTAL TIME: 30 minutes

MAKES: 4 main-dish servings

1½ pounds cleaned squid
1   garlic clove, crushed with garlic press
2   tablespoons plus 2 teaspoons extra-virgin olive oil
½   teaspoon salt
¼   teaspoon coarsely ground black pepper
4   medium peppers (red, orange, and/or yellow)
2   lemons, each cut in half
1   bag (5 ounces) baby arugula

1. With kitchen shears, cut each squid body lengthwise down 1 side and open flat. Cut tentacles in half if large. Rinse squid with cold running water and pat dry with paper towels. Transfer squid to bowl; add garlic, 1 tablespoon oil, ¼ teaspoon salt, and ¼ teaspoon pepper, and toss to coat; set aside. Cut each pepper lengthwise into quarters; discard seeds and stems.

2. Heat large ridged grill pan over medium-high.

3. In large bowl, toss peppers with 2 teaspoons oil. Place peppers on grill pan and cook until charred and tender, 10 to 15 minutes, turning over once. Place lemon halves, cut sides down, on grill pan with peppers and cook until grill marks appear on cut sides and lemons soften, about 5 minutes. Transfer peppers to large bowl. Set lemon halves aside.

4. Place squid on grill pan and cook just until opaque throughout, 1 to 2 minutes, turning over once. Add squid to peppers in bowl and toss with remaining 1 tablespoon oil and ¼ teaspoon salt.

5. Arrange arugula on platter; top with squid mixture. Serve with grilled lemons to squeeze over servings.

EACH SERVING: About 300 calories, 30g protein, 23g carbohydrate, 12g total fat (2g saturated), 3g fiber, 396mg cholesterol, 380mg sodium ⓥ ☺

Poultry & Meat

Italians choose high-quality ingredients and prepare them simply to accentuate their natural flavors, and their poultry and meat entrées are no exception. Whether they're prepared on the stovetop, in the oven, or on the grill, the recipes in this chapter use herbs and an abundance of vegetables, a drizzle of balsamic vinegar or Marsala wine, or a sprinkling of freshly grated Parmesan to create beautiful and satisfying meals.

On busy weeknights, chicken is the solution many of us turn to again and again. Add an Italian accent to your usual repertoire with easy, family-pleasing dishes like Classic Chicken Parmesan, Pecorino Chicken Fingers, or Crispy Balsamic Chicken. Or, if company's coming, impress your guests with slow-cooked specialties like Italian Herb-Roasted Chicken or Cornish Hens Milanese. Turkey is on the menu, too: Try our quick-and-easy Spicy Turkey Sausage and Polenta or holiday-worthy Prosciutto-Wrapped Turkey Roulade.

Red meat lovers will rejoice in traditional Italian favorites like Veal Parmigiana, Osso Bucco with Gremolata, and Braciole with Grape Tomatoes, a thin cut of beef rolled around a tasty bread crumb stuffing seasoned with garlic, Pecorino cheese, and fresh parsley. Our Slow-Cooked Tuscan Pork with Fennel is comfort food at it's best, while inventive dishes like Maple-Glazed Sausages and Figs and Butterflied Leg of Lamb with Mint Pesto bring fresh new flavors to the dinner table.

Grilled Chicken Parm and Vegetables (recipe page 176)

Chicken with Pears and Marsala

Fresh pears and a wine sauce spiked with sage transform basic chicken breasts into an elegant main course.

ACTIVE TIME: 10 minutes
TOTAL TIME: 25 minutes
MAKES: 4 main-dish servings

1	teaspoon vegetable oil
4	small skinless, boneless chicken breast halves (1 pound)
¼	teaspoon salt
⅛	teaspoon ground black pepper
2	Bosc or Anjou pears, each peeled, cored, and quartered
¾	cup canned chicken broth
½	cup dry Marsala wine
1	tablespoon cornstarch
2	teaspoons chopped fresh sage leaves

1. In nonstick 10-inch skillet, heat oil over medium-high. Add chicken; sprinkle with salt and pepper. Cook 10 to 12 minutes, turning over once, until instant-read thermometer inserted horizontally into center of breast registers 165°F. Transfer to plate; keep warm.

2. To skillet, add pears and cook until browned on all sides, 3 to 5 minutes. Meanwhile, in cup, whisk broth, wine, cornstarch, and sage until thoroughly blended.

3. Carefully add broth mixture to skillet; boil 1 minute to thicken slightly. Return chicken with any juices to skillet; heat through.

EACH SERVING: About 195 calories, 27g protein, 12g carbohydrate, 3g total fat (1g saturated), 66mg cholesterol, 410mg sodium 🌿 ☺ 🖤

LET'S TALK MARSALA

Marsala, Italy's most famous fortified wine, is produced by a process similar to the one used in Spain to make sherry. Marsala is made in several different styles: *secco* (dry), *semisecco* (semisweet), and *dolce* (sweet). It is also classified based on its flavor characteristics and aging: *Fino* is usually aged less than one year, while Marsalas designated *Superiore* are aged between two and four years, and those marked *Vergine* are between four and ten years old.

Classic Chicken Parmesan

This make-at-home traditional Italian chicken dish is as flavorful and fast as takeout—at a fraction of the cost.

ACTIVE TIME: 30 minutes
TOTAL TIME: 35 minutes

MAKES: 4 main-dish servings

1	cup plain dried bread crumbs
2/3	cup plus 2 tablespoons freshly grated Parmesan cheese
3	tablespoons olive oil
1	large egg white
4	skinless, boneless chicken breast halves (1 1/2 pounds)
1/2	teaspoon ground black pepper
2	garlic cloves, thinly sliced
2	large yellow summer squashes, cut into 1/4-inch-thick slices
1	cup loosely packed fresh basil leaves, thinly sliced
2	large zucchini, cut into 1/4-inch-thick slices
3/4	cup store-bought reduced-sodium marinara sauce or homemade marinara sauce (page 93)
4	ounces part-skim mozzarella cheese, shredded (1 cup)

1. Arrange one oven rack 4 inches from broiler heat source and one rack in middle of oven. Preheat oven to 450°F. Line 15 1/2" by 10 1/2" jelly-roll pan with foil.

2. In shallow bowl, with fork, combine bread crumbs, 2/3 cup Parmesan, and 1 tablespoon oil. In another shallow bowl, whisk egg white until frothy. With meat mallet or rolling pin, pound chicken (placed between two sheets plastic wrap) to even 1/2-inch thickness. Sprinkle with pepper to season both sides. Dip 1 chicken breast half in egg white, then into bread crumb mixture, coating completely. Place in prepared pan. Repeat with remaining chicken. Bake on middle oven rack 15 to 17 minutes or until chicken is golden and instant-read thermometer inserted horizontally into center registers 165°F.

3. Meanwhile, in 12-inch skillet, heat 1 tablespoon oil over medium-high. Add half of garlic; cook 30 seconds. Add yellow squash, one-fourth of basil, and 1/4 teaspoon pepper and cook 4 to 5 minutes or until soft, stirring. Transfer to large bowl; add remaining oil to pan and cook zucchini, using same amounts of basil and pepper, cooking 6 to 7 minutes, stirring. Transfer to bowl with yellow squash; toss with remaining basil.

4. Remove chicken from oven; reset oven control to broil. Broil chicken on upper rack 1 minute or until crumbs are browned. Reserve 1/4 cup marinara sauce; divide remaining sauce among chicken pieces, spreading evenly. Top with mozzarella and remaining 2 tablespoons Parmesan. Broil 1 to 2 minutes or until cheese melts and bubbles. Microwave reserved marinara on High 30 seconds; divide among plates, then top with chicken and serve with vegetables.

EACH SERVING: About 615 calories, 61g protein, 37g carbohydrate, 25g total fat (8g saturated), 7g fiber, 127mg cholesterol, 925mg sodium

Chicken and Pesto Stacks

These colorful stacks of chicken breasts, veggies, and mozzarella, drizzled with pesto, are as pretty as they are fun to eat.

ACTIVE TIME: 20 minutes
TOTAL TIME: 30 minutes

MAKES: 4 main-dish servings

3   tablespoons pesto, store-bought or homemade (page 82)

3   tablespoons water

1   large sweet onion (12 ounces), cut crosswise into 4 slices

2   yellow peppers, each cut into quarters

4   skinless, boneless chicken breast halves (1½ pounds)

¼   teaspoon salt

¼   teaspoon ground black pepper

2   teaspoons olive oil

4   slices fresh mozzarella (4 ounces)

1   tomato, cut into 4 slices

1. Place rack 6 inches from heat source and preheat broiler. In small bowl, mix pesto with water. Spray 15 ½″ by 10 ½″ jelly-roll pan with nonstick cooking spray. Arrange onion slices on pan; brush with 2 tablespoons pesto mixture. Broil onion slices 5 minutes. Arrange peppers on pan with onion; broil 12 to 15 minutes longer or until vegetables are tender, turning over halfway through cooking.

2. Meanwhile, with meat mallet or rolling pin, pound chicken placed between two sheets plastic wrap to even ½-inch thickness; season with salt and pepper.

3. In 12-inch skillet, heat oil over medium. Add chicken and cook 6 to 8 minutes or until browned on both sides, turning over once.

4. Top chicken in pan with mozzarella slices; cover and cook 2 to 3 minutes or until cheese melts and chicken registers 165°F when instant-read thermometer is inserted into center.

5. To serve, on each dinner plate, stack 1 slice onion, 2 slices pepper, 1 slice tomato, and 1 piece chicken with mozzarella; drizzle with remaining pesto mixture.

EACH SERVING: About 400 calories, 48g protein, 16g carbohydrate, 16g total fat (6g saturated), 3g fiber, 122mg cholesterol, 345mg sodium

Chicken with Caramelized Cauliflower and Green Onions

Cauliflower develops incredible sweet flavor when roasted. To make it a meal, we've added chicken breast tenders and tossed it all in a pesto-like sauce made from olives, almonds, and fresh parsley.

ACTIVE TIME: 10 minutes
TOTAL TIME: 50 minutes

MAKES: 4 main-dish servings

1	head cauliflower (2½ to 3 pounds), trimmed and cut into 1½-inch chunks
2	tablespoons extra-virgin olive oil
⅜	teaspoon salt
¼	teaspoon ground black pepper
1	pound chicken breast tenders, cut into 1½-inch chunks
1	teaspoon freshly grated lemon peel
¼	cup slivered almonds
⅓	cup pitted green olives, rinsed well
¼	cup packed fresh flat-leaf parsley, finely chopped, plus additional for garnish

1. Preheat oven to 450°F. In 18" by 12" jelly-roll pan, combine cauliflower, 2 teaspoons oil, and ⅛ teaspoon each salt and pepper until well mixed. Spread cauliflower in single layer on pan. Roast 20 to 25 minutes or until cauliflower is golden brown.

2. While cauliflower roasts, in large bowl, combine chicken, lemon peel, 1 teaspoon oil, and remaining ¼ teaspoon salt and ⅛ teaspoon pepper. Push cauliflower to one side of pan and arrange chicken in single layer on other side. Roast 10 minutes longer or until chicken just loses pink color throughout.

3. Meanwhile, in food processor with knife blade attached, pulse almonds until finely ground. Add olives and parsley and pulse until almost smooth. With machine running, add remaining 1 tablespoon oil and process until fully incorporated, scraping sides of bowl as needed. Add mixture to pan with hot chicken and cauliflower and stir until well combined. Transfer to serving plates and garnish with additional parsley.

EACH SERVING: About 360 calories, 45g protein, 12g carbohydrate, 15g total fat (2g saturated), 6g fiber, 99mg cholesterol, 660mg sodium ☺

Roman Chicken Sauté with Artichokes

This light and tangy chicken dish, studded with sweet grape tomatoes and garlicky artichoke hearts, is served over a bed of spicy arugula. For a casual summer dinner with friends, pair it with our Antipasti Platter (page 20).

ACTIVE TIME: 15 minutes
TOTAL TIME: 30 minutes

MAKES: 6 main-dish servings

1¼ pounds chicken breast tenders, each cut crosswise, then lengthwise into quarters

¼ teaspoon salt

¼ teaspoon ground black pepper

1 tablespoon olive oil

2 garlic cloves, thinly sliced

1 can (13¾ to 14 ounces) artichoke hearts, drained, each cut into quarters

½ cup dry white wine

½ cup chicken broth

1 pint grape tomatoes

1 teaspoon grated fresh lemon peel plus additional for garnish

1 bag (5 to 6 ounces) baby arugula

1. Sprinkle chicken with salt and pepper to season all sides. In 12-inch skillet, heat 2 teaspoons oil over medium-high until very hot. Add chicken pieces and cook 8 minutes or until browned on outside and cooked through, stirring occasionally. With slotted spoon, transfer chicken to bowl.

2. To same skillet, add remaining 1 teaspoon oil. Reduce heat to medium and add garlic; cook 30 seconds or until golden. Stir in artichokes, and cook 3 to 4 minutes or until browned. Stir in wine, and cook 1 minute over medium-high heat.

3. Add chicken broth and tomatoes; cover and cook 2 to 3 minutes or until most tomatoes burst. Remove skillet from heat. Return chicken to skillet; stir in lemon peel until combined. Arrange arugula on platter; top with sautéed chicken mixture. Garnish with lemon peel.

EACH SERVING: About 165 calories, 25g protein, 5g carbohydrate, 4g total fat (1g saturated), 1g fiber, 55mg cholesterol, 330mg sodium ♥ ☺ ♥

Lemon-Oregano Chicken Cutlets with Mint Zucchini

The bright flavors of lemon and fresh oregano and mint make this easy grilled chicken recipe the perfect option for a hot summer evening.

ACTIVE TIME: 20 minutes
TOTAL TIME: 30 minutes

MAKES: 4 main-dish servings

3	medium zucchini (8 ounces each)
2	tablespoons olive oil
½	teaspoon salt
½	cup loosely packed fresh mint leaves, chopped
4	skinless, boneless chicken breast halves (1½ pounds)
3	lemons
1	tablespoon chopped fresh oregano leaves
½	teaspoon coarsely ground black pepper

1. Prepare outdoor grill for direct grilling over medium heat.

2. With mandoline or sharp knife, slice zucchini very thinly lengthwise. In large bowl, toss zucchini with 1 tablespoon oil, ¼ teaspoon salt, and half of mint.

3. Pound chicken breasts to uniform ¼-inch thickness. From 2 lemons, grate 1 tablespoon peel and squeeze 2 tablespoons juice. Cut remaining lemon into 4 wedges; set aside. In medium bowl, combine lemon peel and juice with oregano, pepper, and remaining 1 tablespoon oil and ¼ teaspoon salt. Add chicken to bowl and toss until evenly coated.

4. Place zucchini slices, in batches, on hot grill grate, and cook 2 to 4 minutes or until grill marks appear and zucchini is tender, turning over once. Remove zucchini from grill; place on large platter and sprinkle with remaining mint.

5. Place chicken on hot grill grate. Cover grill and cook chicken 6 to 8 minutes, turning over once, until instant-read thermometer inserted horizontally into center of breast registers 165°F. Transfer chicken to platter with zucchini; serve with lemon wedges.

EACH SERVING: About 280 calories, 42g protein, 8g carbohydrate, 9g total fat (2g saturated), 3g fiber, 99mg cholesterol, 390mg sodium 🔵 ☺ ♥

POUNDING CHICKEN, TURKEY, OR VEAL CUTLETS

For even cooking, it's a good idea to pound chicken, turkey, and veal cutlets to a uniform thickness. Here's how: Place one piece of chicken or other cutlet between two sheets of plastic wrap. With meat mallet, rolling pin, or heavy skillet, pound three or four times until it is ¼ to ½ inch thick.

Crispy Balsamic Chicken

This quick chicken dish pops with Italian flavor, thanks to the luscious balsamic glaze and fresh arugula and basil salad.

ACTIVE TIME: 10 minutes
TOTAL TIME: 30 minutes
MAKES: 4 main-dish servings

1   pound carrots, peeled and thinly sliced on a diagonal
2   teaspoons extra-virgin olive oil
¼   teaspoon salt
½   teaspoon ground black pepper
1   cup panko (Japanese-style bread crumbs)
1¼   pounds skinless, boneless thin-sliced chicken breast cutlets
1   tablespoon Dijon mustard
½   cup plus 1 tablespoon balsamic vinegar
1   bag (5 ounces) baby arugula
½   cup fresh basil leaves, torn

1. Preheat oven to 450°F. On jelly-roll pan, toss carrots with oil and ⅛ teaspoon each salt and pepper. Roast 8 to 10 minutes or until tender-crisp. Transfer carrots to large bowl to cool.

2. While carrots cook, place panko on large plate. In medium bowl, toss chicken with mustard and ¼ teaspoon pepper until well coated. Coat chicken with panko, pressing so crumbs adhere. Arrange chicken on rack in jelly-roll pan. Bake 12 to 14 minutes or until thermometer inserted horizontally into cutlet registers 165°F (see Tip).

3. Meanwhile, in 1-quart saucepan, heat ½ cup vinegar and remaining ⅛ teaspoon each salt and pepper to boiling over high; reduce heat and simmer 8 to 12 minutes, or until syrupy.

4. To same bowl as carrots, add arugula, basil, and remaining 1 tablespoon vinegar, tossing to mix. Serve salad topped with chicken and balsamic glaze.

EACH SERVING: About 370 calories, 33g protein, 37g carbohydrate, 9g total fat (1g saturated), 4g fiber, 78mg cholesterol, 440mg sodium 💚 ☺ ♥

TIP: *For even crispier chicken, place the cutlets briefly under the broiler after baking.*

Chicken Scarpariello

We adapted this traditional Italian dish for the slow cooker. One secret to its extra-rich taste: coffee-colored cremini mushrooms (or baby portobellos), a more flavorful variety of the common cultivated mushroom.

ACTIVE TIME: 20 minutes
SLOW-COOK TIME: 8 hours on Low or 4 hours on High
MAKES: 6 main-dish servings

8	ounces hot or sweet Italian sausage links, cut crosswise into 1½-inch pieces
1	onion, chopped
2	garlic cloves, crushed with garlic press
2	tablespoons tomato paste
2	tablespoons balsamic vinegar
1	teaspoon Italian seasoning or dried thyme
1	pint grape tomatoes
1	package (8 ounces) sliced cremini mushrooms (see Tip)
1	chicken (3½ to 4 pounds), cut into 8 pieces, skin removed from all but wings
¼	teaspoon salt
¼	teaspoon ground black pepper

1. In 12-inch nonstick skillet, cook sausage pieces over medium heat, turning occasionally, until well browned, about 6 minutes. With tongs or slotted spoon, transfer sausages to 5- to 6-quart slow cooker. Add onion to skillet and cook until slightly softened, about 4 minutes. Add garlic and cook, stirring, 1 minute. Remove skillet from heat; stir in tomato paste, vinegar, and Italian seasoning until blended, then add tomatoes and mushrooms. Spoon vegetable mixture into slow cooker and stir to combine. Do not wash skillet.

2. Sprinkle chicken pieces with salt and pepper. In same skillet, cook chicken (in two batches, if necessary) over medium heat until well browned, about 10 minutes.

3. Place chicken pieces on top of vegetable mixture in slow cooker. Cover with lid and cook 8 hours on Low or 4 hours on High. Skim fat from juices before serving.

EACH SERVING: About 355 calories, 39g protein, 9g carbohydrate, 17g total fat (6g saturated), 2g fiber, 120mg cholesterol, 420mg sodium ☺ 🍲 🍲

TIP: *You can keep fresh mushrooms wrapped in a damp cloth in the refrigerator for about a week.*

Grilled Chicken Parm and Vegetables

Chicken Parmesan takes a light and healthy approach with grilled—rather than breaded and fried—chicken and fresh veggies. For photo, see page 164.

ACTIVE TIME: 20 minutes
TOTAL TIME: 30 minutes

MAKES: 4 main-dish servings

1   slice whole wheat bread
4   teaspoons olive oil
¼   cup packed fresh flat-leaf parsley leaves
1   clove garlic
⅜   teaspoon salt
⅜   teaspoon ground black pepper
1   pound skinless, boneless chicken breast cutlets
1   pound yellow squash, cut into ½-inch-thick slices
1   pound ripe tomatoes, cut into ½-inch-thick slices
1   ounce Parmesan cheese
Basil leaves for garnish

1. Arrange oven rack 6 inches from broiler heat source. Preheat broiler. Line 18" by 12" jelly-roll pan with foil. Preheat large ridged grill pan or prepare outdoor grill for direct grilling over medium-high heat.

2. Tear bread into large chunks. In food processor with knife blade attached, pulse bread into fine crumbs. In small bowl, combine bread crumbs with 1 teaspoon oil.

3. To food processor, add parsley, garlic, ¼ teaspoon each salt and pepper, and remaining 1 tablespoon oil. Pulse until very finely chopped.

4. On large plate, rub half of parsley mixture all over chicken cutlets. Add chicken to hot grill pan or place on hot grill grate; cook 4 minutes. Turn chicken over and cook 3 to 4 minutes longer or until no longer pink in center.

5. Meanwhile, arrange squash in single layer in prepared pan. Toss with remaining parsley mixture. Broil 7 to 9 minutes or until squash is tender and browned. Transfer squash to serving platter in single layer. Place chicken on top.

6. In same baking pan, arrange tomato slices in single layer. Divide crumb mixture evenly among tomatoes. Sprinkle with remaining ⅛ teaspoon each salt and pepper. Broil 30 seconds or until crumbs are golden brown.

7. Arrange crumb-topped tomato slices on top of chicken. With vegetable peeler, shave paper-thin slices of Parmesan directly over tomatoes. Garnish with fresh basil leaves.

EACH SERVING: About 250 calories, 29g protein, 12g carbohydrate, 10g total fat (3g saturated), 69mg cholesterol, 415mg sodium ☺ ♥

Pecorino Chicken Fingers

Serve these lightly breaded chicken fingers with zucchini and marinara dipping sauce for an Italian-style take on every kid's favorite meal.

ACTIVE TIME: 15 minutes
TOTAL TIME: 30 minutes
MAKES: 4 main-dish servings

1 cup panko (Japanese-style bread crumbs), toasted

⅓ cup freshly grated Pecorino-Romano cheese

¼ teaspoon cayenne (ground red) pepper

½ teaspoon salt

2 large egg whites

1 garlic clove, crushed with garlic press

1½ pounds chicken tenders

Olive oil cooking spray

3 medium zucchini (8 ounces each), cut into ¼-inch-thick half-moons

2 tablespoons water

1 tablespoon fresh lemon juice

1 cup marinara sauce, store-bought or homemade (page 93)

¼ cup loosely packed fresh basil leaves, chopped, plus small whole basil leaves for garnish

1. Preheat oven to 475°F. Place rack in 15 ½″ by 10 ½″ jelly-roll pan.

2. On plate, combine panko, Pecorino, cayenne, and ¼ teaspoon salt. Set aside. In pie plate, whisk egg whites and garlic until well mixed.

3. One at a time, dip chicken tenders in egg-white mixture, then into panko mixture to coat evenly; press firmly so mixture adheres. Spray prepared pan and rack with cooking spray, then arrange chicken on rack and spray lightly.

4. Bake chicken 10 to 12 minutes or until crust is golden brown and instant-read thermometer inserted horizontally into center of tender registers 165°F.

5. While chicken cooks, in microwave-safe medium bowl, place zucchini and water. Cover with vented plastic wrap and cook in microwave on High 5 minutes or until zucchini is just fork-tender. Carefully remove plastic wrap and drain zucchini; stir in lemon juice and remaining ¼ teaspoon salt.

6. Meanwhile, in 1-quart saucepot, heat marinara over medium-low 5 minutes or until hot, stirring occasionally. Remove saucepot from heat and stir in chopped basil. Serve dipping sauce with chicken fingers and zucchini; garnish chicken and dipping sauce with basil leaves.

EACH SERVING: About 325 calories, 47g protein, 18g carbohydrate, 6g total fat (2g saturated), 3g fiber, 106mg cholesterol, 790mg sodium ♥ ☺

Chicken Saltimbocca

In Italian, saltimbocca *means "jumps into the mouth." The dish traditionally features veal marinated in wine or olive oil and rolled with prosciutto, sage, and capers. We substituted chicken breasts and added Gorgonzola cheese to create a hearty entrée that contains fewer than 300 calories per serving.*

ACTIVE TIME: 10 minutes
TOTAL TIME: 30 minutes

MAKES: 4 main-dish servings

4	thin slices prosciutto (2 ounces)
1	(2 ounce) chunk Gorgonzola cheese, cut into thin slices
4	skinless, boneless chicken breast halves (1½ pounds)
2	teaspoons olive oil
½	cup dry white wine
1	tablespoon fresh lemon juice
1	bag (5 to 6 ounces) mixed baby greens

1. On large cutting board or cookie sheet, lay prosciutto slices in single layer. Evenly divide Gorgonzola among prosciutto slices, placing it in center. Place 1 chicken breast crosswise on each portion. Wrap each chicken breast with prosciutto, pressing firmly to encase cheese; secure with toothpick if necessary. (Prosciutto will not completely cover chicken.)

2. In 12-inch skillet, heat oil over medium. Add wrapped chicken, Gorgonzola side down, and cook 12 to 15 minutes, turning over once, until chicken is browned on top and bottom and no longer pink inside. (An instant-read thermometer inserted horizontally into center should registers 165°F.) Transfer wrapped chicken breasts to platter; cover with foil to keep warm.

3. To same skillet, add wine and lemon juice and heat to boiling over medium-high; boil 2 minutes to reduce sauce by half, stirring occasionally and scraping up any browned bits. Remove skillet from heat.

4. Place greens in large bowl and toss with sauce. Arrange greens on dinner plates and top with chicken.

EACH SERVING: About 295 calories, 47g protein, 3g carbohydrate, 10g total fat (4g saturated), 1g fiber, 119mg cholesterol, 700mg sodium ⊘ ☺

Italian Herb-Roasted Chicken

This simple and delicious roasted chicken recipe is seasoned with dried Mediterranean herbs and garlic. For a cozy dinner, pair it with Brussels Sprouts with Pancetta and Rosemary (page 210) and Balsamic-Glazed Baby Carrots (page 214).

ACTIVE TIME: 10 minutes
TOTAL TIME: 1 hour 10 minutes plus standing
MAKES: 4 main-dish servings

1	whole chicken (3½ pounds)
1	tablespoon olive oil or softened butter
½	teaspoon dried basil
½	teaspoon dried oregano
½	teaspoon dried rosemary
1	garlic clove, crushed with garlic press
¾	teaspoon salt
1¼	teaspoons coarsely ground black pepper
½	cup water

1. Preheat oven to 450°F. Remove bag with giblets and neck from chicken cavity; discard or reserve for another use.

2. In cup, mix olive oil, herbs, and garlic. With fingertips, gently separate skin from meat on chicken breast. Rub herb mixture on meat under skin. Tie legs together with string. Rub chicken all over with salt and pepper.

3. Place chicken, breast side up, on rack in small roasting pan (13″ by 9″). Pour ¼ cup water into roasting pan. Roast chicken 1 hour or until temperature on instant-read thermometer inserted into thickest part of thigh registers 175°F.

4. Lift chicken from roasting pan and tilt slightly to allow juices inside cavity to run into pan. Place chicken on platter; let stand 10 minutes to allow juices to set for easier carving.

5. Remove rack from roasting pan. Skim and discard fat from pan juices. Add remaining ¼ cup water to pan juices; cook 1 minute over medium heat, stirring constantly to scrape up browned bits from bottom of pan. Serve chicken with pan juices.

EACH SERVING: About 390 calories, 41g protein, 1g carbohydrate, 23g total fat (6g saturated), 1g fiber, 161mg cholesterol, 700mg sodium

IS IT DONE YET?

There's only one way to guarantee that poultry or meat is roasted to the desired doneness: Use a meat thermometer. We like instant-read thermometers, but old-fashioned thermometers that you leave in the meat during cooking will do the job, too.

Always insert a thermometer into the thickest part of the roast; don't touch bone or fatty sections as that will give an inaccurate reading. Remove the roast from the oven when it is 5°F to 10°F cooler than the desired temperature, because the internal temperature will continue to rise as the meat stands.

Cornish Hens Milanese

Gremolata, a tasty blend of fresh parsley, lemon peel, and pungent garlic, is a popular way to finish a meat, poultry, or fish dish in Italy. We also love gremolata scattered over steamed green beans or new potatoes. Serve these roasted hens with a side of our Cauliflower with Golden Raisins and Pine Nuts (page 211).

ACTIVE TIME: 5 minutes
TOTAL TIME: 55 minutes

MAKES: 4 main-dish servings

2	Cornish hens (1½ pounds each)
3	tablespoons chopped fresh parsley
1	teaspoon extra-virgin olive oil
¼	teaspoon salt
⅛	teaspoon ground black pepper
1	small garlic clove, minced
½	teaspoon freshly grated lemon peel

1. Preheat oven to 375°F. Remove giblets and necks from hens; reserve for another use. With poultry shears, cut each hen lengthwise in half; pat dry with paper towels.

2. In small bowl, combine 2 tablespoons parsley, oil, salt, and pepper. With fingertips, carefully separate skin from meat on each hen half; spread parsley mixture under skin. Place hens, skin side up, in large roasting pan (17″ by 11½″).

3. Roast hens, basting with drippings three times, about 50 minutes or until instant-read thermometer inserted into thickest part of thigh registers 165°F.

4. Arrange hens on warm platter. In cup, combine remaining 1 tablespoon parsley, garlic, and lemon peel; sprinkle over hens.

EACH SERVING: About 385 calories, 32g protein, 0g carbohydrate, 27g total fat (7g saturated), 0g fiber, 187mg cholesterol, 236mg sodium

Prosciutto-Wrapped Turkey Roulade

For easier and quicker prep, ask your butcher to butterfly and pound the turkey breast so you can skip step 3.

ACTIVE TIME: 30 minutes
TOTAL TIME: 2 hours
MAKES: 8 main-dish servings

1	lemon
1	cup packed fresh flat-leaf parsley leaves
6	cloves garlic, peeled
3	tablespoons fresh sage leaves
2	tablespoons fresh rosemary leaves
1	tablespoon fennel seeds
½	teaspoon salt
¼	teaspoon freshly ground black pepper
1	whole boneless turkey breast (4 to 5 pounds), skin removed
6	thick slices prosciutto (5 ounces)
2	large red onions (8 to 10 ounces each), peeled and cut into ½-inch-thick rounds
1	tablespoon canola oil
1	cup lower-sodium chicken broth

1. Preheat oven to 375°F. From lemon, grate 1 teaspoon peel, transfer to food processor. Into small bowl, squeeze 1 tablespoon juice; set aside.

2. To food processor, add parsley, garlic, sage, rosemary, fennel seeds, salt, and pepper. Pulse until finely chopped. Transfer to medium bowl.

3. Place turkey on large cutting board, smooth side down. On left breast, cut along right side of tenderloin to separate from breast without cutting tenderloin off completely. Fold tenderloin back until flat but still attached to breast along left side. Repeat on right breast, cutting along left side of tenderloin and folding back. Cover surface of turkey with 2 large sheets plastic wrap. Using flat side of meat mallet or heavy rolling pin, pound turkey until about ¾ inch thick all over. Remove and discard plastic wrap.

4. Spread three-quarters of herb mixture evenly on breast. Starting with short side, roll breast in jelly-roll fashion. Place seam side down.

5. Rub outside of turkey with remaining herb mixture. Cover with prosciutto slices, over-lapping slightly and tucking ends underneath turkey. Using 16-inch pieces of kitchen string, tie turkey tightly in 2-inch intervals. (Turkey can be wrapped in plastic and refrigerated overnight.)

6. Arrange onions in single layer on bottom of medium (14″ by 10″) roasting pan. Place turkey on onions in pan. Brush turkey and onions with oil. Pour broth into pan. Roast for 1½ to 2 hours or until thermometer inserted into center registers 165°F. If pan seems dry after 45 minutes, add 1 cup water.

7. With tongs, transfer turkey to large cutting board and onions to serving platter. Cover turkey loosely with foil. Place roasting pan on burner. Heat to boiling on medium-high; whisk in reserved lemon juice. (If liquid in pan is minimal and tastes too salty, add *½ cup water* along with lemon juice.) Boil 3 to 5 minutes or until reduced slightly, whisking occasionally. Slice turkey; place on platter with onions. Drizzle turkey with reduced pan juices.

EACH SERVING: About 340 calories, 62g protein, 8g carbohydrate, 5g total fat (1g saturated), 2g fiber, 155mg cholesterol ❤ 🍲

Spicy Turkey Sausage and Polenta

Precooked polenta rounds and marinara from a jar speed up this family favorite.

TOTAL TIME: 30 minutes

MAKES: 4 main-dish servings

1	log (16 ounces) plain precooked polenta, cut into 8 rounds
2	tablespoons grated Pecorino-Romano cheese
12	ounces Italian turkey sausage (4 links), casings removed
2	medium zucchini (8 ounces each), cut into 1-inch chunks
1	medium yellow pepper, cut into 1-inch chunks
1	cup marinara sauce
¼	cup water

1. Preheat broiler. Line cookie sheet with foil sprayed with nonstick cooking spray. Place polenta on prepared sheet; place in oven 5 to 6 inches from source of heat. Broil polenta 10 minutes or until golden, without turning over. Sprinkle polenta with cheese; broil 1 minute or until cheese melts.

2. Meanwhile, spray nonstick 12-inch skillet with cooking spray; heat on medium until hot. Add sausage; cook 8 minutes or until browned, breaking up meat with side of spoon. Add zucchini and pepper; cook 3 minutes or until vegetables are tender-crisp, stirring often. Add marinara and water; simmer, covered, 8 minutes.

3. Place 2 polenta rounds on each of 4 plates; top with sausage sauce.

EACH SERVING: About 300 calories, 21g protein, 28g carbohydrate, 11g total fat (3g saturated), 4g fiber, 53mg cholesterol, 1,100mg sodium ☻ ☺

Steak Pizzaiola

Serve this pizza-makers'-style steak on toasted or grilled Italian bread.

ACTIVE TIME: 15 minutes
TOTAL TIME: 30 minutes
MAKES: 4 main-dish servings

2	tablespoons olive oil
1	large onion (12 ounces), thinly sliced
2	garlic cloves, finely chopped
1	large red pepper, thinly sliced
1	large yellow pepper, thinly sliced
4	ounces mushrooms, trimmed and sliced
1	can (15 ounces) crushed tomatoes
¾	teaspoon salt
8	beef minute steaks (2 ounces each)

1. In 12-inch skillet, heat 1 tablespoon oil over medium. Add onion and garlic and cook, stirring, until onion is tender-crisp, about 2 minutes. Add red and yellow peppers and mushrooms and cook, stirring, until peppers are tender-crisp, about 2 minutes.

2. Add tomatoes with their juice and ¼ teaspoon salt; cook just until sauce has slightly thickened, about 2 minutes longer. Transfer to medium bowl; keep warm.

3. Wipe skillet with paper towels, then heat remaining 1 tablespoon oil over medium-high until very hot. Sprinkle beef with remaining ½ teaspoon salt; cook steaks, in batches, until just cooked through, about 2 minutes per side. Transfer steaks to warm platter as they are cooked. Spoon sauce over steaks.

About **SERVING:** About 355 calories, 26g protein, 14g carbohydrate, 22g total fat (7g saturated), 5g fiber, 72mg cholesterol, 668mg sodium ⊙

Veal Parmigiana

Smothered in marinara sauce and topped with mozzarella cheese, this Italian-restaurant favorite is easy to make at home.

ACTIVE TIME: 30 minutes
TOTAL TIME: 55 minutes
MAKES: 6 main-dish servings

1	cup plain dried bread crumbs
½	teaspoon salt
⅛	teaspoon ground black pepper
1	large egg
2	tablespoons water
6	veal cutlets (1½ pounds)
3	tablespoons butter or margarine
2	cups marinara sauce, store-bought or homemade (page 93)
¼	cup freshly grated Parmesan cheese
4	ounces part-skim mozzarella cheese, shredded (1 cup)

1. On waxed paper, combine bread crumbs, salt, and pepper. In pie plate, beat egg and water. Dip cutlets in egg mixture, then in bread crumbs; repeat to coat each cutlet twice.

2. In 12-inch skillet, melt butter over medium heat. Add cutlets, a few at a time, and cook until browned, about 5 minutes per side, using tongs to transfer to platter as they finish cooking.

3. Return all cutlets to skillet. Spoon sauce evenly over cutlets; sprinkle with Parmesan and mozzarella. Reduce heat to low; cover and cook just until cheese has melted, about 5 minutes.

EACH SERVING: About 365 calories, 35g protein, 19g carbohydrate, 17g total fat (8g saturated), 0g fiber, 154mg cholesterol, 913mg sodium ☺

Fire-Grilled Steak
with Fennel

Grilled steak and vegetables get big flavor from heart-healthy olive oil, tangy vinegar, fresh herbs, and capers. Serve Peppers Caprese (page 204) alongside.

ACTIVE TIME: 15 minutes
TOTAL TIME: 35 minutes

MAKES: 4 main-dish servings

1	beef flank steak (1 pound)
3/8	teaspoon salt
1/4	teaspoon ground black pepper
5	teaspoons extra-virgin olive oil
3	large fennel bulbs (1 pound each), cored and cut lengthwise into 1/2-inch-thick slices
1	large red onion (12 ounces), cut into 1/3-inch-thick rounds
1/2	cup fresh mint leaves
1/2	cup fresh flat-leaf parsley leaves
3	tablespoons red wine vinegar
2	tablespoons capers, rinsed and drained
1	small garlic clove, crushed
1	tablespoon water

1. Prepare outdoor grill for direct grilling over medium heat. Sprinkle steak on both sides with 1/4 teaspoon each salt and pepper. Use 2 teaspoons oil to brush both sides of fennel and onion slices; sprinkle with remaining 1/8 teaspoon salt.

2. Grill steak, covered, 8 to 10 minutes for medium-rare or until desired doneness, turning over once. (Instant-read thermometer inserted horizontally into steak should register 145°F.) Grill onion alongside steak 7 to 9 minutes or until tender. Transfer steak to cutting board; let rest 10 minutes. Transfer onion to bowl.

3. Meanwhile, finely chop mint and parsley; place in medium bowl with vinegar, capers, garlic, water, and remaining 1 tablespoon oil. Stir to blend.

4. Place fennel on grill. Cover; cook 3 to 4 minutes or until browned, turning over once. Toss with onion.

5. Thinly slice steak. Serve fennel and onion alongside; top steak with herb sauce.

EACH SERVING: About 290 calories, 26g protein, 16g carbohydrate, 13g total fat (4g saturated), 6g fiber, 67mg cholesterol, 465mg sodium ☺ ❤

Stuffed Breast of Veal

This cut of meat can always be counted on for being moist, flavorful, and easy on the wallet. Here, it is filled with the classic Sicilian combination of spinach and golden raisins. Serve the veal hot or at room temperature; either way, it will be delicious.

ACTIVE TIME: 25 minutes
TOTAL TIME: 2 hours 40 minutes, plus cooling and standing
MAKES: 6 main-dish servings

1	tablespoon olive oil
1	small onion, chopped
3	garlic cloves, finely chopped
2	packages (10 ounces each) frozen chopped spinach, thawed and squeezed dry
1	lemon
1/3	cup golden raisins
3/4	teaspoon salt
1	bone-in veal breast (4 pounds), with pocket for stuffing
1	cup chicken broth

1. Preheat oven to 425°F. In 12-inch skillet, heat oil over medium-low. Add onion and garlic and cook, stirring frequently, until onion is tender, about 5 minutes. Add spinach and cook, stirring frequently, until liquid has evaporated, about 2 minutes. Remove from heat.

2. From lemon, grate 3/4 teaspoon peel and squeeze 2 tablespoons juice; set juice aside. Add lemon peel, raisins, and 1/2 teaspoon salt to skillet. Cool to room temperature. Spoon mixture into pocket of veal.

3. Place breast, meat side up, in medium roasting pan (14" by 10"). Sprinkle remaining 1/4 teaspoon salt on meat side (not rib side) of veal and roast 1 hour. Turn veal rib side up, and pour broth and lemon juice into bottom of roasting pan. Cover veal with loose tent of foil and bake until tender, about 1 hour 15 minutes longer. Instant-read thermometer inserted into center of roast (not touching bone) should register 145°F.

4. Transfer veal, rib side down, to cutting board; let stand 10 minutes to set juices for easier carving. Skim and discard fat from drippings in pan.

5. Carve veal by slicing down along one rib bone. Cut away rib bone and discard, then continue carving. Transfer slices to warm platter and serve with pan juices.

EACH SERVING: About 425 calories, 51g protein, 13g carbohydrate, 18g total fat (6g saturated), 3g fiber, 183mg cholesterol, 637mg sodium

Braciole with Grape Tomatoes

To make braciole, traditionally thin cuts of meat are rolled around a filling and simmered slowly in tomato sauce. This recipe uses a quicker method: roasting the beef at high heat and pairing it with tiny, sweet tomatoes.

ACTIVE TIME: 15 minutes
TOTAL TIME: 40 minutes plus standing
MAKES: 8 main-dish servings

½ cup Italian-style bread crumbs

1 garlic clove, crushed with garlic press

¼ cup finely grated Pecorino-Romano cheese

½ cup packed fresh flat-leaf parsley leaves, finely chopped

4 teaspoons olive oil

½ teaspoon ground black pepper

1 beef flank steak (1¾ to 2 pounds)

¼ teaspoon salt

2 pints grape tomatoes

1. Preheat oven to 475°F. In small bowl, combine bread crumbs, garlic, Pecorino, parsley, 1 tablespoon oil, and ¼ teaspoon pepper.

2. On large sheet of waxed paper, with flat side of meat mallet or heavy skillet, pound steak to even ½-inch thickness. Spread crumb mixture over steak in even layer; press into meat. Starting at 1 long side, roll steak into cylinder (about 2½ inches in diameter) to enclose filling completely. (Some bread crumbs may spill out.) With butcher's twine or kitchen string, tie roll tightly at 1-inch intervals. Place roll in center of 18" by 12" jelly-roll pan. Rub salt and remaining 1 teaspoon oil and ¼ teaspoon pepper all over steak. Scatter tomatoes around steak.

3. Roast 25 to 27 minutes or until temperature on meat thermometer inserted into thickest part of roll registers 130°F. Let steak stand in pan 10 minutes to set juices for easier slicing. Remove and discard twine; cut roll crosswise into ½-inch-thick slices. Transfer meat and tomatoes with their juices to serving platter.

EACH SERVING: About 255 calories, 22g protein, 10g carbohydrate, 14g total fat (5g saturated), 1g fiber, 54mg cholesterol, 290mg sodium ☺ ♥

Osso Bucco with Gremolata

This aromatic recipe from northern Italy is especially wonderful served with Creamy Polenta (page 136), another regional specialty.

ACTIVE TIME: 40 minutes
TOTAL TIME: 2 hours 40 minutes

MAKES: 4 main-dish servings

4	meaty veal shank cross-cuts (osso bucco), each about 2 inches thick (1 pound each)
½	teaspoon salt
¼	teaspoon ground black pepper
1	tablespoon olive oil
2	medium onions, chopped
3	carrots, peeled and chopped
2	stalks celery, chopped
4	garlic cloves, finely chopped
1	can (14½ to 16 ounces) tomatoes in puree
1	cup dry white wine
1	cup chicken broth
1	bay leaf
2	tablespoons chopped fresh parsley
½	teaspoon freshly grated lemon peel

1. Preheat oven to 350°F. Sprinkle shanks with salt and pepper. In nonreactive 5-quart Dutch oven, heat oil over medium-high until very hot. Add shanks and cook until browned, about 10 minutes, transferring to plate as they are done.

2. Add onions to Dutch oven and cook over medium heat, stirring occasionally, until slightly browned, about 5 minutes. Add carrots, celery, and three-fourths of garlic; cook 2 minutes.

3. Return veal to Dutch oven. Stir in tomatoes with their puree, wine, broth, and bay leaf; increase heat and bring to boiling. Cover and place in oven. Bake until veal is tender when pierced with fork, about 2 hours.

4. Meanwhile, prepare gremolata: In small bowl, mix parsley, lemon peel, and remaining garlic. Cover and refrigerate until ready to serve.

5. Transfer veal to serving platter. Heat cooking juices remaining in Dutch oven to boiling over high heat; boil until reduced to 4 cups, about 10 minutes. Pour sauce over veal and sprinkle with gremolata.

EACH SERVING: About 275 calories, 53g protein, 20g carbohydrate, 8g total fat (2g saturated), 3g fiber, 183mg cholesterol, 874mg sodium 😊 🍲

LET'S TALK GREMOLATA

A finishing touch, gremolata is a classic Italian herb mixture best known as a garnish for braised veal shanks (osso bucco). It can also be stirred into sauces or sprinkled over grilled fish, roast chicken, and bean dishes just before serving. You can make gremolata from mint, parsley, or a mix of parsley and a small amount of a stronger herb like rosemary or sage. Other variations: Try orange or lime zest instead of lemon.

Slow-Cooked Tuscan Pork with Fennel

Lean pork and an assortment of fresh Italian vegetables make for a flavorful yet healthy slow-cooker dinner.

ACTIVE TIME: 25 minutes
SLOW-COOK TIME: 7 hours on High or 10 hours on Low
MAKES: 12 main-dish servings

2   teaspoon fennel seeds
1   teaspoon dried rosemary
¾   teaspoon salt
¾   teaspoon ground black pepper
1   boneless pork shoulder (Boston butt; 4 to 5 pounds)
¾   cup chicken broth
2   teaspoons chicken base/demi-glace
2   pound red potatoes, sliced
2   medium bulbs fennel, cored and cut into wedges (reserve fronds; optional)
3   garlic cloves, chopped

1. In small bowl, combine fennel seeds, rosemary, and ½ teaspoon each salt and pepper. Cut pork shoulder into 4 equal pieces. Season pork with spice rub mixture on all sides.

2. In 6- to 7-quart slow-cooker bowl, whisk broth, demi-glace, and remaining ¼ teaspoon each salt and pepper; add potatoes, fennel, and garlic. Place meat on top of vegetables.

3. Cover and cook 7 hours on High or 10 hours on Low, until very tender. Transfer meat to cutting board. Skim and discard fat from cooking liquid. Chop fennel fronds, if using.

4. To serve, slice pork and arrange on platter with vegetables. Drizzle with cooking liquid and garnish with chopped fennel fronds, if desired.

EACH SERVING: About 355 calories, 29g protein, 16g carbohydrate, 19g total fat (7g saturated), 3g fiber, 104mg cholesterol, 350mg sodium ☺ 🍱 🍱

PERFECT VEGETABLES IN A SLOW COOKER

No one loves mushy mystery vegetables. Here's where to place them to preserve their flavor and texture.

- **Bottom Layer:** Position the densest, toughest vegetables at the bottom of the cooker, where temperatures are hightest. Think: Turnips, parsnips, carrots, potatoes, sweet potatoes, winter squash.
- **Middle Layer:** The middle is the go-to zone for semi-hardy veggies: They'll cook through there without going soft. Think: Fennel, green beans, bell peppers, celery.
- **Top Layer:** These more delicate vegetables can't hold up through hours of heat, so add them in the last 30 minutes of cooking. Think: Peas, broccoli, fresh herbs, spinach, zucchini.

Pork Chops Marsala

A lush but light wine sauce flavors these lean chops for restaurant-style richness minus the fat and calories (see "Let's Talk Marsala" on page 166). Cremini mushrooms and asparagus complete the meal.

TOTAL TIME: 25 minutes

MAKES: 4 main-dish servings

4	boneless pork loin chops (4 ounces each), trimmed of fat
½	teaspoon salt
¼	teaspoon ground black pepper
1	tablespoon olive oil
1	package (10 ounces) sliced cremini or white mushrooms
1	large shallot, chopped
½	teaspoon dried thyme, or 1½ teaspoons fresh thyme leaves
1	pound asparagus, ends trimmed
2	tablespoons water
½	cup reduced-sodium chicken broth
⅓	cup Marsala wine, preferably *semisecco*

1. Season pork chops on both sides with salt and pepper.

2. In 12-inch nonstick skillet, heat 2 teaspoons oil over medium. Add pork chops and cook 6 minutes or until browned outside and still slightly pink in center, turning over once. Instant-read thermometer inserted horizontally into chop should register 145°F. Transfer chops to platter; keep warm.

3. In same skillet, heat remaining 1 teaspoon oil 1 minute. Add mushrooms, shallot, and thyme; cook 5 minutes or until mushrooms are browned and shallot is softened.

4. Meanwhile, place asparagus in glass pie plate with water; cover and microwave on High 3 to 3½ minutes or until fork-tender. Set aside.

5. Add broth and wine to mushroom mixture in skillet; cook 2 minutes. Place chops on dinner plates; top with wine sauce. Serve with asparagus alongside.

EACH SERVING: About 230 calories, 29g protein, 6g carbohydrate, 9g total fat (2g saturated), 3g fiber, 67mg cholesterol, 460mg sodium ♥ ☺ ♥

Balsamic Roasted Pork with Berry Salad

We've paired roasted pork loin with berries, licorice-flavored fennel, and baby spinach for a colorful and satisfying no-fuss meal.

ACTIVE TIME: 25 minutes
TOTAL TIME: 35 minutes

MAKES: 4 main-dish servings

¼ cup balsamic vinegar

2 tablespoons extra-virgin olive oil

1 tablespoon Dijon mustard

2 teaspoons packed fresh oregano leaves, finely chopped

2 medium fennel bulbs (12 ounces each), each cut into ¼-inch-thick slices

1 small red onion, thinly sliced

1 pork tenderloin (1 pound)

⅝ teaspoon salt

⅛ teaspoon ground black pepper

1 pound strawberries

¼ cup packed fresh basil leaves

1 bag (5 ounces) baby spinach

½ pint blackberries

1. Preheat oven to 450°F.

2. In large bowl, with wire whisk, stir together 3 tablespoons balsamic vinegar, 1 tablespoon oil, 2 teaspoons mustard, and oregano. Add fennel, tossing until well coated. Transfer fennel to 18" by 12" jelly-roll pan, arranging on outer edges; leave remaining dressing in bowl. Add onions to bowl and toss until well coated. Transfer onions to center of pan. Add pork to same bowl and toss until coated; place on top of onions.

3. Sprinkle pork and vegetables with ¼ teaspoon salt and pepper. Roast 18 to 22 minutes or until instant-read thermometer inserted in thickest part of pork registers 140°F. Let pork stand 5 minutes.

4. While pork roasts, hull and slice strawberries. Finely chop basil; place in large bowl.

5. In bowl with basil, whisk together remaining 1 tablespoon balsamic vinegar, 1 tablespoon oil, 1 teaspoon mustard, and remaining ⅛ teaspoon salt until well combined. Thinly slice pork. Add fennel, onion, spinach, and strawberries to bowl with dressing, tossing until well mixed. Divide among serving plates. Top with berries and pork.

EACH SERVING: About 315 calories, 26g protein, 30g carbohydrate, 11g total fat (2g saturated), 10g fiber, 62mg cholesterol, 480mg sodium ☺ ♥

Maple-Glazed Sausages and Figs

Here's an easy Italian meal that combines both sweet and savory. You prepare the side of chard in the microwave.

ACTIVE TIME: 30 minutes
TOTAL TIME: 40 minutes
MAKES: 4 main-dish servings

2	tablespoons maple syrup
2	tablespoons balsamic vinegar
8	fully cooked chicken and roasted garlic sausages (two 12-ounce packages; see Tip)
8	ripe fresh figs, each cut lengthwise in half
½	large sweet onion (12 ounces), chopped
1½	pounds Swiss chard, stems sliced and leaves chopped
2	teaspoons olive oil
¼	teaspoon salt
¼	teaspoon ground black pepper

1. Preheat oven to 450°F and line cookie sheet with foil. In small bowl, stir syrup and 1 table-spoon vinegar until blended. Place sausages and figs in single layer on cookie sheet, and lightly brush with half of syrup mixture.

2. Roast sausages and figs 8 to 10 minutes or until heated through and golden, turning over and brushing with remaining syrup mixture halfway through roasting.

3. Meanwhile, place onion in microwave-safe large bowl. Cover with vented plastic wrap and microwave on High 3 minutes. Add chard to bowl; cover and microwave 9 minutes or until vegetables are tender, stirring once. Stir in oil, salt, pepper, and remaining 1 tablespoon vinegar.

4. Place 2 sausages on each plate and serve chard and figs alongside.

EACH SERVING: About 450 calories, 34g protein, 42g carbohydrate, 17g total fat (4g saturated), 7g fiber, 140mg cholesterol, 1,455mg sodium ☺

TIP: *To lower the sodium in recipe by 650 milligrams (and the calories, too), serve one sausage per person instead of two.*

Butterflied Leg of Lamb with Mint Pesto

We top this juicy, chargrilled leg of lamb with a fresh mint-and-almond pesto—a flavor match made in heaven!

ACTIVE TIME: 10 minutes
TOTAL TIME: 30 minutes plus marinating
MAKES: 12 main-dish servings

4½ cups loosely packed fresh mint leaves
2 garlic cloves, crushed with garlic press
½ cup water
⅓ cup olive oil
1 teaspoon salt
1 teaspoon coarsely ground black pepper
1 butterflied boneless leg of lamb (4 pounds), trimmed
¾ cup blanched almonds

1. In food processor with knife blade attached, pulse mint, garlic, water, oil, salt, and pepper until well blended.

2. Place lamb in 13" by 9" glass baking dish. Remove ¼ cup mint mixture from food processor; spread on lamb to coat both sides. Cover and refrigerate at least 1 hour or up to 6 hours.

3. Meanwhile, add almonds to mint mixture remaining in food processor and pulse until almonds are finely chopped. Spoon pesto into serving bowl; cover and refrigerate until ready to serve.

4. Remove lamb from refrigerator about 15 minutes before cooking. Prepare outdoor grill for direct grilling over medium heat.

5. Place lamb on hot grill rack; cover and cook 20 to 35 minutes (depending on thickness) for medium-rare, turning over once halfway through cooking and removing pieces to cutting board as they are done (see Tip). An instant-read thermometer inserted into thickest part of lamb (not touching bone) should register 140°F. (Internal temperature of lamb will rise to 145°F upon standing.)

6. When remaining lamb is done, transfer to same cutting board and let stand 10 minutes to allow juices to set for easier slicing. Serve lamb with pesto.

EACH SERVING: About 380 calories, 32g protein, 5g carbohydrate, 26g total fat (8g saturated), 4g fiber, 99mg cholesterol, 270mg sodium

TIP: *The thickness of a butterflied leg of lamb will vary; check thinner pieces early for doneness, cut off those sections as they are cooked, and place them on a cutting board. Cover with foil to keep warm.*

Pork Loin with Lemon, Thyme, and Garlic

Prepare the grilled grapes and fennel while the pork rests and the grill is still hot. The fragrance alone will bring everyone to the table.

ACTIVE TIME: 15 minutes
TOTAL TIME: 1 hour 5 minutes plus standing
MAKES: 8 main-dish servings

4	lemons
4	garlic cloves, crushed with press
2	tablespoons fresh thyme leaves, chopped
1	tablespoon olive oil
½	teaspoon salt
½	teaspoon coarsely ground black pepper
1	boneless pork loin roast (3 pounds)

1. Prepare outdoor grill for indirect grilling over medium heat.

2. From 2 lemons, grate 1 tablespoon peel and squeeze 1 tablespoon juice. Cut 2 remaining lemons into 4 wedges.

3. In small bowl, combine lemon peel and juice, garlic, thyme, oil, salt, and pepper.

4. Make 10 to 12 slits in pork about 1 inch long and ½ inch deep. Rub pork all over with lemon mixture, pushing some into slits.

5. Place pork on hot grill grate and cook over direct heat 10 minutes, turning to sear all sides. Move pork to unheated side of grill; cover and cook about 40 minutes or until meat thermometer inserted into center of pork reaches 150°F. Transfer pork to cutting board; let stand 10 minutes for easier slicing. (Internal temperature will rise 5°F to 10°F upon standing.)

6. Serve sliced pork with lemon wedges and any juices from cutting board.

EACH SERVING: About 350 calories, 35g protein, 3g carbohydrate, 21g total fat (7g saturated), 1g fiber, 112mg cholesterol, 240mg sodium

Grilled Grapes

Prepare outdoor grill for direct grilling over medium heat. Place *2 large bunches (1 pound each) red grapes*, broken into clusters if you like, on hot grill grate. Cover grill and cook grapes 4 to 5 minutes or until grapes begin to char and soften, turning occasionally. Serves 8.

EACH SERVING: About 75 calories, 1g protein, 19g carbohydrate, 1g total fat (0g saturated), 1g fiber, 0mg cholesterol, 2mg sodium ✓ ☺ ♥

Grilled Fennel

Prepare outdoor grill for direct grilling over medium heat. Trim tops from *4 large fennel bulbs*. Cut each bulb into 8 wedges; place half of wedges in microwave-safe large bowl. Cover with vented plastic wrap. Microwave on High 5 minutes. Drain liquid from bowl. Repeat with remaining fennel. (Fennel can be microwaved up to 1 day ahead and refrigerated). Place all fennel pieces in bowl; toss with 2 tablespoons olive oil and sprinkle with *½ teaspoon salt* and *½ teaspoon coarsely ground black pepper*. Place fennel on hot grill grate. Grill fennel, covered, 10 minutes or until lightly charred and tender, turning over once. Serves 8.

EACH SERVING: About 95 calories, 3g protein, 15g carbohydrate, 4g total fat (1g saturated), 6g fiber, 0mg cholesterol, 250mg sodium ✓ ☺ ♥

Leg of Lamb with Oregano and Onion

This roasted leg of lamb recipe is perfect for large family meals—and the prep is easier than you may think.

ACTIVE TIME: 30 minutes
TOTAL TIME: 2 hours 20 minutes plus standing
MAKES: 16 main-dish servings

3	lemons
3	tablespoons chopped fresh oregano leaves, plus oregano sprigs for garnish
1	tablespoon extra-virgin olive oil
3	garlic cloves, crushed with garlic press
1	teaspoon salt
½	teaspoon ground black pepper
1	whole bone-in leg of lamb (7 to 8 pounds), well trimmed
½	cup dry white wine
3	tablespoons all-purpose flour
1	can (14 ½ ounces) chicken broth

1. Preheat oven to 450°F. From 1 lemon, grate 1 tablespoon peel and squeeze 2 teaspoons juice. In small bowl, combine lemon peel and juice, oregano, oil, garlic, 1 teaspoon salt, and ½ teaspoon pepper.

2. Pat lamb dry and place, fat side up, on rack in large roasting pan (17" by 11½"). With knife, cut ½-inch-wide slits all over lamb. Rub lamb with lemon-oregano mixture, pressing into slits. Roast lamb 20 minutes. Turn oven control to 350°F, and roast 1 hour 20 minutes longer or until meat thermometer inserted into thickest part of lamb (not touching bone) reaches 140°F. (Internal temperature of lamb will rise to 145°F upon standing.)

3. Transfer lamb from roasting pan to large platter and cover with foil; let stand 15 minutes.

4. Meanwhile, prepare gravy: Remove rack from roasting pan; pour pan drippings into 2-cup measuring cup. Place roasting pan on range over two burners on medium. Add wine to roasting pan; cook 1 to 2 minutes or until brown bits are loosened, stirring. Pour wine mixture into meat juice in cup; let stand until fat separates. Spoon 2 tablespoons fat from drippings into roasting pan; skim and discard any remaining fat.

5. With wire whisk, whisk flour into fat in roasting pan and cook over medium-high, stirring constantly, until blended and almost smooth. Gradually whisk in wine mixture and chicken broth, and cook, stirring constantly, until gravy thickens slightly and begins to boil; boil 1 minute. Stir any meat juices remaining on platter into gravy. Makes about 2 cups gravy.

6. Garnish platter with lemon wedges and oregano sprigs. Carve lamb into thin slices; serve lamb with gravy and lemon wedges.

EACH SERVING: About 325 calories, 29g protein, 2g carbohydrate, 21g total fat (9g saturated), 0g fiber, 104mg cholesterol, 280mg sodium

Glazed Rosemary Lamb Chops

Try this apple-jelly and balsamic-vinegar glaze on pork, too.

ACTIVE TIME: 10 minutes
TOTAL TIME: 20 minutes
MAKES: 4 main-dish servings

8	lamb loin chops, 1 inch thick (4 ounces each)
1	large garlic clove, cut in half
2	teaspoons chopped fresh rosemary, or ½ teaspoon dried rosemary, crumbled
¼	teaspoon salt
¼	teaspoon coarsely ground black pepper
¼	cup apple jelly
1	tablespoon balsamic vinegar

1. Position rack close to heating element and preheat broiler. Rub both sides of each lamb chop with garlic; discard garlic. Sprinkle lamb with rosemary, salt, and pepper. In cup, combine apple jelly and balsamic vinegar.

2. Place chops on rack in broiling pan; broil 4 minutes. Brush chops with half of apple-jelly mixture; broil 1 minute. Turn chops over and broil 4 minutes longer. Brush chops with remaining jelly mixture and broil 1 minute longer for medium-rare or continue cooking to desired doneness. Instant-read thermometer inserted horizontally into center of chop should register at least 145°F.

3. Transfer lamb to warm platter. Skim and discard fat from drippings in pan. Serve chops with pan juices drizzled on top.

EACH SERVING: About 240 calories, 26g protein, 14g carbohydrate, 8g total fat (3g saturated), 0g fiber, 82mg cholesterol, 223mg sodium ● ☺ ♥

Vegetables & Sides

Italians love their vegetables, as evidenced by the fresh and flavorful recipes in this chapter. Classic seasonings like fresh herbs and balsamic vinegar and toppings like Parmesan cheese and toasted pine nuts make everyday vegetables extraordinary. Whether they're steamed, braised, roasted, or grilled, these side dishes are as mouthwatering as the entrées that will accompany them.

We've included Italian takes on popular vegetables, like Green Beans with Hazelnuts, Zucchini and Ham Ribbons, and Stuffed Parmesan Potatoes. If you like vegetables prepared on the grill, Grilled Eggplant Caponata or Grilled Summer Vegetables with Parmesan are sure to please—and be sure to check out our chart on how to grill and season a garden full of other vegetables, Italian style.

If you're not familiar with Italian vegetables like broccoli rabe, fennel, or escarole, we encourage you to try Garlic Broccoli Rabe, Zucchini and Pepper Ciambotta, and Garlicky Escarole with White Beans. We predict that you'll come to appreciate their flavor and versatility. For kids (or adults) in your household who are reluctant vegetable eaters, try serving Crispy Parmesan Broccoli or Balsamic-Glazed Baby Carrots. We guarantee they will clean their plates.

And, of course, we haven't forgotten the garlic bread—you'll need it when you make our Spaghetti and Meatballs (page 99). Also included is a recipe for Tomato-Herb Foccacia. Pair it with soup or salad and dinner is served.

Brussels Sprouts with Pancetta and Rosemary (recipe page 210)

Peppers Caprese

This twist on the classic Caprese salad uses peppers instead of tomatoes—it's the perfect addition to any summer meal.

TOTAL TIME: 10 minutes plus standing or chilling

MAKES: 4 side-dish servings

2	tablespoons red wine vinegar
2	tablespoons extra-virgin olive oil
½	teaspoon salt
¼	teaspoon ground black pepper
3	peppers, preferably red, orange, and yellow, cut into thin slices
⅓	cup fresh basil leaves
4	ounces *bocconcini* (small mozzarella balls)

1. Whisk vinegar, oil, salt, and black pepper in medium bowl.

2. Add peppers. Toss until well coated. Let stand 10 minutes, or refrigerate up to 4 hours.

3. Meanwhile, thinly slice basil leaves and cut *bocconcini* into 1-inch pieces.

4. Toss basil and *bocconcini* with peppers just before serving.

EACH SERVING: About 175 calories, 6g protein, 7g carbohydrate, 13g total fat (5g saturated), 1g fiber, 22mg cholesterol, 314mg sodium

Garlicky Escarole with White Beans

This Mediterranean-inspired side dish pairs crisp, mildly bitter escarole with white beans, garlic, and capers. Serve on top of toasted Italian bread for a delightful appetizer.

ACTIVE TIME: 5 minutes
TOTAL TIME: 15 minutes

MAKES: 6 side-dish servings

1	tablespoon extra-virgin olive oil
2	garlic cloves, finely chopped
¼	teaspoon crushed red pepper
2	heads escarole, chopped
⅛	teaspoon salt
⅛	teaspoon ground black pepper
1	can (14½ ounces) white kidney beans (cannellini), rinsed and drained
1	tablespoon capers, drained and chopped

Heat oil in 12-inch skillet over medium. Add garlic and crushed red pepper. Cook 1 minute, stirring. Add escarole, salt, and pepper. Cook 3 to 4 minutes or until wilted, stirring and tossing. Stir in beans and capers; cook 2 minutes.

EACH SERVING: About 80 calories, 5g protein, 16g carbohydrate, 3g total fat (0g saturated), 8g fiber, 0mg cholesterol, 234mg sodium

Zucchini and Ham Ribbons

Shave zucchini into thin ribbons for this no-cook summer salad, which is flavored with a fresh pistachio pesto.

TOTAL TIME: 20 minutes

MAKES: 4 main-dish servings

2	pounds zucchini (5 small), ends trimmed
4	slices deli ham (1 ounce each), sliced into ½-inch ribbons
1	lemon
⅔	cup salted pistachios, shells removed
⅓	cup packed fresh basil leaves
⅓	cup packed fresh mint leaves
1	garlic clove
⅛	teaspoon salt
3	tablespoons extra-virgin olive oil
2	tablespoons water
8	slices whole-wheat baguette, toasted
1½	ounces goat cheese, softened
⅛	teaspoon ground black pepper

1. With vegetable peeler, peel zucchini into wide ribbons. Transfer zucchini ribbons to large bowl and add ham. If making ahead, cover and refrigerate up to 1 day. From lemon, grate 1 teaspoon peel and squeeze 2 tablespoons juice. Cover and refrigerate lemon peel.

2. In food processor with knife blade attached, pulse pistachios until finely chopped. Add basil, mint, garlic, lemon juice, and salt. Process until finely chopped. With machine running, slowly drizzle in oil and water. Puree until smooth, scraping down sides if necessary. If making pesto ahead, cover and refrigerate up to 1 day.

3. To serve, spread each slice toasted baguette with about 1 teaspoon goat cheese. Sprinkle reserved lemon peel and pepper over toasts. Add pesto to zucchini and ham; toss until well combined. Serve with goat cheese toasts.

EACH SERVING: About 380 calories, 15g protein, 25g carbohydrate, 27g total fat (5g saturated), 3g fiber, 20mg cholesterol, 650mg sodium ☑ ☺ 🍴

Asparagus Gremolata

For this fresh-as-spring side, blanched asparagus is blanketed with a lemony herbed bread crumb mix.

ACTIVE TIME: 20 minutes
TOTAL TIME: 30 minutes
MAKES: 6 side-dish servings

2	pounds jumbo asparagus
2¼	teaspoons salt
1	garlic clove, finely chopped
4	teaspoons extra-virgin olive oil
1	teaspoon freshly grated lemon peel
¼	cup panko (Japanese-style bread crumbs)
¼	cup finely chopped fresh flat-leaf parsley leaves
¼	teaspoon freshly ground black pepper

1. Trim asparagus and peel if necessary. Heat large covered saucepot of *water* to boiling on high. Fill large bowl with ice and water.

2. Add 1 teaspoon salt, then asparagus, to boiling water. Cook uncovered 5 to 6 minutes or until asparagus is bright green and knife pierces thickest part of stalk easily. With tongs, transfer directly to bowl of ice water. When asparagus is cool, drain well. Roll between paper towels to dry completely. Asparagus can be refrigerated in an airtight container or resealable plastic bag up to overnight.

3. In 12-inch skillet, combine garlic, 1 tablespoon oil, and ½ teaspoon lemon peel. Cook over medium heat 2 minutes or until golden, stirring occasionally. Add panko and cook 1 to 2 minutes or until golden and toasted, stirring frequently. Transfer to small bowl; wipe out skillet.

4. In same skillet, combine boiled asparagus, *1 tablespoon water*, and remaining 1 teaspoon oil. Cook on medium 2 to 5 minutes or until heated through, turning frequently. Transfer to platter.

5. Stir parsley, remaining ½ teaspoon lemon peel, remaining ¼ teaspoon salt, and pepper into panko mixture. Spoon over asparagus.

EACH SERVING: About 65 calories, 2g protein, 7g carbohydrate, 4g total fat (1g saturated), 2g fiber, 0mg cholesterol, 140mg sodium ♥ ☺ ♥ ▤

Garlic Broccoli Rabe

Here's a classic preparation for a leafy green vegetable that's a favorite in Italy. If broccoli rabe is too bitter for your taste, stir in a little balsamic vinegar when you add the salt.

TOTAL TIME: 15 minutes

MAKES: 4 side-dish servings

1	pound broccoli rabe
2	tablespoons extra-virgin olive oil
2	garlic cloves, thinly sliced
¼	teaspoon crushed red pepper
½	teaspoon kosher salt

1. Trim ends of broccoli rabe and cut each stem into 2 or 3 pieces. Bring large pot of *water* to boil; add broccoli rabe. Cook 2 to 3 minutes, until firm-tender and bright green; drain.

2. Wipe out pot; add oil, garlic, and crushed red pepper. Cook over medium heat, stirring, until garlic is lightly golden, about 2 minutes. Add broccoli rabe and salt; cook 2 minutes longer, tossing with tongs, until just tender.

EACH SERVING: About 95 calories, 4g protein, 5g carbohydrate, 7g total fat (1g saturated), 2g fiber, 0mg cholesterol, 279mg sodium 🌿 😋 🖤

LET'S TALK BROCCOLI RABE

Related to both the cabbage and the turnip families, leafy dark green rabe has long stalks and scattered clusters of tiny broccoli-like buds. Although it's pungent flavor is not particularly popular in the U.S., Italians are fond of this vegetables and cook it in a variety of ways, from steaming to braising. It is also featured in soups and pastas.

Available year-round in specialty food markets and increasingly in supermarkets, broccoli rabe should be wrapped in a plastic bag with a few holes poked in it and refrigerated in the crisper drawer for up to three days. To prepare, trim steams and discard any tough leaves. Wash in several changes of cold water to remove any grit. Cook it like any other leafy green.

Green Beans
with Hazelnuts

A hint of lemon and lots of crunchy hazelnuts lend Italian flair to this classic side dish.

ACTIVE TIME: 20 minutes
TOTAL TIME: 35 minutes

MAKES: 8 side-dish servings

1½ teaspoons salt
2   pounds green beans, trimmed
2   tablespoons butter or margarine
½   cup hazelnuts (filberts), toasted and skinned (see Tip), chopped
1   teaspoon freshly grated lemon peel
¼   teaspoon ground black pepper

1. In 12-inch skillet, heat *1 inch water* and 1 teaspoon salt to boiling over high. Add green beans and heat to boiling. Cover and cook until tender-crisp, 6 to 8 minutes. Drain; wipe skillet dry with paper towels.

2. In same skillet, melt butter over medium heat. Add hazelnuts and cook, stirring, until butter just begins to brown, about 3 minutes. Add green beans, lemon peel, remaining ½ teaspoon salt, and pepper. Cook, stirring, until heated through, about 5 minutes.

EACH SERVING: About 145 calories, 3g protein, 9g carbohydrate, 12g total fat (4g saturated), 3g fiber, 16mg cholesterol, 356mg sodium ☺ ▭

TIP: *Spread hazelnuts in single layer on rimmed baking pan. Bake in 350°F oven until any portions without skin begin to brown, 10 to 15 minutes, stirring occasionally. Transfer nuts to a clean, dry kitchen towel and rub them until skins come off.*

Swiss Chard,
Sicilian Style

A simple side dish of leafy greens and onions gets a burst of salty-sweet flavor from raisins and toasted pine nuts, which are known as pignoli *in Italy.*

TOTAL TIME: 30 minutes

MAKES: 6 side-dish servings

1   large bunch (1¼ pounds) Swiss chard, rinsed well
1   tablespoon olive oil
1   small onion, chopped
¼   cup golden raisins
¼   teaspoon salt
2   tablespoons pine nuts *(pignoli)*, toasted

1. Trim and discard tough stem ends from chard. Cut center ribs and tender stems from leaves, then slice ribs and stems into ½-inch pieces; set aside. Slice leaves into 2-inch pieces; transfer to colander to drain well.

2. In 7- to 8-quart Dutch oven, heat oil over medium. Add onion and chard ribs and stems, and cook 7 to 9 minutes or until tender, stirring occasionally. Add drained chard leaves, raisins, and salt; cover and cook 2 to 3 minutes or until leaves are tender. Remove Dutch oven from heat; stir in pine nuts.

EACH SERVING: About 80 calories, 3g protein, 10g carbohydrate, 4g total fat (1g saturated), 2g fiber, 0mg cholesterol, 275mg sodium ◕ ☺ ♥

Brussels Sprouts with Pancetta and Rosemary

This mini member of the cabbage family gains stature when partnered with robust Italian ingredients like pancetta and fresh rosemary. For photo, see page 202.

ACTIVE TIME: 20 minutes
TOTAL TIME: 25 minutes
MAKES: 8 side-dish servings

3   containers (10 ounces each) Brussels sprouts
1½   teaspoons salt
1   tablespoon olive oil
2   ounces pancetta, chopped (½ cup)
1   teaspoon chopped fresh rosemary
½   teaspoon ground black pepper
¼   cup pine nuts (*pignoli*), toasted

1. Pull off yellow or wilted leaves from Brussels sprouts; trim stem ends. Cut each sprout in half. In covered 5- to 6-quart saucepot, heat *3 quarts water* and 1 teaspoon salt to boiling on high. Fill large bowl with ice water and place nearby.

2. Add Brussels sprouts to boiling water and cook, uncovered, 5 minutes. Drain. Plunge Brussels sprouts into ice water bath to chill quickly. Drain well. If not continuing with recipe right away, place sprouts in resealable plastic bags and refrigerate until ready to use.

3. In 12-inch skillet, heat oil over medium. Add pancetta and cook 2 to 3 minutes or until beginning to brown. Stir in rosemary and cook 1 minute.

4. To mixture in skillet, add Brussels sprouts, pepper, and remaining ½ teaspoon salt, and cook on medium-high 5 minutes or until heated through, stirring frequently. Add pine nuts; toss to combine.

EACH SERVING: About 110 calories, 5g protein, 9g carbohydrate, 7g total fat (2g saturated), 4g fiber, 4mg cholesterol, 230mg sodium 🟢 ☺ ♥ 🗂

BRUSSELS SPROUTS WITH BROWN BUTTER AND CHESTNUTS: Prepare Brussels sprouts as described above in steps 1 and 2. In step 3, omit olive oil, pancetta, and rosemary; melt *2 tablespoons butter* (no substitutions) in skillet over medium heat. Add *1 finely chopped small onion* and cook until translucent, about 4 minutes, stirring frequently. Add *1 ½ cups coarsely chopped roasted, peeled chestnuts* (from about 1 pound whole chestnuts), or *1 jar (7 to 7½ ounces) roasted chestnuts*, chopped, and cook 5 minutes longer or until butter just begins to brown, stirring occasionally. Complete recipe as in step 4, substituting *¼ cup chopped fresh parsley* and *2 teaspoons fresh lemon juice* for pine nuts.

EACH SERVING: About 110 calories, 4g protein, 18g carbohydrate, 4g total fat (2g saturated), 5g fiber, 8mg cholesterol, 245mg sodium 🟢 ☺ ♥ 🗂

Cauliflower with Golden Raisins and Pine Nuts

This Sicilian-inspired side dish has just a touch of anchovy for authentic flavor. If you prefer to omit the anchovy, add a little more salt.

ACTIVE TIME: 20 minutes
TOTAL TIME: 35 minutes

MAKES: 6 side-dish servings

8	cups water
1	large head cauliflower (2½ pounds), cut into 1½-inch flowerets
2¼	teaspoons salt
2	tablespoons olive oil
2	garlic cloves, crushed with side of chef's knife
1	teaspoon anchovy paste (optional)
¼	teaspoon crushed red pepper
¼	cup golden raisins
2	tablespoons pine nuts (*pignoli*), lightly toasted
1	tablespoon chopped fresh parsley

1. In 5-quart Dutch oven, bring water to boiling over high heat. Add cauliflower and 2 teaspoons salt; return to boiling. Cook until tender, 5 to 7 minutes; drain. Wipe Dutch oven dry.

2. In same Dutch oven, heat oil over medium. Add garlic and cook until golden. Add anchovy paste, if using, and crushed red pepper; cook 15 seconds. Add cauliflower, raisins, pine nuts, and remaining ¼ teaspoon salt; cook, stirring, until heated through, about 2 minutes. To serve, sprinkle with parsley.

EACH SERVING: About 95 calories, 2g protein, 9g carbohydrate, 6g total fat (1g saturated), 2g fiber, 0mg cholesterol, 401mg sodium ☺

LET'S TALK CAULIFLOWER

Cauliflower is composed of bunches of tiny creamy white flowerets on clusters of stalks the same color. The entire white portion is edible. Available year round, purple or green cauliflower occasionally shows up at farmers' markets. Choose a firm cauliflower with compact flowerets with no brown spots or flowering buds; the leaves should be crisp and green with no signs of yellowing.

To store, place cauliflower in a plastic bag with a few holes poked in it. Refrigerate in the crisper drawer for up to 5 days. To prepare, remove the leaves and cut out the core. Separate the head into flowerets or leave whole. Rinse under cold water. Often steamed or boiled, cauliflower is also delicious roasted until caramelized on the outside and meltingly tender inside.

Zucchini and Pepper Ciambotta

Ciambotta is a versatile vegetable stew—ingredients can vary according to what you have on hand. We love it with some prosciutto and crusty bread served alongside. It also makes a delicious accompaniment to roasted chicken, fish, or meat.

ACTIVE TIME: 35 minutes
TOTAL TIME: 1 hour

MAKES: 6 main-dish servings

2	tablespoons extra-virgin olive oil
1	large onion (12 ounces), chopped
2	large fennel bulbs (1 pound each), trimmed of stems and tough outer layers, thinly sliced
3	garlic cloves, finely chopped
1	large red pepper (10 ounces), cut into 1-inch pieces
1	can (28 ounces) whole tomatoes in juice
4	medium zucchini (8 ounces each), cut into ½-inch chunks
1	pound green beans, trimmed and cut into 1-inch pieces
½	teaspoon salt
⅔	cup loosely packed fresh basil leaves, thinly sliced

1. In 5- to 6-quart Dutch oven, heat oil on medium until hot. Add onion and fennel; cook 15 minutes or until vegetables are lightly browned and tender, stirring occasionally. Add garlic and red pepper, and cook 5 to 7 minutes or until pepper is tender-crisp.

2. Add tomatoes with their juice, zucchini, green beans, and salt; heat to boiling on medium-high, stirring and breaking up tomatoes with side of spoon. Reduce heat to medium-low; cover and simmer 25 to 30 minutes or until all vegetables are very tender. Stir in all but 2 tablespoons basil; top with remaining basil to serve.

EACH SERVING: About 160 calories, 6g protein, 28g carbohydrate, 6g total fat (1g saturated), 10g fiber, 0mg cholesterol, 430mg sodium ☺ ♥ ▭

LET'S TALK FENNEL

Known as *finochio* in Italy, fennel has a celerylike texture and a mild licorice flavor that is accentuated by roasting. A delicious addition to pastas and braises or shaved raw and tossed into salads, it is readily available from September through April. Chose firm, compact, unblemished bulbs. The fronds, if attached, should be bright green and sprightly; they can be used as a garnish. Refrigerate fennel in the crisper drawer for up to three days.

To prepare this vegetable, start by trimming off the fronds, if attached. Rinse the bulb under cold running water, then trim the root end and remove the stalks. Cut the bulb lengthwise into wedges or slices as recipe directs, discarding the central core.

Crispy Parmesan Broccoli

Salty Parmesan cheese and a hit of citrus boost the flavor of simple roasted broccoli.

ACTIVE TIME: 5 minutes
TOTAL TIME: 25 minutes
MAKES: 4 side-dish servings

1	pound broccoli flowerets
1	tablespoon olive oil
¼	teaspoon salt
¼	teaspoon ground black pepper
¼	cup freshly grated Parmesan cheese
¼	cup panko (Japanese-style bread crumbs)
2	teaspoons olive oil
1	teaspoon finely grated lemon peel

1. On jelly-roll pan, toss broccoli with 1 tablespoon oil, salt, and pepper.

2. Roast in 450°F oven 15 minutes. Meanwhile, combine Parmesan, panko, oil, and lemon peel.

3. Sprinkle panko mixture over broccoli; roast 3 to 5 minutes longer or until broccoli is tender and crumbs are golden brown.

EACH SERVING: About 130 calories, 6g protein, 11g carbohydrate, 8g total fat (2g saturated), 3g fiber, 4mg cholesterol, 265mg sodium 🌣 ☺ ♥

Balsamic-Glazed Baby Carrots

This recipe is perfect for a family dinner or a large dinner party; the balsamic glaze adds a burst of Italian flavor to everyday carrots.

ACTIVE TIME: 15 minutes
TOTAL TIME: 45 minutes
MAKES: 8 side-dish servings

2	pounds trimmed baby carrots, with 1 inch green steam left on, if you like (see Tip)
1	tablespoon olive oil
¼	teaspoon salt
½	teaspoon ground black pepper
2	tablespoons white or traditional balsamic vinegar
1	tablespoon sugar

1. Preheat oven to 400°F. With vegetable brush, scrub carrots and rinse under cold water. Pat dry with paper towels.

2. In 15½" by 10½" jelly-roll pan, toss carrots with oil, salt, and pepper. Roast 25 minutes. Stir in vinegar and sugar until carrots are coated. Roast 6 to 8 minutes longer or until carrots are tender and sugar has dissolved.

EACH SERVING: About 65 calories, 1g protein, 11g carbohydrate, 2g total fat (0g saturated), 2g fiber, 0mg cholesterol, 110mg sodium ☺ ♥

TIP: *In springtime, bunches of fresh baby carrots should be readily available at supermarkets and farmers' markets. If not, use 2 pounds medium carrots, quartered lengthwise, then halved crosswise. We don't recommend using prepackaged "baby" carrots; they require a much longer roasting time, and we've found they don't caramelize as well.*

Spaghetti Squash with Olives and Pecorino

Cook spaghetti squash the no-fuss way using the microwave—then just scrape it into strands, garnish, and serve.

ACTIVE TIME: 10 minutes
TOTAL TIME: 25 minutes plus cooling
MAKES: 4 side-dish servings

1   small spaghetti squash (2½ pounds)
¼   cup Kalamata olives, pitted and chopped
3   tablespoons freshly grated Pecorino-Romano cheese
2   tablespoons chopped fresh parsley
1   tablespoon olive oil
2   teaspoons red wine vinegar

1. With fork, pierce squash all over. On plate, microwave squash on High 14 minutes or until tender; let cool. Cut squash in half lengthwise; discard seeds.

2. With fork, scrape squash lengthwise to separate into strands; place strands in medium bowl. Mix in olives, Pecorino, parsley, oil, and vinegar.

EACH SERVING: About 125 calories, 4g protein, 12g carbohydrate, 8g total fat (2g saturated), 3g fiber, 8mg cholesterol, 252mg sodium ☺ ♥

Stuffed Parmesan Potatoes

Seasoned with fresh basil and Parmesan, these twice-cooked potatoes are crowd-pleasers.

ACTIVE TIME: 5 minutes
TOTAL TIME: 35 minutes
MAKES: 6 side-dish servings

3   medium russet potatoes (8 ounces each), scrubbed and pierced with a fork
½   cup heavy cream
½   cup freshly grated Parmesan cheese
5   fresh basil leaves, chopped
⅛   teaspoon dried thyme
½   teaspoon salt
½   teaspoon ground black pepper

1. Place potatoes in 2-quart baking dish; cover with vented plastic wrap. Microwave on High 17 minutes or until tender. Cut each in half; scoop flesh into bowl. Cut slices off bottoms.

2. Preheat oven to 425°F. Mash potato flesh with cream, ¼ cup Parmesan, basil, thyme, salt, and pepper. Spoon into potato halves; place in baking dish.

3. Top with remaining ¼ cup grated Parmesan. Bake 15 minutes.

EACH SERVING: About 180 calories, 5g protein, 19g carbohydrate, 9g total fat (6g saturated), 2g fiber, 33mg cholesterol, 312mg sodium 🍲

Grilled Summer Vegetables with Parmesan

This mélange of best-of-summer vegetables is lightly brushed with a red-wine vinaigrette before it hits the grill. Fresh basil and Parmesan shavings top off the dish.

ACTIVE TIME: 20 minutes
TOTAL TIME: 30 minutes

MAKES: 8 side-dish servings

3	tablespoons red wine vinegar
1	garlic clove, crushed with garlic press
¾	teaspoon salt
¼	teaspoon coarsely ground black pepper
¼	cup olive oil
2	pounds plum tomatoes, each cut lengthwise in half
2	red peppers, each cut lengthwise into quarters
2	medium zucchini (8 ounces each), cut crosswise into ½-inch-thick slices
1	large eggplant (1½ pounds), cut crosswise into ½-inch-thick slices
1	large onion (12 ounces), cut into ½-inch-thick slices
½	cup loosely packed fresh basil leaves, chopped
2	ounces Parmesan cheese

1. Prepare outdoor grill for covered, direct grilling on medium heat.

2. Prepare vinaigrette: In small bowl, whisk together vinegar, garlic, salt, and pepper. In slow, steady stream, whisk in oil until blended.

3. On two jelly-roll pans, lightly brush tomatoes, peppers, zucchini, eggplant, and onion slices with some vinaigrette. With tongs, transfer vegetables to hot grill grate. Cover grill and cook until all vegetables are tender and lightly charred on both sides. Cook tomatoes about 6 minutes; peppers, zucchini, and eggplant about 8 minutes; and onion about 12 minutes. Return cooked vegetables to jelly-roll pans.

4. To serve, on platter, arrange grilled vegetables; drizzle with remaining vinaigrette and sprinkle with basil. With vegetable peeler, shave Parmesan into large pieces over vegetables.

EACH SERVING: About 155 calories, 4g protein, 16g carbohydrate, 10g total fat (3g saturated), 5g fiber, 8mg cholesterol, 320mg sodium

VEGETABLES ON THE GRILL

For a summery side dish, nothing's easier than grilling peak-season produce. All you do: Prep veggies as directed, lightly brush with olive oil, and sprinkle with salt. Arrange in a single layer on a medium-high grill, cook for the time indicated, and season Italian-style as directed.

	PREP, GRILL . . .	. . . THEN SEASON
Bell Peppers (4 medium)	Remove seeds, cut lengthwise into eighths; grill 6 to 8 minutes per side.	Toss with 1 tablespoon balsamic vinegar and 1 tablespoon capers.
Red or Yellow Onions (4 medium)	Cut crosswise into ½-inch-thick slices; grill 8 to 10 minutes per side.	Sprinkle with 3 tablespoons finely chopped roasted red pepper and 8 basil leaves, sliced.
Green Beans (8 ounces)	Trim, then wrap in double layer of heavy-duty foil and seal edges tightly; grill 8 to 10 minutes per side.	Before grilling, to packet, sprinkle 1 garlic clove, chopped, and ¼ teaspoon ground black pepper.
Radicchio (1 large head)	Cut lengthwise into eight wedges; grill 4 to 5 minutes per side.	Sprinkle with 2 tablespoons grated Parmesan cheese and 1 tablespoon lemon juice.
Red Baby Potatoes (8 ounces)	Cut in half, then wrap in double layer of heavy-duty foil and seal edges tightly; grill 15 minutes per side.	Toss with 3 tablespoons Parmesan cheese and 2 tablespoons finely chopped parsley.
Eggplant (1 medium)	Cut crosswise into ½-inch-thick slices; grill 4 to 5 minutes per side.	Drizzle with 1 tablespoon balsamic vinegar and sprinkle with 2 tablespoons chopped fresh mint.
Yellow Squash, Zucchini (4 medium)	Cut lengthwise into ½-inch-thick slices; grill 5 minutes per side.	Toss with 1 teaspoon grated orange peel.

Grilled Eggplant Caponata

Fresh tomatoes, sweet raisins, and briny capers combined with grilled onions, celery, and eggplant make this a dish you'll go back to again and again. For photo, see page 5.

ACTIVE TIME: 25 minutes
TOTAL TIME: 35 minutes

MAKES: 6 side-dish servings

2	small red onions, cut into ½-inch-thick slices
2	small eggplants (1 to 1¼ pounds each), cut into ¾-inch-thick slices

Nonstick cooking spray

4	medium stalks celery
½	teaspoon salt
2	tablespoons red wine vinegar
2	tablespoons extra-virgin olive oil
1	teaspoon sugar
¼	teaspoon coarsely ground black pepper
1½	pounds ripe plum tomatoes, cut into ½-inch chunks
1	cup Kalamata, Gaeta, or green Sicilian olives, pitted and chopped
¼	cup golden raisins
3	tablespoons drained capers
½	cup loosely packed fresh flat-leaf parsley leaves

1. Prepare outdoor grill for direct grilling over medium heat.

2. Meanwhile, for easier handling, insert metal skewers through onion slices, if you like. Lightly spray both sides of eggplant slices with cooking spray. Sprinkle onions, eggplants, and celery with salt.

3. Place onions, eggplants, and celery on hot grill rack. Cover and cook until tender and lightly browned, 8 to 10 minutes, turning over once; as vegetables are done, transfer to plate. Cool slightly until easy to handle.

4. Cut eggplants and celery into ¾-inch chunks; coarsely chop onions. In large bowl, mix vinegar, oil, sugar, and pepper until blended. Stir in tomatoes, olives, raisins, capers, and parsley. Add eggplants, onions, and celery; gently toss to coat.

5. Serve immediately, or cover and refrigerate up to one day, then return salad to room temperature before serving.

EACH SERVING: About 75 calories, 1g protein, 11g carbohydrate, 3g total fat (1g saturated), 2g fiber, 0mg cholesterol, 240mg sodium ☺ ♥ ▤

Garlic and Herb Bread

Here's a classic Italian favorite to pair with pasta. We call for dried oregano in this recipe, but if you have it, swap in 1 tablespoon chopped fresh oregano instead.

ACTIVE TIME: 5 minutes
TOTAL TIME: 20 minutes

MAKES: 10 slices

1   loaf Italian bread
2   tablespoons olive oil
2   garlic cloves, finely chopped
1   teaspoon dried oregano
1   tablespoon freshly grated Parmesan cheese

1. Preheat oven to 350°F. Slice loaf in half lengthwise. On cut sides of bread, sprinkle oil, garlic, oregano, and Parmesan.

2. Wrap bread in aluminum foil; bake 15 minutes or until top of bread is lightly browned.

EACH SLICE: About 110 calories, 3g protein, 16g carbohydrate, 4g total fat (1g saturated), 1g fiber, 0mg cholesterol, 188mg sodium 🟢 ☺ 🖤

Tomato-Herb Focaccia

A round of pizza dough is used in this recipe to make a simple focaccia bread. Serve it with some olive oil seasoned with cracked black pepper for dipping.

ACTIVE TIME: 10 minutes
TOTAL TIME: 40 minutes

MAKES: 6 side-dish servings

3   plum tomatoes, very thinly sliced
¼   teaspoon salt
2   tablespoons olive oil
2   garlic cloves, crushed with garlic press
2   teaspoons chopped fresh rosemary
1   pound pizza dough, store-bought or homemade (page 61)

1. Preheat oven to 450°F. Arrange tomatoes in single layer on paper towel. Sprinkle with ⅛ teaspoon salt. In small bowl, combine oil, garlic, rosemary, and remaining ⅛ teaspoon salt.

2. Press dough into 9" by 12" jelly-roll pan. Spread herb oil on top.

3. Blot tomatoes; place on top of dough. Bake for 30 to 40 minutes or until crust is golden brown.

EACH SERVING: About 225 calories, 7g protein, 36g carbohydrate, 6g total fat (1g saturated), 0g fiber, 0mg cholesterol, 484mg sodium 🍲

Dolci Desserts

If you love nothing better than a luscious square of tiramisù for dessert or a bag of crunchy biscotti from an Italian bakery, then this chapter is for you. You can make these traditional Italian desserts and other favorites at home. Our recipes aren't fussy or time-consuming, but the results will have you singing *amore*.

We start with cookies that you can dunk in an espresso or cappuccino, if you prefer. We offer recipes for two kinds of biscotti, walnut (with an optional white chocolate dip) and chocolate (good news: they're low fat!). The light, crisp waffle cookies known as Pizzelles are also perfect for dunking.

To beat the heat, you can make your own granita, an Italian ice that doesn't require any special equipment. Or, for a sophisticated refresher, try lemon sorbet topped with mint and Prosecco, an Italian sparkling wine. Fresh figs are the basis for two more elegant sweet treats: Drunken Chocolate Figs, which include a drizzle of port wine syrup, and Stuffed Fresh Figs, which feature ricotta sweetened with a dollop of honey.

Fresh fruit is the star of other dolci desserts, including a Peach Crostata, a rustic free-form tart that's bursting with sweet baked fruit. Or try other fruity classics like Chianti-Roasted Pears and Almond Panna Cotta with Strawberries.

For the chocolate lovers, we serve up a rich Flourless Chocolate Hazelnut Cake and a decadent Ganache Tart with a Salted Almond Crust. Grab a fork and indulge!

Berry Cheesecake (recipe page 240)

Pizzelles

These paper-thin waffle cookies are an Italian holiday tradition for both Christmas and Easter. To bake up hot stacks of them, you'll need a pizzelle iron (see Tip). For a sweet finish, sprinkle them with confectioners' sugar.

ACTIVE TIME: 30 minutes
BAKE TIME: 1 minute per batch
MAKES: about 30 pizzelles

¾   cup granulated sugar
½   cup butter or margarine (1 stick), softened
3   large eggs
2   teaspoons vanilla extract
1¾ cups all-purpose flour
1   teaspoon baking powder
Confectioners' sugar for sprinkling (optional)

1. Preheat pizzelle iron as manufacturer directs. In large bowl, with mixer on medium speed, beat sugar and butter until creamy. Reduce speed to low; beat in eggs and vanilla until blended. Beat in flour and baking powder just until well mixed, occasionally scraping bowl with rubber spatula.

2. Pour 1 rounded tablespoon batter at a time onto center of each pizzelle mold. Cover and bake as manufacturer directs (do not lift cover during baking).

3. When done, lift cover of iron and loosen pizzelles with fork. Transfer to wire racks to cool completely. Trim cookie edges with scissors if necessary. Just before serving, sprinkle with confectioners' sugar, if desired.

4. Store cookies in an airtight container up to 2 weeks, or freeze up to 3 months.

EACH PIZZELLE: About 80 calories, 1g protein, 11g carbohydrate, 4g total fat (2g saturated), 0g fiber, 30mg cholesterol, 55mg sodium ☺ ♥ ▨

TIP: *Pizzelle irons are available in various sizes in electric and stovetop models. Be sure to follow manufacturer's directions for the correct amount of batter to use in your iron.*

Pignoli Cookies

Thanks to the food processor—and prepared almond paste—making these classic Italian cookies, with their topping of pine nuts, is a breeze. Use a pastry bag to form the rounds and keep your fingers from getting sticky.

ACTIVE TIME: 25 minutes
BAKE TIME: 10 minutes per batch
MAKES: About 24 cookies

1	tube or can (7 to 8 ounces) almond paste
¾	cup confectioners' sugar
1	large egg white
4	teaspoons honey
½	cup pine nuts (*pignoli*; 3 ounces)

LET'S TALK ALMOND PASTE

This firm but pliable confection is made of blanched ground almonds and confectioner's sugar mixed with glucose, corn syrup, or egg white. It's used in many Italian cookies, from macaroons to pignoli to amarettis, which feature a bitter-almond paste. Available in 6- to 8-ounce cans or tubes, almond paste is similar to marzipan, which is sweeter and softer. If your almond paste is too hard to work with, microwave on High for a few seconds to soften. Once opened, it should be wrapped tightly and refrigerated.

1. Preheat oven to 350°F. Line two large cookie sheets with parchment paper.

2. Crumble almond paste into food processor with knife blade attached. Add sugar and process until paste has texture of fine meal; transfer to large bowl. Add egg white and honey. With mixer on low speed, beat until dough is blended. Increase speed to medium-high and beat until very smooth, about 5 minutes.

3. Spoon batter into pastry bag fitted with ½-inch round tip. Pipe 1¼-inch rounds, 2 inches apart, onto prepared cookie sheets. Brush cookies lightly with *water* and cover completely with pine nuts, pressing gently to make nuts stick.

4. Bake until golden brown, 10 to 12 minutes, rotating cookie sheets between upper and lower oven racks halfway through. Slide parchment onto wire racks and let cookies cool before peeling off paper. Repeat with remaining dough and pine nuts.

5. Store pignoli in an airtight container up to 5 days, or freeze up to 3 months.

EACH COOKIE: About 75 calories, 2g protein, 9g carbohydrate, 4g total fat (0g saturated), 0g fiber, 0mg cholesterol, 5mg sodium ☺ ♥ ⬚

Angeletti

Try eating just one of these luscious glazed cookies festooned with red, green, and white décors in honor of the Italian flag.

ACTIVE TIME: 40 minutes plus cooling and standing
BAKE TIME: 7 minutes per batch

MAKES: about 60 cookies

½   cup butter or margarine (1 stick), melted
¾   cup granulated sugar
¼   cup whole milk
1½ teaspoons vanilla extract
3   large eggs
3   cups all-purpose flour
1   tablespoon baking powder
¼   teaspoon salt
2   cups confectioners' sugar
3½ tablespoons water
½   cup assorted red, white, and green candy décors

1. Preheat oven to 375°F. Grease two large cookie sheets.

2. In large bowl, whisk butter, granulated sugar, milk, vanilla, and eggs until blended. In medium bowl, mix flour, baking powder, and salt. Stir flour mixture into egg mixture until evenly blended. Cover dough with plastic wrap or waxed paper; let stand 5 minutes.

3. With floured hands, shape dough into 1-inch balls. Place balls, 2 inches apart, on prepared cookie sheets. Bake until puffed and light brown on bottoms, 7 to 8 minutes, rotating cookie sheets between upper and lower oven racks halfway through. With wide metal spatula, transfer cookies to wire rack to cool. Repeat with remaining dough.

4. When cookies are cool, in small bowl, whisk confectioners' sugar and water until blended. Dip top of each cookie into glaze. Place cookies on wire rack set over waxed paper to catch any drips. Immediately sprinkle cookies with décors. Allow glaze to set, about 20 minutes.

5. Store cookies in an airtight container, with waxed paper between layers, up to 5 days, or freeze up to 3 months.

EACH COOKIE: About 75 calories, 1g protein, 13g carbohydrate, 2g total fat (1g saturated), 0g fiber, 15mg cholesterol, 55mg sodium ☺ ♥ ▤

Walnut Biscotti

Crisp and nutty, these twice-baked cookies are an Italian classic. First the dough is baked in a loaf, then it's sliced and baked again to create crisp treats that are just the thing for dipping in coffee or dessert wine. To dress them up, dunk the biscotti in melted white chocolate, if you like.

ACTIVE TIME: 40 minutes
BAKE TIME: 50 minutes plus cooling
MAKES: about 3 dozen biscotti

2   cups all-purpose flour
1½   teaspoons baking powder
¼   teaspoon salt
½   cup (1 stick) butter, no substitutions, softened
⅓   cup granulated sugar
⅓   cup packed brown sugar
2   large eggs
1   tablespoon vanilla extract
1   cup walnuts, toasted and chopped
12   ounces white chocolate (optional), melted

1. Preheat oven to 325°F. Line large cookie sheet with parchment paper.

2. On waxed paper, combine flour, baking powder, and salt.

3. In large bowl, with mixer on medium speed, beat butter and both sugars until creamy. Add eggs, one at a time, beating well after each addition. Beat in vanilla. Reduce speed to low; gradually beat in flour mixture just until blended, occasionally scraping bowl. Stir in walnuts.

4. Divide dough in half. Form each half into 1½-inch-wide log and place logs on prepared sheet, 3 inches apart.

5. Bake 30 minutes or until golden brown. Cool on pan on wire rack 5 minutes.

6. Slide logs onto cutting board. With serrated knife, cut each log crosswise into ½-inch-thick diagonal slices; place, cut side down, on same cookie sheet. Bake 20 to 25 minutes or until golden brown and crisp. Cool completely on pan on wire rack.

7. If you like, dip half of each cookie into melted chocolate. Let harden on waxed paper. Store cookies in airtight containers, with waxed paper between layers if dipped, up to 1 week, or freeze up to 1 month.

EACH BISCOTTO: About 90 calories, 2g protein, 10g carbohydrate, 5g total fat (2g saturated), 0g fiber, 17mg cholesterol, 45mg sodium 😊 ♥ 🍴

SHAPING BISCOTTI

Here's how to shape and bake these crunchy Italian cookies.

1. Drop the dough by spoonfuls down the length of the cookie sheet. With lightly floured hands, flatten and shape it into a log of even thickness.
2. After the first baking, slice the slightly cooled loaf with a serrated knife, using a gentle but confident sawing motion.

Crunchy Low-Fat Chocolate Biscotti

Don't skip dessert just because you've enjoyed a hearty Italian meal: Here, we use egg whites instead of whole eggs and vegetable oil instead of butter to create a lighter biscotti with a satisfying crunch.

ACTIVE TIME: 30 minutes
BAKE TIME: 50 minutes plus cooling
MAKES: about 48 biscotti

3	large egg whites
⅓	cup vegetable oil
2	tablespoons strong brewed coffee
1	teaspoon vanilla extract
1⅔	cups all-purpose flour
¾	cup sugar
½	cup unsweetened cocoa
1	teaspoon baking powder
¼	teaspoon baking soda
¼	teaspoon salt
⅓	cup chopped hazelnuts or other nuts, toasted (see Tip, page 208)
⅓	cup dried tart cherries

1. Preheat oven to 350°F. Lightly grease large cookie sheet.

2. In small bowl, beat together egg whites, oil, coffee, and vanilla.

3. In large bowl, stir together flour, sugar, cocoa, baking powder, baking soda, salt, nuts, and cherries until well mixed. Pour egg mixture over dry ingredients and stir until combined. Shape dough into two 12" by 1" logs; place both on prepared cookie sheet and flatten slightly. Bake 30 minutes or until toothpick inserted in center comes out clean. Cool logs on cookie sheet on wire rack 10 minutes.

4. Transfer 1 log to cutting board. Cut diagonally into scant ½-inch-thick slices. Lay slices out flat on ungreased cookie sheet. Repeat with remaining log, using second sheet if necessary. Bake until dry, 20 minutes, rotating cookie sheets between upper and lower oven racks halfway through, if using two sheets. Using wide metal spatula, transfer biscotti to wire racks to cool.

5. Store biscotti in an airtight container up to 2 weeks, or freeze up to 3 months.

EACH BISCOTTO: 50 calories, 1g protein, 8g carbohydrate, 2g total fat (1g saturated), 1g fiber, 0mg cholesterol, 30mg sodium ☺ ♥ ▭

Drunken Chocolate Figs

Dipped in dark chocolate and drizzled with a made-in-minutes port syrup, fiber-rich fresh figs instantly transform into a simple-meets-sophisticated finale to summer supper.

ACTIVE TIME: 10 minutes
TOTAL TIME: 25 minutes plus chilling
MAKES: 4 servings

1	cup ruby port wine
½	cup sugar
1	cinnamon stick
3	ounces bittersweet chocolate (see box, page 243)
12	fresh ripe green or black figs

1. In heavy-bottomed 2-quart saucepan, bring port, sugar, and cinnamon stick to boiling over high heat. Reduce heat to medium and cook 13 minutes, stirring frequently to prevent syrup from boiling over (syrup will reduce by half). Let cool to room temperature (syrup will thicken).

2. Meanwhile, line cookie sheet with waxed paper. Place chocolate in microwave-safe small bowl or cup. Heat, covered with waxed paper, in microwave on High 1 minute or until chocolate is almost melted. Stir until smooth.

3. Hold 1 fig by stem and dip into melted chocolate, leaving top half uncovered. Shake off excess chocolate. Place chocolate-covered fig on prepared cookie sheet. Repeat with remaining figs and chocolate.

4. Place chocolate-covered figs in refrigerator 15 minutes or until chocolate is set. Figs will keep at room temperature up to 2 hours. If not serving right away, refrigerate up to 12 hours. To serve, arrange figs on dessert plates and drizzle with port syrup.

EACH SERVING: About 350 calories, 3g protein, 73g carbohydrate, 8g total fat (5g saturated), 7g fiber, 8mg cholesterol, 5mg sodium

Stuffed Fresh Figs

If you're lucky enough to have a fig tree, or to find ripe figs at your market, try this recipe.

TOTAL TIME: 25 minutes

MAKES: 6 servings

19	small ripe figs (1¼ pounds)
¼	cup pure honey
½	cup part-skim ricotta cheese, store-bought or homemade (page 15)
¼	cup natural almonds, toasted and chopped

1. On plate, with fork, mash ripest fig with honey; set aside.

2. With sharp knife, trim stems from remaining figs, then cut a deep X in top of each, making sure not to cut through to bottom. Gently spread each fig open to make "petals."

3. In small bowl, combine ricotta and almonds. With back of spoon, press fig and honey mixture through sieve into 1-cup measure.

4. To serve, spoon ricotta mixture into figs. Arrange figs on platter. Drizzle with fig honey.

EACH SERVING: About 170 calories, 4g protein, 32g carbohydrate, 4g total fat (1g saturated), 4g fiber, 6mg cholesterol, 25mg sodium 🌿 ♥

LET'S TALK HONEY

There are hundreds of different honeys from around the world, most of them named for the flower from which they originate. The color and flavor of each honey is derived from the flowers' nectar, used by bees to make the honey. In general, the darker the honey, the stronger the flavor. Clover honey is popular in the U.S. for its light delicate fragrance and flavor.

Bold Berry Granita

Coffee Granita

This simple Italian dessert is similar to sorbet but has a coarser texture. This coffee-flavored version is a Neapolitan tradition. Substitute decaffeinated coffee, if you prefer.

TOTAL TIME: 5 minutes plus freezing

MAKES: 4 servings

⅔	cup sugar
2	cups hot coffee

1. Dissolve sugar in hot coffee. Pour mixture into 9-inch square metal pan. Cover; freeze 2 hours. Stir to break up chunks. Freeze 3 hours longer.

2. To serve, with fork, scrape granita into coffee cups or bowls.

EACH SERVING: About 130 calories, 0g protein, 34g carbohydrate, 0g total fat, 0g fiber, 0mg cholesterol, 3mg sodium ☺ ♥ ▅

GRANITA KNOW-HOW

The heat-beating Italian ice known as granita doesn't require any special equipment—just a metal baking pan. Cover and freeze the mixture until partially frozen, about 2 hours. Stir it with a fork to break up the chunks. Cover it again and freeze until the mixture is completely frozen, at least 3 hours or up to overnight. To serve granita, let it stand at room temperature until slightly softened, about 15 minutes. Use a metal spoon or fork to scrape across surface, transferring the flavorful ice shards to chilled dishes or wine goblets.

Bold Berry Granita

Frosty, fruity, and fat-free, this mix of pureed raspberries and strawberries is the ultimate summer dessert.

TOTAL TIME: 20 minutes plus freezing

MAKES: 10 servings

½	cup sugar
1	cup water
2	lemons
1	pound strawberries, hulled
1½	cups raspberries

1. In saucepan, heat sugar and water to boiling, stirring until sugar dissolves. Reduce heat to low and simmer, uncovered, 5 minutes. Set aside to cool slightly.

2. Meanwhile, from lemons, grate 2 teaspoons peel and squeeze ¼ cup juice. In food processor with knife blade attached, blend berries until pureed. With back of spoon, press puree through sieve into bowl; discard seeds.

3. Stir sugar syrup, lemon juice, and lemon peel into berry puree. Pour into 9-inch square metal baking pan.

4. Cover and freeze mixture 2 hours or until frozen around edges. With fork, scrape ice at edges into center. Cover and freeze until solid, at least 3 hours or overnight.

5. To serve, let granita stand at room temperature 15 minutes. With fork, scrape across surface to form ice shards and spoon into chilled bowls.

EACH SERVING: About 60 calories, 1g protein, 15g carbohydrate, 0g total fat (0g saturated), 2g fiber, 0mg cholesterol, 0mg sodium ☺ ♥ ▅

Chianti-Roasted Pears

Bosc pears become tender and caramelized on the outside when baked with a butter-and-sugar coating and basted with red wine. This is also delicious with Marsala wine (see box, page 166).

ACTIVE TIME: 15 minutes
TOTAL TIME: 1 hour plus cooling
MAKES: 6 servings

1	large navel orange
6	Bosc pears
½	cup hearty red wine, such as Chianti
¼	cup water
¼	cup sugar
1	tablespoon butter or margarine, melted

1. Preheat oven to 450°F. With vegetable peeler, remove peel from orange in 2″ by ½″ strips. Reserve orange for another use.

2. With melon baller or small knife, remove cores and seeds from pears by cutting through blossom end (bottom) of pears; do not remove stems or peels.

3. In shallow 1½- to 2-quart glass or ceramic baking dish, combine orange peel, wine, and water. Place sugar in medium bowl. Hold pears, one at a time, over bowl of sugar with one hand. With other hand, use pastry brush to brush pears with melted butter, then sprinkle pears with sugar until coated. Stand pears in baking dish. Sprinkle any remaining sugar into baking dish around pears.

4. Bake pears 35 to 40 minutes or until tender when pierced with tip of small knife, basting occasionally with syrup in baking dish.

5. Cool pears about 30 minutes to serve warm. Or cool completely; cover and refrigerate up to 1 day. Reheat to serve warm, if you like.

EACH SERVING: About 135 calories, 1g protein, 29g carbohydrate, 3g total fat (1g saturated), 4g fiber, 5mg cholesterol, 20mg sodium ☺ ♥ 🗑

LET'S TALK PEARS

Sweet, juicy, crisp, and aromatic, pears are the star of many Italian desserts like our Chianti-Roasted Pears (above) and play supporting roles in stuffings, salads, and sides. Available year-round, pears are picked unripe, then ripen during shipping and storage. Select well-shaped, fairly firm fruit; the color depends on the variety. Avoid shriveled, discolored, cut, or bruised fruit.

For cooking, Bosc, Bartlett, or Anjou are good choices. The elegant shape of the Bosc pear makes it especially appealing for poaching. Knowing when a particular pear is ripe depends on the variety. Bartletts go from green to soft yellow; greenish brown Boscs turn the color of milk chocolate; and Anjous yield to firm pressure. Let firm pears ripen at room temperature in a brown paper bag for a few days (it may even take a week), then refrigerate and use within three to five days. Never refrigerate pears in an airtight plastic bag; the centers will turn dark brown. To prevent peeled or cut-up pears from browning, sprinkle with lemon juice.

Sgroppino Sorbet with Prosecco and Mint

Sgroppino is a classic after-dinner beverage from the Veneto region in northern Italy. It's usually made by whipping up lemon sorbet and Prosecco; a splash of vodka is sometimes added. Here we've left the sorbet intact to create a light and refreshing sparkling wine float—and topped it with a sprig of fresh mint.

TOTAL TIME: 5 minutes

MAKES: 6 servings

1	pint lemon sorbet
2	cups Prosecco (Italian sparkling wine)

Fresh mint sprigs for garnish

Divide sorbet among wineglasses or dessert bowls. Pour ⅓ cup Prosecco into each glass; garnish with mint. Serve immediately.

EACH SERVING: About 135 calories, 0g protein, 22g carbohydrate, 0g total fat, 0g fiber, 0mg cholesterol, 10mg sodium 🌀 ☺ ♥

Peach Crostata

Similar to the French galette, a crostata is a rustic freeform tart. It is traditionally formed by rolling out the dough, arranging the fruit and other fillings in the center, and folding the edges of the dough over the filling so the fruit is on display. Using a ready-to-use pie crust makes this summer dessert super-easy to prepare. For photo, see page 8.

ACTIVE TIME: 15 minutes
TOTAL TIME: 40 minutes

MAKES: 4 servings

1	pound peaches, peeled and thinly sliced
3	tablespoons packed brown sugar
1	tablespoon cornstarch
⅛	teaspoon ground ginger
1	pinch salt
1	refrigerated ready-to-use pie crust for 9-inch pie

1. Preheat oven to 425°F.

2. In large bowl, toss peaches with brown sugar, cornstarch, ginger, and salt.

3. Unroll crust on cookie sheet.

4. Arrange peach mixture on crust, leaving 2-inch border; fold border over filling. Bake 25 to 30 minutes or until crust is golden.

EACH SERVING: About 290 calories, 3g protein, 44g carbohydrate, 13g total fat (6g saturated), 1g fiber, 6mg cholesterol, 297mg sodium 🗑

Almond Panna Cotta with Strawberries

Sweet almond flavors this cool Italian custard, which is topped with vibrant red berries tossed in an optional almond liqueur for an extra layer of nutty flavor.

ACTIVE TIME: 20 minutes
TOTAL TIME: 40 minutes plus chilling

MAKES: 8 servings

1	envelope unflavored gelatin
3	tablespoons cold water
1½	cups whole milk
1	cup heavy cream
⅓	cup plus 2 tablespoons sugar
¼	teaspoon almond extract
¼	teaspoon vanilla extract
⅛	teaspoon salt
2	cups (8 ounces) strawberries, hulled and thinly sliced
2	tablespoons almond-flavored liqueur such as Amaretto (optional)
3	tablespoons sliced toasted almonds

1. In small bowl, sprinkle gelatin over water; set aside. Lightly oil eight 4-ounce custard cups or ramekins.

2. In 2-quart saucepan, heat milk, cream, ⅓ cup sugar, both extracts, and salt over high until just bubbling around edges of pan, stirring to dissolve sugar. Remove from heat and stir in gelatin mixture until dissolved.

3. Divide cream mixture among prepared cups. Refrigerate at least 4 hours or up to 1 day.

4. Meanwhile, in medium bowl, stir together strawberries, liqueur, if using, and remaining 2 tablespoons sugar.

5. Run thin-bladed knife around sides of cups; invert each cup onto small serving plate. Top with strawberries; garnish with almonds.

EACH SERVING: About 210 calories, 4g protein, 18g carbohydrate, 14g total fat (8g saturated), 1g fiber, 46mg cholesterol, 70mg sodium

LET'S TALK BERRIES

Whether you're making our Almond Panna Cotta with Strawberries (above) or Berry Cheesecake (page 240), choose ripe berries during peak season, from June through October. Berries should be plump, uniformly colored, and (with the exception of strawberries) free of stems and leaves. Avoid bruised berries and cartons that are stained with berry juice. Beware of moldy berries and don't be tempted by dewy-looking water-sprayed berries at the market; the moisture will only accelerate the decay of the berries. Frozen berries are an acceptable substitution for granitas and dessert sauces.

Berries are very perishable. You can store them in their baskets for a brief period, but to keep them for more than two days, place the (unwashed) berries in a paper towel–lined baking pan, cover loosely with paper towels, and refrigerate. Rinse fresh berries just before using.

Buttermilk Panna Cotta with Blackberry Sauce

A mixture of milk, sugar, flavorings, and gelatin, this traditional Italian custard is simple to make at home. In this recipe, we used buttermilk and blackberries to create an especially luscious and creamy dessert.

ACTIVE TIME: 15 minutes
TOTAL TIME: 25 minutes plus chilling
MAKES: 8 servings

1	envelope unflavored gelatin
¼	cup plus 2 tablespoons water
2¾	cups buttermilk
½	cup plus 4 teaspoons sugar
10	ounces frozen blackberries, thawed
1	teaspoon fresh lemon juice

1. In cup, evenly sprinkle gelatin over ¼ cup water. Let stand 2 minutes to allow gelatin to absorb liquid and soften.

2. In 3-quart saucepan, heat ½ cup buttermilk and ½ cup sugar over medium heat 2 to 3 minutes or until sugar dissolves, stirring occasionally. Reduce heat to low; whisk in gelatin. Cook 1 to 2 minutes or until gelatin dissolves, stirring. Remove saucepan from heat; stir in remaining 2¼ cups buttermilk.

3. Pour buttermilk mixture into eight 4-ounce ramekins or 6-ounce custard cups. Place ramekins in jelly-roll pan for easier handling. Cover pan with plastic wrap and refrigerate panna cotta at least 4 hours or overnight, until well chilled and set.

4. Reserve ⅓ cup blackberries for garnish. In blender, puree remaining blackberries with lemon juice and remaining 2 tablespoons water and 4 teaspoons sugar. Pour puree through sieve set over small bowl, stirring to press out fruit sauce; discard seeds. Cover and refrigerate sauce if not serving right away.

5. To unmold panna cotta, run tip of small knife around edge of ramekins. Sharply tap side of each ramekin to break seal; invert onto dessert plates. Spoon sauce around each panna cotta. Garnish with reserved berries.

EACH SERVING: 115 calories, 4g protein, 24g carbohydrate, 1g total fat (1g saturated), 1g fiber, 3mg cholesterol, 90mg sodium ☺ ♥ ▤

Flourless Chocolate Hazelnut Cake

This fudgy flourless cake boasts a creaminess reminiscent of truffles. Toasted hazelnuts folded into the batter add a delectable depth of flavor.

ACTIVE TIME: 30 minutes
TOTAL TIME: 1 hour 10 minutes
MAKES: 12 servings

1   cup hazelnuts (filberts)
1¼   cups sugar
8   squares (8 ounces) semisweet chocolate, chopped (see box, page 243)
4   tablespoons butter or margarine
5   large eggs
¾   cup heavy cream

1. Preheat oven to 350°F. Lightly grease 9-inch springform pan. Line bottom with waxed or parchment paper; grease paper.

2. Place hazelnuts in 15½" by 10½" jelly-roll pan. Bake 10 to 15 minutes or until toasted and fragrant, shaking pan occasionally. Remove pan from oven. Wrap hot hazelnuts in clean cloth towel; with hands, roll hazelnuts back and forth until as much skin as possible rubs off. Cool hazelnuts completely.

3. In food processor with knife blade attached, place ¾ cup nuts and ¼ cup sugar; pulse until finely ground. With chef's knife, roughly chop remaining nuts; set aside separately.

4. In 3-quart saucepan, melt chocolate and butter over medium-low heat, stirring occasionally. Meanwhile, in large bowl, with mixer on medium-high speed, beat eggs and ½ cup sugar 7 minutes or until tripled in volume. With rubber spatula, fold in chocolate mixture, then fold in ground-nut mixture. Pour batter into prepared pan and bake 35 minutes or until top is dry and cracked and toothpick inserted in center comes out slightly wet. Cool in pan on wire rack 10 minutes. Remove side of pan and cool 30 minutes longer on wire rack.

5. Meanwhile, line 9-inch round cake pan with foil. In pan, spread reserved chopped hazelnuts in single layer. In 12-inch skillet, spread remaining ½ cup sugar in even layer. Cook on medium-high 3 to 5 minutes or until sugar is melted and golden amber, swirling sugar in pan to cook evenly. (Do not stir.) Immediately drizzle melted sugar over nuts in pan to coat evenly. Cool praline completely in pan.

6. Meanwhile, in large bowl, with mixer on medium speed, beat cream until soft peaks form, 3 to 5 minutes.

7. To serve, break cooled praline into 12 large pieces. Cut cake and divide slices among serving plates. Top each slice with dollop of whipped cream and shard of hazelnut praline.

EACH SERVING: About 360 calories, 6g protein, 33g carbohydrate, 25g total fat (11g saturated), 2g fiber, 120mg cholesterol, 75mg sodium

Classic Tiramisù

Tiramisù is an Italian favorite—and with good reason! It's rich, delicious, and a cinch to put together.

TOTAL TIME: 35 minutes plus chilling

MAKES: 12 servings

1	cup hot espresso or very strong brewed coffee
3	tablespoons brandy
2	tablespoons plus ½ cup sugar
18	crisp Italian ladyfingers (5 ounces)
½	cup milk
1	container (16 to 17½ ounces) marscarpone cheese
¾	cup heavy or whipping cream
1½	tablespoons unsweetened cocoa

Semisweet or bittersweet chocolate curls (see Tip)

1. In 9-inch pie plate, stir coffee, brandy, and 2 tablespoons sugar until sugar has dissolved; cool to room temperature. Dip both sides of 9 ladyfingers into coffee mixture, one at a time, to soak completely; arrange in single layer in 8-inch square baking dish.

2. In large bowl, stir milk and remaining ½ cup sugar until sugar has dissolved. Stir in mascarpone until blended.

3. In small bowl, with mixer on high speed, beat cream until soft peaks form. With rubber spatula, gently fold whipped cream into mascarpone mixture until blended. Spread half of mixture over ladyfingers in baking dish.

4. Dip remaining 9 lady fingers into coffee mixture and arrange on top of mascarpone mixture. Refrigerate 3 hours or overnight.

5. Meanwhile, prepare chocolate curls.

6. Just before serving, dust tiramisù with cocoa. Cut into squares and serve garnished with chocolate curls.

EACH SERVING: About 325 calories, 4g protein, 22g carbohydrate, 23g total fat (15g saturated), 0g fiber, 55mg cholesterol, 59mg sodium 🍽

TIP: *Chocolate curls are easy to make with a Y-shaped vegetable peeler. Just scrape the peeler across the top of a block of chocolate.*

Berry Cheesecake

Cool, creamy, and topped with mixed summer berries, this lemony cheesecake is the perfect finale to a dinner party. For photo, see page 220.

ACTIVE TIME: 25 minutes
TOTAL TIME: 1 hour 30 minutes plus cooling, standing, and chilling
MAKES: 16 servings

1½ cups graham cracker crumbs

6   tablespoons butter or margarine, melted

1½ cups plus 1 tablespoon granulated sugar

2   lemons

2   packages (8 ounces each) reduced-fat cream cheese (Neufchâtel), softened

1   container (15 ounces) part-skim ricotta cheese or 1 recipe Homemade Ricotta (page 15)

3   tablespoons cornstarch

¼   teaspoon salt

2   cups half-and-half

2   teaspoons vanilla extract

1   teaspoon almond extract

4   large eggs, lightly beaten

2½ cups mixed berries (such as blackberries, raspberries, and blueberries)

1   tablespoon confectioners' sugar

1. Preheat oven to 375°F. Wrap outside of 9-inch springform pan with heavy-duty foil to prevent batter from leaking out. Spray pan with nonstick baking spray.

2. In medium bowl, combine crumbs, butter, and 1 tablespoon granulated sugar. Press firmly onto bottom of prepared pan. Bake 8 to 10 min-utes or until brown around edge. Cool on wire rack. Reset oven temperature to 325°F.

3. While crust cools, from lemons, grate 1 table-spoon peel and squeeze ¼ cup juice; set aside.

4. In stand mixer or large bowl, with mixer on high speed, beat both cheeses until smooth. Add cornstarch, remaining 1½ cups granulated sugar, and salt, scraping bowl occasionally with rubber spatula; beat on low until well incor-porated. On low speed, beat in half-and-half, vanilla and almond extracts, and lemon peel and juice. Add eggs; beat until just blended. Pour batter onto cooled crust. Bake 1 hour. Turn oven off. Let stand in oven 1 hour.

5. Place cheesecake on wire rack. Run thin knife between edge of cheesecake and pan. Cool in pan on rack 1 hour. Cover; refrigerate at least 6 hours or up to 2 days.

6. To serve, top with berries; sprinkle confec-tioners' sugar through sieve over berries.

EACH SERVING: About 345 calories, 9g protein, 34g carbohydrate, 20g total fat (11g saturated), 1g fiber, 104mg cholesterol, 260mg sodium 🍲

TIP: *For perfect slices of cheesecake—that don't stick to your knife—dip knife into warm water and wipe dry before the first cut. Then wipe knife clean, dip in warm water, and dry between slices.*

Ganache Tart with Salted-Almond Crust

Silky smooth and sprinkled with sea salt, this truffle-like tart gets its richness from deep dark chocolate and heavy cream.

ACTIVE TIME: 45 minutes
TOTAL TIME: 55 minutes plus freezing, cooling, and chilling
MAKES: 12 servings

- ½ cup roasted salted almonds
- ¾ cup (1½ sticks) butter (no substitutions), cut into tablespoons and softened
- ½ cup confectioners' sugar
- ¼ teaspoon salt
- 1 large egg yolk
- ½ teaspoon vanilla extract
- 1¼ cups all-purpose flour
- 1 cup heavy cream
- 1 pound highest-quality bittersweet chocolate (60% to 70% cacao), very finely chopped

Flaky sea salt for garnish (optional)

1. Preheat oven to 350°F.

2. In food processor, pulse almonds until finely ground. Transfer to cup. In same processor (no need to clean), pulse 6 tablespoons butter until creamy. With rubber spatula, scrape bottom and side of bowl, then add sugar and salt and pulse until smooth. Scraping down bowl after each addition, add egg yolk and vanilla and pulse until smooth. Add flour and ground almonds and pulse until mixture forms fine crumbs. Pour into 11-inch tart pan with removable bottom.

3. With fingers, firmly press crumb mixture into bottom and up side of pan to form even crust. Freeze 10 minutes. Bake crust 25 minutes or until golden brown. Cool completely on wire rack.

4. In 3-quart saucepan, heat cream to bubbling over medium. Remove from heat. Add chocolate and let stand 1 minute. With rubber spatula, stir gently until smooth. Add remaining 6 tablespoons butter, 1 tablespoon at a time, gently stirring after each addition until blended. Pour mixture into cooled crust. Gently shake tart pan to create smooth, even top.

5. Refrigerate 30 minutes to set, then let stand at room temperature until ready to serve, up to 6 hours. Garnish with sea salt if desired.

EACH SERVING: About 485 calories, 6g protein, 29g carbohydrate, 39g total fat (22g saturated), 3g fiber, 72mg cholesterol, 95mg sodium

Metric Equivalents

The recipes in this book use the standard United States method for measuring liquid and dry or solid ingredients (teaspoons, tablespoons, and cups). The information in these charts is provided to help cooks outside the U.S. successfully use these recipes. All equivalents are approximate.

METRIC EQUIVALENTS FOR DIFFERENT TYPES OF INGREDIENTS

A standard cup measure of a dry or solid ingredient will vary in weight depending on the type of ingredient. A standard cup of liquid is the same volume for any type of liquid. Use the following chart when converting standard cup measures to grams (weight) or milliliters (volume).

Standard Cup	Fine Powder (e.g., flour)	Grain (e.g., rice)	Granular (e.g., sugar)	Liquid Solids (e.g., butter)	Liquid (e.g., milk)
1	140 g	150 g	190 g	200 g	240 ml
³/₄	105 g	113 g	143 g	150 g	180 ml
²/₃	93 g	100 g	125 g	133 g	160 ml
¹/₂	70 g	75 g	95 g	100 g	120 ml
¹/₃	47 g	50 g	63 g	67 g	80 ml
¹/₄	35 g	38 g	48 g	50 g	60 ml
¹/₈	18 g	19 g	24 g	25 g	30 ml

USEFUL EQUIVALENTS FOR COOKING / OVEN TEMPERATURES

	Fahrenheit	Celsius	Gas Mark
Freeze water	32° F	0° C	
Room temperature	68° F	20° C	
Boil water	212° F	100° C	
Bake	325° F	160° C	3
	350° F	180° C	4
	375° F	190° C	5
	400° F	200° C	6
	425° F	220° C	7
	450° F	230° C	8
Broil			Grill

USEFUL EQUIVALENTS FOR LIQUID INGREDIENTS BY VOLUME

¹/₄ tsp	=					1 ml
¹/₂ tsp	=					2 ml
1 tsp	=					5 ml
3 tsp	=	1 tblsp	=	¹/₂ fl oz	=	15 ml
2 tblsp	=	¹/₈ cup	=	1 fl oz	=	30 ml
4 tblsp	=	¹/₄ cup	=	2 fl oz	=	60 ml
5¹/₃ tblsp	=	¹/₃ cup	=	3 fl oz	=	80 ml
8 tblsp	=	¹/₂ cup	=	4 fl oz	=	120 ml
10²/₃ tblsp	=	²/₃ cup	=	5 fl oz	=	160 ml
12 tblsp	=	³/₄ cup	=	6 fl oz	=	180 ml
16 tblsp	=	1 cup	=	8 fl oz	=	240 ml
1 pt	=	2 cups	=	16 fl oz	=	480 ml
1 qt	=	4 cups	=	32 fl oz	=	960 ml
				33 fl oz	=	1000 ml

USEFUL EQUIVALENTS FOR DRY INGREDIENTS BY WEIGHT

(To convert ounces to grams, multiply the number of ounces by 30.)

1 oz	=	¹/₁₆ lb	=	30 g
4 oz	=	¹/₄ lb	=	120 g
8 oz	=	¹/₂ lb	=	240 g
12 oz	=	³/₄ lb	=	360 g
16 oz	=	1 lb	=	480 g

USEFUL EQUIVALENTS FOR LENGTH

(To convert inches to centimeters, multiply the number of inches by 2.5.)

1 in	=				2.5 cm	
6 in	=	¹/₂ ft	=		15 cm	
12 in	=	1 ft	=		30 cm	
36 in	=	3 ft	=	1 yd	90 cm	
40 in	=				100 cm	= 1 m

General Index

Note: Page numbers in *italics* indicate photos of recipes located separately from respective recipes.

Almond Panna Cotta
with Strawberries, 234
Angeletti, 224
Antipasti and
other appetizers, 19–37
about: overview of, 19; quick
and easy antipasti tips, 21
Antipasti Platter, 20
Artichoke and Mint Dip, 34
Baked Ricotta with
Tomato Vinaigrette, 29
Caramelized Onion and
Goat Cheese Topping, 26
Creamy Spinach-Leek
Filling, 30
Crostini Platter, 26
Fig and Walnut Cheese Balls, 33
Giardiniera, 23
Herbed Goat Cheese Filling, 30
Honeyed Figs and Brie, 32
Lasagna Toasts, 28
Prosciutto with Melon, 37
Ricotta and Roasted
Pepper Filling, 31
Roasted Apricots and
Pistachios, 36
Roasted Prosciutto-
Wrapped Asparagus, 20
Roman-Style Artichokes, 24
Savory Tartlets with
Three Fillings, 30–31
Spiced Citrus Olives, 22–23
Spring Pea Dip, 34–35
Tomato and Mozzarella
Bites, *18*, 31
Tomato and Ricotta
Salata Bruschetta, 27
Tuna and Tomato Topping, 26
Tuscan White Bean
Bruschetta, 27
White Bean Topping, 26
Apple Coleslaw with Golden
Raisins and Pine Nuts, 79
Apricots, roasted,
and pistachios, 36

Artichokes
about: selecting
and prepping, 25
Artichoke and Mint Dip, 34
Farfalle with Baby Artichokes
and Mushrooms, 88
Roman Chicken Sauté with
Artichokes, 170–171
Roman-Style Artichokes, 24
Veggie Focaccia, 74
Arugula
Arugula and Olive Salad, 40
Lemony Mushroom
and Arugula Salad, 48
Pizza with Arugula
and Prosciutto, *58*, 67
Asparagus
Asparagus-Fontina Pizzettes
with Bacon, 64–65
Asparagus Gremolata, 206
Chicken Pasta
Primavera, 108–109
Roasted Prosciutto-
Wrapped Asparagus, 20
Spring Vegetable Risotto
with Shrimp, 128–129

Baby Romaine with
Fennel and Citrus, 79
Bacon and pancetta
about: pancetta, 103
Asparagus-Fontina Pizzettes
with Bacon, 64–65
Brussels Sprouts with Pancetta
and Rosemary, *202*, 210
Linguine with Frisée,
Bacon, and Egg, 95
Spaghetti All'Amatriciana, 107
Spaghetti Carbonara, 103
Baked Cavatelli with Sausage
and Broccoli Rabe, 116–117
Baked Eggs and Polenta with
Chunky Vegetable Sauce, 139
Baked Ricotta with
Tomato Vinaigrette, 29

Baked Snapper with Peppers
and Mushrooms, 148–149
Balsamic-Glazed Baby Carrots, 214
Balsamic Roasted Pork with
Berry Salad, 194–195
Balsamic vinaigrette, 40
Balsamic vinegar, 12
Barley
Barley Minestrone, 132–133
Butternut Squash Barley
Risotto, *124*, 131
Basil
about: preserving, 201
Classic Italian Pesto, 82
Mozzarella, Tomato,
and Basil Panini, 73
Pestos, 82, 85, 86, 133
Spaghetti with
Pesto Verde, 84–85
Bass with Tomato Paste, 156
Beans and legumes. *See
also* Green beans; Peas
about: canned, 14; cooking
dry beans, 55; Italian
use of, 14; types of, 14
Garlicky Escarole with
White Beans, 204
Italian Tuna and White
Bean Salad, 47
Lentil Stew with
Butternut Squash, 49
Mixed Vegetable
Minestrone, 50–51
Osso Bucco with
Gremolata, 190–191
Pasta e Fagioli Bake, 119
Pasta with Broccoli Rabe
and Garbanzos, 89
Tuscan White Bean
Bruschetta, 27
White Bean Panzanella
Salad, 44–45
White Bean Topping, 26
Whole-Wheat Penne
Genovese, 94

Beef. *See also* Veal
  about: thermometers for, 179
  Beef Ragu with Minted
    Penne, 100
  Braciole with Grape
    Tomatoes, 189
  Classic Bolognese
    Sauce, 105
  Fire-Grilled Steak
    with Fennel, 186–187
  Northern-Style
    Lasagna, 114–115
  Quick Bolognese, 105
  Spaghetti and Meatballs, 98–99
  Steak Pizzaiola, 185
Berries
  about, 234
  Almond Panna Cotta with
    Strawberries, 234
  Balsamic Roasted Pork with
    Berry Salad, 194–195
  Berry Cheesecake, *220*, 240
  Bold Berry Granita, *230*, 231
  Buttermilk Panna Cotta with
    Blackberry Sauce, 236
Biscotti, 225–227
Blackberries and
  blueberries. *See* Berries
Bocconcini, about, 41
Bolognese sauces, 104–105
Braciole with Grape
  Tomatoes, 189
Breads
  in appetizers. *See* Antipasti
    and other appetizers
  Garlic and Herb Bread, 219
  Tomato-Herb Focaccia, 219
Broccoli
  Broccoli and
    Mushroom Pizza, 62
  Chicago Deep-Dish-Style
    Veggie Pizza, 68–69
  Crispy Parmesan Broccoli, 214
  Shrimp Gemelli, 161
  Spaghetti with Pesto
    Verde, 84–85
Broccoli rabe
  about, 207
  Baked Cavatelli with Sausage
    and Broccoli Rabe, 116–117
  Garlic Broccoli Rabe, 207
  Pasta with Broccoli Rabe
    and Garbanzos, 89

Broiled Rosemary
  Polenta Wedges, 137
Broths, 53. *See also*
  Soups and stews
Bruschetta, 27
Brussels sprouts
  Brussels Sprouts with Pancetta
    and Rosemary, *202*, 210
  Brussels Sprouts with
    Sausage and Grapes on
    Creamy Polenta, 143
Buttermilk Panna Cotta
  with Blackberry Sauce, 236
Butternut squash. *See* Zucchini
  and other squash

Caesar salad, grilled, 43
Calamari (squid), 146, 163
Campanelle with Chicken
  and Pea-Mint Pesto, 110
Cantaloupe, in Prosciutto
  with Melon, 37
Caramelized Onion and
  Goat Cheese Topping, 26
Carrots, balsamic glazed, 214
Cauliflower
  about, 211
  Cauliflower with Golden
    Raisins and Pine Nuts, 211
  Chicken with Caramelized
    Cauliflower and
    Green Onions, 169
  Giardiniera, 23
Cheese
  about: bocconcini, 41;
    quick and easy antipasti
    tips, 21; types of, 14–15
  Antipasti Platter, 20
  Baked Ricotta with
    Tomato Vinaigrette, 29
  Berry Cheesecake, *220*, 240
  Caramelized Onion and
    Goat Cheese Topping, 26
  Fig and Walnut Cheese Balls, 33
  Herbed Goat Cheese Filling, 30
  Homemade Ricotta, 15
  Honeyed Figs and Brie, 32
  Lasagna Toasts, 28
  pasta with. *See* Pasta
  pizzas with. *See* Pizzas
    and calzones
  Red Potato, Spinach,
    and Fontina Frittata, 77

Ricotta and Roasted
  Pepper Filling, 31
salads with. *See* Salads
sandwiches with. *See*
  Panini and frittatas
Tomato and Mozzarella
  Bites, *18*, 31
Tomato and Ricotta
  Salata Bruschetta, 27
Chicago Deep-Dish-Style
  Veggie Pizza, 68–69
Chicken. *See* Poultry
Chilled Tuscan-Style
  Tomato Soup, *38*, 52
Chocolate
  Crunchy Low-Fat Chocolate
    Biscotti, 226–227
  Drunken Chocolate Figs, 228
  Flourless Chocolate
    Hazelnut Cake, 237
  Ganache Tart with Salted-
    Almond Crust, 241
Citrus
  Lemon-Oregano Chicken Cut-
    lets with Mint Zucchini, 172
  Lemony Mushroom
    and Arugula Salad, 48
  Sgroppino Sorbet with
    Prosecco and Mint, 233
  Sicilian Citrus Salsa, 159
  Spiced Citrus Olives, 22–23
Cod, 57, 151
Coffee Granita, 231
Cookies, 222–227
Corn, in Fresh Tomato, Corn,
  and Basil Risotto, 130.
  See also Polenta
Cornish Hens Milanese, 180–181
Creamy Polenta, 137
Creamy Spinach-Leek Filling, 30
Crispy Parmesan Broccoli, 214
Crostini Platter, 26
Crustless Tomato Ricotta Pie, 71

Desserts, 221–243
  about: making granitas, 231;
    overview of, 221; shaping
    biscotti, 225
  Almond Panna Cotta with
    Strawberries, 234
  Angeletti, 224
  Berry Cheesecake, *220*, 240
  Bold Berry Granita, *230*, 231

Buttermilk Panna Cotta with
    Blackberry Sauce, 236
Chianti-Roasted Pears, 232
Classic Tiramisù, 238–239
Coffee Granita, 231
Crunchy Low-Fat Chocolate
    Biscotti, 226–227
Drunken Chocolate Figs, 228
Flourless Chocolate
    Hazelnut Cake, 237
Ganache Tart with Salted-
    Almond Crust, 241
Peach Crostata, 8, 233
Pignoli Cookies, 223
Pizzelles, 222
Sgroppino Sorbet with
    Prosecco and Mint, 233
Stuffed Fresh Figs, 229
Walnut Biscotti, 225
Dips, toppings, and fillings. See
    Antipasti and other appetizers
Dressings. See Sauces and dressings
Drunken Chocolate Figs, 228

Easy Pea Risotto, 127
Eggplant
    about: grilling tips, 217
    Eggplant and Ricotta
        Baked Ziti, 123
    Grilled Eggplant
        Caponata, 7, 218
    Grilled Summer Vegetables
        and Parmesan, 216
    Ratatouille Rigatoni, 96
Eggs
    Baked Eggs and Polenta with
        Chunky Vegetable Sauce, 139
    Florentine Frittata, 78–79
    Linguine with Frisée,
        Bacon, and Egg, 95
    Spaghetti Carbonara, 103
    Stracciatella with Escarole, 53
Escarole
    Chicken and Escarole Soup, 49
    Escarole Frisée Salad, 41
    Garlicky Escarole with
        White Beans, 204
    Stracciatella with Escarole, 53

Farfalle. See Pasta
Farro
    about, 134

Farro and Mushroom
    Sauté, 135
Warm Farro Salad
    with Roasted
    Vegetables, 134
Fennel
    about, 213
    Fire-Grilled Steak with
        Fennel, 186–187
    Grilled Fennel, 198
    Roasted Halibut with Fennel
        and Potatoes, 154–155
    Shrimp and Fennel
        Spaghetti, 144, 162
Figs
    about, 32
    Drunken Chocolate Figs, 228
    Fig and Walnut Cheese Balls, 33
    Honeyed Figs and Brie, 32
    Maple-Glazed Sausages
        and Figs, 196
    Prosciutto-Wrapped
        Grilled Fig Salad, 46
    Stuffed Fresh Figs, 229
Fire-Grilled Steak with
    Fennel, 186–187
Fish and shellfish, 145–163
    about: cooking whole fish, 153;
        overview of, 145; quick
        and easy antipasti tips, 21;
        removing pin bones, 151;
        scrubbing, debearding
        mussels, 147; sea scallop
        prep, 150; shelling, deveining
        shrimp, 162
    Baked Snapper with Peppers
        and Mushrooms, 148–149
    Bass with Tomato Pesto, 156
    Cod Livornese, 151
    Farfalle Livornese
        with Tuna, 152
    Fried Calamari Fra Diavolo, 146
    Grilled Squid and Peppers
        with Arugula, 163
    Italian Tuna and
        White Bean Salad, 47
    Linguine with Red
        Clam Sauce, 157
    Mediterranean Seafood
        Stew, 56–57
    Mussels with Tomatoes
        and White Wine, 147
    Pasta with Tuna Puttanesca, 82

Roasted Halibut with Fennel
    and Potatoes, 154–155
Roast Salmon with Capers
    and Parsley, 157
Salmon and Summer Squash
    in Parchment, 158
Salt-Baked Fish, 153
Seared Scallops with Olive and
    Tomato Compote, 150
Shrimp and Fennel
    Spaghetti, 144, 162
Shrimp Gemelli, 161
Sicilian Citrus Salsa, 159
Sicilian Tuna with
    Puttanesca Sauce, 159
Spring Vegetable Risotto
    with Shrimp, 128–129
Trattoria-Style Shrimp
    Fettuccine, 160
Tuna and Tomato Topping, 26
Florentine Frittata, 78–79
Flourless Chocolate
    Hazelnut Cake, 237
Focaccia, 74, 219
Fresh Tomato, Corn,
    and Basil Risotto, 130
Fried Calamari Fra Diavolo, 146
Frittatas
    Florentine Frittata, 78–79
    Red Potato, Spinach, and
        Fontina Frittata, 77

Ganache Tart with
    Salted-Almond Crust, 241
Garlic and Herb Bread, 219
Garlic Broccoli Rabe, 206
Garlicky Escarole with
    White Beans, 204
Giardiniera, 23
Glazed Rosemary Lamb Chops, 201
Gnocchi with brown butter
    and fresh herbs, 111
Grains. See also Polenta; Risotto
    about: farro, 134;
        overview of, 125
    Farro and Mushroom
        Sauté, 135
    Orzo Salad with Grape
        Tomatoes and Mint, 136
    Warm Farro Salad with Roasted
        Vegetables, 134
Granitas, 230–231

Grapes
    Brussels Sprouts with
        Sausage and Grapes on
        Creamy Polenta, 143
    Grilled Grapes, 198
Green beans
    about: grilling tips, 217
    Green Beans with
        Hazelnuts, 208
    Sopressata and Roma
        Bean Salad, 47
    Zucchini and Pepper
        Ciambotta, 212–213
Gremolata, about, 191
Grilled Caesar Salad, 43
Grilled Chicken Parm and
    Vegetables, *164*, 176
Grilled Eggplant Caponata, *7*, 218
Grilled Fennel, 198
Grilled Grapes, 198
Grilled Pizza with Zucchini
    plus variations, *58*, 66–67
Grilled Squid and Peppers
    with Arugula, 163
Grilled Summer Vegetables
    and Parmesan, 216

Halibut, roasted, 154–155
Ham. *See* Prosciutto (ham)
Herbed Goat Cheese Filling, 30
Herbs
    buying and storing, 17
    chopping fresh, 17
    fresh, preserving, 201
    gremolata, 191
    using fresh vs. dried, 17
Homemade Marinara Sauce, 93
Homemade Pizza Dough, 61
Homemade Ricotta, 15
Honey, about, 229
Honeyed Figs and Brie, 32
Hummus, 20

Ingredients, essential Italian, 11–16.
    *See also specific
    main ingredients*
Italian food
    appeal and simplicity of, 10
    Mediterranean diet habits, 11
    naturally healthy nature of, 10
    relaxing and enjoying, 9
Italian Herb-Roasted Chicken, 179

Italian Tuna and White
    Bean Salad, 47
Italian Wedding
    Pasta, 112–113

Lamb
    Butterflied Leg of Lamb
        with Mint Pesto, 197
    Glazed Rosemary
        Lamb Chops, 201
    Leg of Lamb with
        Oregano and Onion, 200
    Spiced Lamb Ragu Shells, 106
Lasagna. *See* Pasta
Lasagna Toasts, 28
Leeks, in Creamy Spinach-
    Leek Filling, 30
Lemon. *See* Citrus
Lentil Stew with
    Butternut Squash, 49
Linguine. *See* Pasta

Maple-Glazed Sausages
    and Figs, 196
Marsala, about, 166
Meats. *See also specific meats*
    about: overview of, 165
    quick and easy antipasti tips, 21
    thermometers for, 179
Mediterranean diet habits, 11
Mediterranean Salad with Goat
    Cheese and Olives, 79
Mediterranean Seafood
    Stew, 56–57
Melon, prosciutto with, 37
Microwave Polenta, 137
Minestrone, 50–51, 132–133
Mint
    Artichoke and Mint Dip, 34
    Beef Ragu with Minted
        Penne, 100
    Mint Pesto, 197
    Mint Zucchini, 172
Mixed Winter Greens, 40
Mushrooms
    about: quick and easy
        antipasti tips, 21
    Broccoli and Mushroom
        Pizza, 62
    Farfalle with Baby Artichokes
        and Mushrooms, 88
    Farro and Mushroom Sauté, 135

Lemony Mushroom
    and Arugula Salad, 48
Penne with Three Cheeses and
    Porcini Mushrooms, 120–121
Pizza with Sausage and
    Mushrooms, *58*, 67
Sausage and Mushroom
    Penne, 93
Tomato, Portobello,
    and Mozzarella Melts, 76
Veal and Mushroom Stew, 54
Mussels, 57, 147

Northern-Style Lasagna, 114–115
Nuts
    about: almond paste, 223;
        pine nuts, 85
    Almond Panna Cotta with
        Strawberries, 234
    Fig and Walnut Cheese Balls, 33
    Flourless Chocolate
        Hazelnut Cake, 237
    Pignoli Cookies, 223
    Roasted Apricots
        and Pistachios, 36
    Walnut Biscotti, 225

Olive oil, 11
Olives
    about, 15–16
    Arugula and Olive Salad, 40
    Chicago Deep-Dish-Style
        Veggie Pizza, 68–69
    Giardiniera, 23
    Muffulettas, 75
    Spiced Citrus Olives, 22–23
Onions
    about: grilling tips, 217
    Caramelized Onion and Goat
        Cheese Panini, 72–73
    Caramelized Onion and Goat
        Cheese Topping, 26
    Chicken, Peppers, and Onions
        on Polenta, 140–141
    Grilled Summer Vegetables
        and Parmesan, 216
Orecchiette Shells with
    Veal Bolognese, 104
Orzo Salad with Grape
    Tomatoes and Mint, 136
Osso Bucco with
    Gremolata, 190–191
Oven-Dried Tomatoes, 16

Pancetta. *See* Bacon and pancetta

Panini and frittatas
about: overview of, 69
Caramelized Onion and Goat Cheese Panini, 72–73
Florentine Frittata, 78–79
Mozzarella, Tomato, and Basil Panini, 73
Muffulettas, 75
Red Pepper and Provolone Panini, 73
Red Potato, Spinach, and Fontina Frittata, 77
Tomato, Portobello, and Mozzarella Melts, 76
Veggie Focaccia, 74

Panna cotta, 234–236

Panzanella salads, 42, 44–45

Pasta, 81–123
about: freezing/reheating casseroles, 13; ingredients and types, 12–13; lasagna noodles, 115; overview of, 81; storing, 13; substituting shapes of, 97; testing doneness, 92; types of, 97
Baked Cavatelli with Sausage and Broccoli Rabe, 116–117
Beef Ragu with Minted Penne, 100
Butternut Squash and Pesto Rotini, *4*, 86
Campanelle with Chicken and Pea-Mint Pesto, 110
Cheese Ravioli with Fresh Tomatoes, 87
Chicken Pasta Primavera, 108–109
Classic Bolognese Sauce, 105
Classic Italian Pesto, 82
Eggplant and Ricotta Baked Ziti, 123
Farfalle Livornese with Tuna, 152
Farfalle with Baby Artichokes and Mushrooms, 88
Farfalle with Gorgonzola and Peas, 107
Fusilli with Herbed Ricotta and Grape Tomatoes, 86
Homemade Marinara Sauce, 93
Italian Wedding Pasta, 112–113
Linguine with Frisée, Bacon, and Egg, 95

Linguine with Red Clam Sauce, 157
Mixed Vegetable Minestrone, 50–51
Northern-Style Lasagna, 114–115
Orecchiette Shells with Veal Bolognese, 104
Pasta e Fagioli Bake, 119
Pasta e Fagioli with Sausage, 55
Pasta with Broccoli Rabe and Garbanzos, 89
Pasta with Tuna Puttanesca, 82
Penne alla Vodka, 92
Penne with Three Cheeses and Porcini Mushrooms, 120–121
Quick Bolognese, 105
Ratatouille Rigatoni, 96
Ricotta Gnocchi with Brown Butter and Fresh Herbs, 111
Sausage and Mushroom Penne, 93
Sausage and Pepper Baked Ziti, 118
Sausage Lover's Pasta, 102
Shrimp and Fennel Spaghetti, *144*, 162
Six-Herb Linguine, 83
Spaghetti All'Amatriciana, 107
Spaghetti and Meatballs, 98–99
Spaghetti Carbonara, 103
Spaghetti Pie, 90–91
Spaghetti with Pesto Verde, 84–85
Spiced Lamb Ragu Shells, 106
Summer Vegetable Garden Lasagna, 122
Tomato-Ricotta Rigatoni, *80*, 101
Trattoria-Style Shrimp Fettuccine, 160
Whole-Wheat Penne Genovese, 94

Peach Crostata, *8*, 233

Pears
about, 232
Chianti-Roasted Pears, 232
Chicken with Pears and Marsala, 166

Peas
Campanelle with Chicken and Pea-Mint Pesto, 110

Easy Pea Risotto, 127
Farfalle Livornese with Tuna, 107
Spaghetti Pie, 90–91
Spring Pea Dip, 34–35

Pecorino Chicken Fingers, 177

Penne. *See* Pasta

Peppers
about: grilling tips, 217; roasting, 69
Chicago Deep-Dish-Style Veggie Pizza, 68–69
Chicken, Peppers, and Onions on Polenta, 140–141
Grilled Summer Vegetables and Parmesan, 216
Peppers Caprese, 204
Red Pepper and Provolone Panini, 73
Ricotta and Roasted Pepper Filling, 31
Ricotta, Yellow Pepper, and Asparagus Pizza, 60
Sausage and Pepper Baked Ziti, 118
Veggie Focaccia, 74
Zucchini and Pepper Ciambotta, 212–213

Pestos, 82, 85, 86, 133, 197

Pickled vegetables, 19, 21, 23

Pignoli Cookies, 223

Pine nuts, about, 85

Pizzas and calzones
about: grilling tips, 67; overview of, 69; rolling and shaping dough, 61
Asparagus-Fontina Pizzettes with Bacon, 64–65
Broccoli and Mushroom Pizza, 62
Cheese and Salad Pizza, 63
Chicago Deep-Dish-Style Veggie Pizza, 68–69
Crustless Tomato Ricotta Pie, 71
Grilled Pizza with Zucchini plus variations, *58*, 66–67
Homemade Pizza Dough, 61
Pizza with Arugula and Prosciutto, *58*, 67
Pizza with Sausage and Mushrooms, *58*, 67
Ricotta-Spinach Calzone, 70
Ricotta, Yellow Pepper, and Asparagus Pizza, 60

Sausage Calzones, 71
Veggie Whole-Wheat Pizza, 62
Pizzelles, 222
Polenta
about: freezing/reheating
casseroles, 13; overview
of, 125; types of (course,
medium, fine), 13
Baked Eggs and Polenta with
Chunky Vegetable Sauce, 139
Broiled Rosemary
Polenta Wedges, 137
Brussels Sprouts with
Sausage and Grapes on
Creamy Polenta, 143
Chicken, Peppers, and Onions
on Polenta, 140–141
Creamy Polenta, 137
Microwave Polenta, 136
Polenta and Spinach Gratin, 138
Spicy Sausage and Polenta
Casserole, 142
Spicy Turkey Sausage
and Polenta, 184
Pork. *See also* Bacon and pancetta;
Prosciutto (ham); Sausage
about: thermometers for, 179
Balsamic Roasted Pork with
Berry Salad, 194–195
Classic Bolognese Sauce, 105
Northern-Style
Lasagna, 114–115
Pork Chops Marsala, 193
Pork Loin with Lemon, Thyme,
and Garlic, 198–199
Quick Bolognese, 105
Slow-Cooked Tuscan Pork
with Fennel, 192
Potatoes
about: grilling tips, 217
Red Potato, Spinach, and
Fontina Frittata, 77
Roasted Halibut with Fennel
and Potatoes, 154–155
Stuffed Parmesan Potatoes, 215
Poultry
about: overview of, 165;
thermometers for, 179
Campanelle with Chicken
and Pea-Mint Pesto, 110
Chicken and Escarole Soup, 49
Chicken and Pesto Stacks, 168
Chicken, Peppers, and Onions
on Polenta, 140–141

Chicken Saltimbocca, 178
Chicken Scarpariello, 174–175
Chicken with Caramelized
Cauliflower and
Green Onions, 169
Chicken with Pears
and Marsala, 166
Classic Chicken Parmesan, 167
Cornish Hens Milanese, 180–181
Crispy Balsamic Chicken, 173
Grilled Chicken Parm and
Vegetables, *164*, 176
Italian Herb-Roasted
Chicken, 179
Italian Wedding Pasta, 112–113
Lemon-Oregano Chicken Cut-
lets with Mint Zucchini, 172
Panzanella Salad with
Grilled Chicken, 42
Pecorino Chicken Fingers, 177
Prosciutto-Wrapped Turkey
Roulade, 182–183
Quick Bolognese, 105
Roman Chicken Sauté with
Artichokes, 170–171
Spaghetti and Meatballs, 98–99
Spicy Turkey Sausage
and Polenta, 184
Prosciutto (ham)
Antipasti Platter, 20
Muffulettas, 75
Pizza with Arugula and
Prosciutto, *58*, 67
Prosciutto with Melon, 37
Prosciutto-Wrapped Grilled
Fig Salad, 46
Prosciutto-Wrapped Turkey
Roulade, 182–183
Roasted Prosciutto-Wrapped
Asparagus, 20
Zucchini and Ham Ribbons, 205
Prosecco, sorbet with, 233

Raddichio, grilling, 217
Radishes, in Antipasti Platter, 20
Ratatouille Rigatoni, 96
Ravioli, 87
Red Potato, Spinach,
and Fontina Frittata, 77
Ricotta. *See* Cheese; Pizzas
and calzones

Risotto
about: overview of, 125; rice
types and risotto prep, 13–14
Butternut Squash Barley
Risotto, *124*, 131
Easy Pea Risotto, 127
Fresh Tomato, Corn,
and Basil Risotto, 130
Risotto Milanese, 126
Spring Vegetable Risotto
with Shrimp, 128–129
Roasted Apricots and Pistachios, 36
Roasted Halibut with Fennel
and Potatoes, 154–155
Roasted Prosciutto-
Wrapped Asparagus, 20
Roast Salmon with Capers
and Parsley, 157
Roman Chicken Sauté
with Artichokes, 170–171
Roman-Style Artichokes, 24
Rosemary polenta wedges,
broiled, 137

Saffron-scented risotto, 126
Salads
about: overview of, 39;
quick side salads, 79
Apple Coleslaw with Golden
Raisins and Pine Nuts, 79
Arugula and Olive Salad, 40
Baby Romaine with
Fennel and Citrus, 79
Balsamic Roasted Pork with
Berry Salad, 194–195
Cheese and Salad Pizza, 63
Escarole Frisée Salad, 41
Grilled Caesar Salad, 43
Italian Tuna and
White Bean Salad, 47
Lemony Mushroom and
Arugula Salad, 48
Mediterranean Salad with
Goat Cheese and Olives, 79
Mixed Winter Greens, 40
Orzo Salad with Grape
Tomatoes and Mint, 136
Panzanella Salad with
Grilled Chicken, 42
Prosciutto-Wrapped
Grilled Fig Salad, 46
Sopressata and Roma
Bean Salad, 47

Spinach and Endive with
Pears and Walnuts, 79

Tomato and Mozzarella
Salad, 41

Warm Farro Salad with
Roasted Vegetables, 134

White Bean Panzanella
Salad, 44–45

Salmon, 157, 158

Salt-Baked Fish, 153

Sauces and dressings
Béchamel Sauce, 114–115
Blackberry Sauce, 236
Chunky Vegetable Sauce, 139
Classic Balsamic Vinaigrette, 40
Classic Bolognese Sauce, 105
Classic Italian Pesto, 82
Homemade Marinara Sauce, 93
Light Pesto, 133
Mint Pesto, 197
Pestos, 82, 85, 86, 133, 197
Pesto Verde, 85
Puttanesca Sauce, 159
Quick Bolognese, 105
Red Clam Sauce, 157
Sicilian Citrus Salsa, 159
Tomato Sauce, 99
Tomato Vinaigrette, 29

Sausage
Baked Cavatelli with Sausage
and Broccoli Rabe, 116–117

Brussels Sprouts with
Sausage and Grapes on
Creamy Polenta, 143

Maple-Glazed Sausages
and Figs, 196

Pasta e Fagioli with Sausage, 55

Pizza with Sausage and
Mushrooms, 58, 67

Sausage and Mushroom
Penne, 93

Sausage and Pepper
Baked Ziti, 118

Sausage Calzones, 71

Sausage Lover's Pasta, 102

Spicy Sausage and Polenta
Casserole, 142

Spicy Turkey Sausage
and Polenta, 184

Savory Tartlets with
Three Fillings, 30–31

Scallops, 150

Seared Scallops with Olive
and Tomato Compote, 150

Sgroppino Sorbet with
Prosecco and Mint, 233

Shrimp. See Fish and shellfish

Sicilian Citrus Salsa, 159

Six-Herb Linguine, 83

Slow-Cooked Tuscan
Pork with Fennel, 192

Slow cookers, cooking
vegetables in, 192

Snapper, 148–149, 153

Sopressata and Roma
Bean Salad, 47

Soups and stews
about: broths for, 53;
overview of, 39
Barley Minestrone, 132–133
Chicken and Escarole Soup, 49
Chilled Tuscan-Style
Tomato Soup, 38, 52
Lentil Stew with
Butternut Squash, 49
Mediterranean Seafood
Stew, 56–57
Mixed Vegetable
Minestrone, 50–51
Pasta e Fagioli with Sausage, 55
Stracciatella with Escarole, 53
Summery Vegetable Soup, 52
Veal and Mushroom Stew, 54
Zucchini and Pepper
Ciambotta, 212–213

Spaghetti. See Pasta

Spaghetti Squash with
Olives and Pecorino, 215

Spiced Citrus Olives, 22–23

Spiced Lamb Ragu Shells, 106

Spicy Sausage and Polenta
Casserole, 142

Spicy Turkey Sausage
and Polenta, 184

Spinach
Creamy Spinach-Leek
Filling, 30
Pasta e Fagioli with Sausage, 55
Polenta and Spinach Gratin, 138
Red Potato, Spinach,
and Fontina Frittata, 77
Ricotta-Spinach Calzone, 70
Spinach and Endive with
Pears and Walnuts, 79
Veggie Focaccia, 74

Spring Pea Dip, 34–35

Spring Vegetable Risotto
with Shrimp, 128–129

Squash. See Zucchini
and other squash

Squid (calamari), 146, 163

Steak. See Beef

Stracciatella with Escarole, 53

Strawberries. See Berries

Stuffed Breast of Veal, 188

Stuffed Fresh Figs, 229

Stuffed Parmesan Potatoes, 215

Summer Vegetable Garden
Lasagna, 122

Summery Vegetable Soup, 52

Swiss chard
Maple-Glazed Sausages
and Figs, 196
Summer Vegetable
Garden Lasagna, 122
Swiss Chard, Sicilian
Style, 208–209

Tiramisù, 238–240

Tomatoes
about, 16–17; canned, 17, 139;
chopping canned, 139;
peeling, 17; quick and
easy antipasti tips, 21;
selecting, 16; storing, 17
Fresh Tomato, Corn,
and Basil Risotto, 130
Grilled Summer Vegetables
and Parmesan, 216
Lasagna Toasts, 28
Oven-Dried Tomatoes, 16
pasta with. See Pasta
salads with. See Salads
sandwiches with. See
Panini and frittatas
sauces with. See Sauces
and dressings
soups with. See Soups and stews
Tomato and Mozzarella
Bites, 18, 31
Tomato and Ricotta
Salata Bruschetta, 27
Tomato-Herb Focaccia, 219
Tuna and Tomato Topping, 26

Trattoria-Style Shrimp
Fettuccine, 160

Tuna. See Fish and shellfish

Turkey. See Poultry

Tuscan White Bean Bruschetta, 27

Veal
    Classic Bolognese Sauce, 105
    Northern-Style
        Lasagna, 114–115
    Orecchiette Shells with
        Veal Bolognese, 104
    Quick Bolognese, 105
    Stuffed Breast of Veal, 188
    Veal and Mushroom Stew, 54
    Veal Parmigiana, 185
Vegetables, 210–219. *See also*
    Salads; *specific vegetables*
    about: grilling tips, 217;
        overview of sides and, 210;
        slow cookers for, 192
    Chicago Deep-Dish-Style
        Veggie Pizza, 68–69
    Chunky Vegetable Sauce, 139
    Grilled Summer Vegetables
        and Parmesan, 216
    Spring Vegetable Risotto
        with Shrimp, 128–129

    Summer Vegetable
        Garden Lasagna, 122
    Summery Vegetable Soup, 52
    Veggie Focaccia, 74
    Veggie Whole-Wheat Pizza, 62
Vinegar, 11–12

Walnut Biscotti, 225
Warm Farro Salad with
    Roasted Vegetables, 134
White beans. *See* Beans
    and legumes
Whole-Wheat Penne
    Genovese, 94
Wine, 11, 166

Zucchini and other squash
    about: grilling tips, 217; prepar-
        ing butternut squash, 131
    Butternut Squash and
        Pesto Rotini, *4*, 86

Butternut Squash
    Barley Risotto, *124*, 131
Grilled Chicken Parm and
    Vegetables, *164*, 176
Grilled Pizza with Zucchini
    plus variations, *58*, 66–67
Grilled Summer Vegetables
    and Parmesan, 216
Lasagna Toasts, 28
Lentil Stew with
    Butternut Squash, 49
Mint Zucchini, 172
Salmon and Summer Squash
    in Parchment, 158
Spaghetti Squash with Olives
    and Pecorino, 215
Spaghetti with Pesto
    Verde, 84–85
Summery Vegetable Soup, 52
Zucchini and Ham Ribbons, 205
Zucchini and Pepper Ciambotta,
    212–213

Index of Recipes by Icon

Note: Page numbers in *italics* indicate photos of recipes located separately from respective recipes.

◔ 30 MINUTES OR LESS

Each of these recipes requires 30 minutes or less to prepare—from kitchen to table!

Antipasti Platter, 20
Artichoke and Mint Dip, 34
Arugula and Olive Salad, 40
Asparagus Gremolata, 206
Barley Minestrone, 132–133
Bass with Tomato Paste, 156
Beef Ragu with Minted Penne, 100
Broiled Rosemary
    Polenta Wedges, 137
Brussels Sprouts with Brown
    Butter and Chestnuts, 210

Brussels Sprouts with Pancetta
    and Rosemary, *202*, 210
Butternut Squash and
    Pesto Rotini, *4*, 86
Campanelle with Chicken
    and Pea-Mint Pesto, 110
Caramelized Onion and
    Goat Cheese Topping, 26
Cheese and Salad Pizza, 63
Cheese Ravioli with
    Fresh Tomatoes, 87
Chicken and Pesto Stacks, 168
Chicken Pasta Primavera, 108–109
Chicken, Peppers, and Onions
    on Polenta, 140–141
Chicken Saltimbocca, 178

Chicken with Pears
    and Marsala, 166
Classic Italian Pesto, 82
Cod Livornese, 151
Creamy Polenta, 137
Crispy Balsamic Chicken, 173
Crispy Parmesan Broccoli, 214
Crostini Platter, 26
Crunchy Low-Fat Chocolate
    Biscotti, 226–227
Easy Pea Risotto, 127
Escarole Frisée Salad, 41
Farfalle Livornese with Tuna, 152
Florentine Frittata, 78–79
Fusilli with Herbed Ricotta
    and Grape Tomatoes, 86
Garlic and Herb Bread, 219

Garlic Broccoli Rabe, 207

Garlicky Escarole with
White Beans, 204

Glazed Rosemary Lamb Chops, 201

Grilled Caesar Salad, 43

Grilled Fennel, 198–199

Grilled Grapes, 198

Grilled Pizza with Zucchini, *58*, 66

Grilled Squid and Peppers
with Arugula, 163

Homemade Marinara Sauce, 93

Honeyed Figs and Brie, 32

Italian Tuna and White
Bean Salad, 47

Lemon-Oregano Chicken Cutlets
with Mint Zucchini, 172

Lemony Mushroom
and Arugula Salad, 48

Lentil Stew with
Butternut Squash, 49

Linguine with Frisée,
Bacon, and Egg, 95

Microwave Polenta, 137

Mixed Winter Greens, 40

Muffulettas, 75

Orecchiette Shells with
Veal Bolognese, 104

Orzo Salad with Grape
Tomatoes and Mint, 136

Panzanella Salad with
Grilled Chicken, 42

Pecorino Chicken Fingers, 177

Peppers Caprese, 204

Pizza with Arugula and
Prosciutto, *58*, 67

Pizza with Sausage
and Mushrooms, *58*, 67

Pork Chops Marsala, 193

Prosciutto with Melon, 37

Prosciutto-Wrapped
Grilled Fig Salad, 46

Red Potato, Spinach,
and Fontina Frittata, 77

Ricotta-Spinach Calzone, 70

Roasted Apricots and Pistachios, 36

Roman Chicken Sauté with
Artichokes, 170–171

Salt-Baked Fish, 153

Sausage and Mushroom Penne, 93

Seared Scallops with Olive
and Tomato Compote, 150

Sgroppino Sorbet with
Prosecco and Mint, 233

Shrimp and Fennel
Spaghetti, *144*, 162

Shrimp Gemelli, 161

Sicilian Citrus Salsa, 159

Sopressata and Roma Bean Salad, 47

Spaghetti with Pesto Verde, 84–85

Spiced Lamb Ragu Shells, 106

Spicy Turkey Sausage
and Polenta, 184

Spring Pea Dip, 34–35

Steak Pizzaiola, 185

Stracciatella with Escarole, 53

Stuffed Fresh Figs, 229

Swiss Chard, Sicilian
Style, 208–209

Tomato and Mozzarella Bites, *18*, 31

Tomato and Mozzarella Salad, 41

Tomato and Ricotta
Salata Bruschetta, 27

Tomato, Portobello, and
Mozzarella Melts, 76

Tomato-Ricotta Rigatoni, *80*, 101

Trattoria-Style Shrimp
Fettuccine, 160

Tuna and Tomato Topping, 26

Tuscan White Bean Bruschetta, 27

Veggie Focaccia, 74

Veggie Whole-Wheat Pizza, 62

White Bean Panzanella
Salad, 44–45

White Bean Topping, 26

Whole-Wheat Penne Genovese, 94

Zucchini and Ham Ribbons, 205

♥ HEART HEALTHY

Each main dish contains no
more than 5 grams of saturated fat, 150 milligrams of
cholesterol, and 480 mil-
ligrams of sodium. Each
appetizer, side dish, and dessert is limited to no more than
2 grams of saturated fat, 50
milligrams of cholesterol, and
360 milligrams of sodium.

Angeletti, 224

Artichoke and Mint Dip, 34

Asparagus Gremolata, 206

Baked Snapper with Peppers
and Mushrooms, 148–149

Balsamic-Glazed Baby Carrots, 214

Balsamic Roasted Pork with
Berry Salad, 194–195

Barley Minestrone, 132–133

Beef Ragu with Minted Penne, 100

Blueberry-Lemon Tiramisù, 240

Bold Berry Granita, *230*, 231

Braciole with Grape Tomatoes, 189

Brussels Sprouts with Brown
Butter and Chestnuts, 210

Brussels Sprouts with Pancetta
and Rosemary, *202*, 210

Buttermilk Panna Cotta with
Blackberry Sauce, 236

Campanelle with Chicken
and Pea-Mint Pesto, 110

Caramelized Onion and Goat
Cheese Topping, 26

Chianti-Roasted Pears, 232

Chicken with Pears
and Marsala, 166

Classic Italian Pesto, 82

Cod Livornese, 151

Coffee Granita, 231

Creamy Spinach-Leek Filling, 30

Crispy Balsamic Chicken, 173

Crispy Parmesan Broccoli, 214

Crostini Platter, 26

Crunchy Low-Fat Chocolate
Biscotti, 226–227

Escarole Frisée Salad, 41

Farro and Mushroom Sauté, 135

Fire-Grilled Steak with
Fennel, 186–187

Fresh Tomato, Corn,
and Basil Risotto, 130

Fusilli with Herbed Ricotta
and Grape Tomatoes, 86

Garlic and Herb Bread, 219

Garlic Broccoli Rabe, 207

Garlicky Escarole with
White Beans, 204

Glazed Rosemary Lamb Chops, 201

Grilled Chicken Parm and
Vegetables, *164*, 176

Grilled Eggplant Caponata, *7*, 218

Grilled Fennel, 198–199

Grilled Grapes, 198

Herbed Goat Cheese Filling, 30

Homemade Ricotta, 15

Italian Wedding Pasta, 112–113

Lasagna Toasts, 28

Lemon-Oregano Chicken Cutlets
with Mint Zucchini, 172

Lemony Mushroom and
    Arugula Salad, 48
Lentil Stew with
    Butternut Squash, 49
Mussels with Tomatoes
    and White Wine, 147
Oven-Dried Tomatoes, 16
Pignoli Cookies, 223
Pizzelles, 222
Pork Chops Marsala, 193
Prosciutto-Wrapped Turkey
    Roulade, 182–183
Quick Bolognese, 105
Ricotta and Roasted
    Pepper Filling, 31
Ricotta, Yellow Pepper,
    and Asparagus Pizza, 60
Roasted Prosciutto-
    Wrapped Asparagus, 20
Roman Chicken Sauté with
    Artichokes, 170–171
Salmon and Summer Squash
    in Parchment, 158
Savory Tartlets with
    Three Fillings, 30
Sgroppino Sorbet with
    Prosecco and Mint, 233
Sicilian Citrus Salsa, 159
Sicilian Tuna with Puttanesca
    Sauce, 159
Spaghetti Squash with
    Olives and Pecorino, 215
Spiced Citrus Olives, 22–23
Spring Pea Dip, 34–35
Stuffed Fresh Figs, 229
Swiss Chard, Sicilian
    Style, 208–209
Tomato and Ricotta
    Salata Bruschetta, 27
Tuna and Tomato Topping, 26
Tuscan White Bean Bruschetta, 27
Veal and Mushroom Stew, 54
Walnut Biscotti, 225
White Bean Topping, 26
Whole-Wheat Penne Genovese, 94
Zucchini and Pepper
    Ciambotta, 212–213

☺ LOW CALORIE

These main-dish meals are 450 calories or less. The appetizers, sides, and desserts are limited to 150 calories.

Angeletti, 224
Artichoke and Mint Dip, 34
Arugula and Olive Salad, 40
Asparagus Gremolata, 206
Baked Eggs and Polenta with
    Chunky Vegetable Sauce, 139
Baked Snapper with Peppers
    and Mushrooms, 148–149
Balsamic-Glazed Baby Carrots, 214
Balsamic Roasted Pork with
    Berry Salad, 194–195
Barley Minestrone, 132–133
Beef Ragu with Minted Penne, 100
Bold Berry Granita, *230*, 231
Braciole with Grape Tomatoes, 189
Broccoli and Mushroom Pizza, 62
Broiled Rosemary Polenta
    Wedges, 137
Brussels Sprouts with Brown
    Butter and Chestnuts, 210
Brussels Sprouts with Pancetta
    and Rosemary, *202*, 210
Buttermilk Panna Cotta with
    Blackberry Sauce, 236
Butternut Squash Barley
    Risotto, *124*, 131
Caramelized Onion and
    Goat Cheese Topping, 26
Cauliflower with Golden Raisins
    and Pine Nuts, 211
Cheese Ravioli with
    Fresh Tomatoes, 87
Chianti-Roasted Pears, 232
Chicken and Escarole Soup, 49
Chicken and Pesto Stacks, 168
Chicken, Peppers, and Onions
    on Polenta, 140–141
Chicken Saltimbocca, 178
Chicken Scarpariello, 174–175
Chicken with Caramelized Cauli-
    flower and Green Onions, 169
Chicken with Pears and
    Marsala, 166
Chilled Tuscan-Style
    Tomato Soup, *38*, 52
Classic Italian Pesto, 82
Cod Livornese, 151
Coffee Granita, 231
Creamy Spinach-Leek Filling, 30
Crispy Balsamic Chicken, 173
Crispy Parmesan Broccoli, 214
Crostini Platter, 26
Crustless Tomato Ricotta Pie, 71
Escarole Frisée Salad, 41
Farfalle Livornese with Tuna, 152
Farfalle with Baby Artichokes
    and Mushrooms, 88
Fig and Walnut Cheese Balls, 33
Fire-Grilled Steak with
    Fennel, 186–187
Florentine Frittata, 78–79
Fresh Tomato, Corn,
    and Basil Risotto, 130
Fusilli with Herbed Ricotta
    and Grape Tomatoes, 86
Garlic and Herb Bread, 219
Garlic Broccoli Rabe, 207
Garlicky Escarole with
    White Beans, 204
Giardiniera, 23
Glazed Rosemary Lamb Chops, 201
Green Beans with Hazelnuts, 208
Grilled Chicken Parm and
    Vegetables, *164*, 176
Grilled Eggplant Caponata, *7*, 218
Grilled Fennel, 198–199
Grilled Grapes, 198
Grilled Squid and Peppers
    with Arugula, 163
Herbed Goat Cheese Filling, 30
Homemade Marinara Sauce, 93
Homemade Ricotta, 15
Italian Tuna and White
    Bean Salad, 47
Italian Wedding Pasta, 112–113
Lasagna Toasts, 28
Lentil Stew with Butternut Squash, 49
Lemon-Oregano Chicken Cutlets
    with Mint Zucchini, 172
Linguine with Red Clam Sauce, 157
Maple-Glazed Sausages
    and Figs, 196
Mediterranean
    Seafood Stew, 56–57
Mozzarella, Tomato, and
    Basil Panini, 73
Mussels with Tomatoes
    and White Wine, 147
Osso Bucco with
    Gremolata, 190–191

Oven-Dried Tomatoes, 16

Panzanella Salad with
Grilled Chicken, 42

Pasta e Fagioli Bake, 119

Pasta with Broccoli Rabe
and Garbanzos, 89

Pasta with Tuna Puttanesca, 82

Pecorino Chicken Fingers, 177

Penne alla Vodka, 92

Pignoli Cookies, 223

Pizzelles, 222

Polenta and Spinach Gratin, 138

Pork Chops Marsala, 193

Prosciutto with Melon, 37

Prosciutto-Wrapped
Grilled Fig Salad, 46

Quick Bolognese, 105

Ratatouille Rigatoni, 96

Red Potato, Spinach,
and Fontina Frittata, 77

Ricotta and Roasted
Pepper Filling, 31

Ricotta Gnocchi with Brown
Butter and Fresh Herbs, 111

Ricotta-Spinach Calzone, 70

Ricotta, Yellow Pepper, and
Asparagus Pizza, 60

Roasted Halibut with Fennel
and Potatoes, 154–155

Roasted Prosciutto-
Wrapped Asparagus, 20

Roast Salmon with Capers
and Parsley, 157

Roman Chicken Sauté
with Artichokes, 170–171

Salmon and Summer Squash
in Parchment, 158

Salt-Baked Fish, 153

Savory Tartlets with
Three Fillings, 30

Seared Scallops with Olive
and Tomato Compote, 150

Sgroppino Sorbet with
Prosecco and Mint, 233

Sicilian Citrus Salsa, 159

Sicilian Tuna with
Puttanesca Sauce, 159

Six-Herb Linguine, 83

Slow-Cooked Tuscan
Pork with Fennel, 192

Sopressata and Roma
Bean Salad, 47

Spaghetti and Meatballs, 98–99

Spaghetti Squash with
Olives and Pecorino, 215

Spiced Citrus Olives, 22–23

Spicy Sausage and Polenta
Casserole, 142

Spicy Turkey Sausage
and Polenta, 184

Spring Pea Dip, 34–35

Spring Vegetable Risotto
with Shrimp, 128–129

Stracciatella with Escarole, 53

Summer Vegetable Garden
Lasagna, 122

Summery Vegetable Soup, 52

Swiss Chard, Sicilian
Style, 208–209

Tomato and Mozzarella Bites, 18, 31

Tomato, Portobello, and
Mozzarella Melts, 76

Tomato-Ricotta Rigatoni, 80, 101

Trattoria-Style Shrimp
Fettuccine, 160

Tuna and Tomato Topping, 26

Tuscan White Bean Bruschetta, 27

Veal and Mushroom Stew, 54

Veal Parmigiana, 185

Veggie Whole-Wheat Pizza, 62

Walnut Biscotti, 225

Warm Farro Salad with
Roasted Vegetables, 134

White Bean Topping, 26

Whole-Wheat Penne Genovese, 94

Zucchini and Ham Ribbons, 205

Zucchini and Pepper
Ciambotta, 212–213

🍲 MAKE AHEAD

You can make all (or a portion) of these recipes ahead of time.

Almond Panna Cotta with
Strawberries, 234–235

Angeletti, 224

Artichoke and Mint Dip, 34

Asparagus Gremolata, 206

Baked Cavatelli with Sausage
and Broccoli Rabe, 116–117

Barley Minestrone, 132–133

Berry Cheesecake, 220, 240

Bold Berry Granita, 230, 231

Brussels Sprouts with Brown
Butter and Chestnuts, 210

Brussels Sprouts with Pancetta
and Rosemary, 202, 210

Buttermilk Panna Cotta with
Blackberry Sauce, 236

Butternut Squash Barley
Risotto, 124, 131

Caramelized Onion and
Goat Cheese Topping, 26

Chianti-Roasted Pears, 232

Chicken and Escarole Soup, 49

Chicken Scarpariello, 174–175

Chilled Tuscan-Style
Tomato Soup, 38, 52

Classic Italian Pesto, 82

Classic Tiramisù, 238–239

Coffee Granita, 231

Creamy Spinach-Leek Filling, 30

Crostini Platter, 26

Crunchy Low-Fat Chocolate
Biscotti, 226–227

Drunken Chocolate Figs, 228

Eggplant and Ricotta
Baked Ziti, 123

Farro and Mushroom Sauté, 135

Fig and Walnut Cheese Balls, 33

Flourless Chocolate
Hazelnut Cake, 237

Ganache Tart with Salted-
Almond Crust, 241

Garlicky Escarole with
White Beans, 204

Giardiniera, 23

Green Beans with Hazelnuts, 208

Grilled Eggplant Caponata, 7, 218

Grilled Summer Vegetables
and Parmesan, 216

Herbed Goat Cheese Filling, 30

Homemade Marinara Sauce, 93

Homemade Ricotta, 15

Italian Tuna and White
Bean Salad, 47

Italian Wedding Pasta, 112–113

Lentil Stew with Butternut
Squash, 49

Mediterranean Seafood
Stew, 56–57

Mixed Vegetable
Minestrone, 50–51

Muffulettas, 75

Northern-Style Lasagna, 114–115

Orzo Salad with Grape
Tomatoes and Mint, 136

Osso Bucco with
    Gremolata, 190–191
Oven-Dried Tomatoes, 16
Pasta e Fagioli Bake, 119
Pasta e Fagioli with Sausage, 55
Peach Crostata, *8*, 233
Penne with Three Cheeses and
    Porcini Mushrooms, 120–121
Pignoli Cookies, 223
Pizzelles, 222
Polenta and Spinach Gratin, 138
Prosciutto-Wrapped Turkey
    Roulade, 182–183
Quick Bolognese, 105
Ricotta and Roasted
    Pepper Filling, 31
Sausage and Pepper Baked Ziti, 118
Savory Tartlets with
    Three Fillings, 30
Slow-Cooked Tuscan Pork
    with Fennel, 192
Spaghetti and Meatballs, 98–99
Spaghetti Pie, 90–91
Spiced Citrus Olives, 22–23
Spicy Sausage and Polenta
    Casserole, 142
Spring Pea Dip, 34–35
Stuffed Parmesan Potatoes, 215
Summery Vegetable Soup, 52
Tomato-Herb Focaccia, 219
Tuna and Tomato Topping, 26
Veal and Mushroom Stew, 54
Walnut Biscotti, 225
Warm Farro Salad with
    Roasted Vegetables, 134
White Bean Topping, 26
Zucchini and Ham Ribbons, 205
Zucchini and Pepper
    Ciambotta, 212–213

🍲 SLOW COOKER

These slow-cooked dishes make it easy to get dinner on the table.

Butternut Squash Barley
    Risotto, *124*, 131
Chicken Scarpariello, 174–175
Lentil Stew with Butternut
    Squash, 49
Mediterranean
    Seafood Stew, 56–57
Slow-Cooked Tuscan Pork
    with Fennel, 192

Photography Credits

Front cover: Ann Stratton
Spine: Ivan Mateev/ iStock Photo
Back cover: Ngoc Minh Ngo (upper left); Kate Mathis (upper right); Kate Sears (lower left and right)

Antonis Achilleos: 35, 76

James Baigrie: 5, 6, 38, 42, 80, 151, 154, 199, 206, 216, 228, 230

Monica Buck: 118, 132, 142

Corbis Images: Andrew Scrivani/the food passionates, 69

Tara Donne: 163

Getty images: Image Source, Dennis Gottlieb, 227, 17; Richard Jung, 137; StockFood, 61

Brian Hagiwara: 147, 162, 165, 180

Lisa Hubbard: 229

iStockphoto: 214; Bedo, 43; Joe Biafore, 207; Mariya Bibikova, 11; Bluestocking, 60; Kelly Cline, 222; Egal, 131; Eyewave, 172; Only Fabrizio, 134; Floortje, 54, 97 (fusilli); Fotogal, 77; Intraprese, 217 (radicchio); Alasdair James, 67; Robert Kirk, 143; Uyen Le, 217 (eggplant); Viktor Lugovsky, 40; Layland Masuda, 37; Maxg71, 31; Juan Monino, 20; Orchid Poet, 12; Ragnarocks, 135; Milo Sluz, 179; Syolacan, 209; Laura Stanley, 93

Frances Janisch: 21, 136, 158

Yunhee Kim: 225

Rita Maas: 25, 27, 224

Kate Mathis: 2, 15, 18, 22, 24, 29, 32, 33, 36, 46, 58, 63, 67, 68, 83, 84, 91, 98, 100, 104, 106, 122, 129, 145, 164, 183, 184, 187, 195, 202, 205, 234, 236

Ngoc Minh Ngo: 78

Con Poulos: 8, 74, 75, 96, 102, 110, 113, 116, 119, 121, 156, 161, 189, 242

David Prince: 30, 175s

Alan Richardson: 10, 89

Kate Sears: 28, 48, 72, 87, 94, 95, 109, 127, 140, 148, 152, 160, 168, 177, 196, 209, 212, 220, 233

Shutterstock: Bienchen's, 201; Norman Chan, 70; Irina Fischer, 193; Fortish, 181; Oliver Hoffmann, 217 (zucchini); Rido, 218, Stargazer, 149

Stock Food: George Crudo, 219; Buchanan Studios, 146

Ann Stratton: 114

Studio D: Philip Friedman, 9, 53, 192; J. Muckle, 97 (all pasta except fusilli); Lara Robby, 217 (onion, potatoes)

Mark Thomas: 123, 190

Anna Williams: 45, 56, 64, 124, 130, 173

The Good Housekeeping Triple-Test Promise

At *Good Housekeeping*, we want to make sure that every recipe we print works in any oven, with any brand of ingredient, no matter what. That's why, in our test kitchens at the **Good Housekeeping Research Institute**, we go all out: We test each recipe at least three times—and, often, several more times after that.

When a recipe is first developed, one member of our team prepares the dish and we judge it on these criteria: It must be **delicious, family-friendly, healthy,** and **easy to make.**

1 The recipe is then tested several more times to fine-tune the flavor and ease of preparation, always by the same team member, using the same equipment.

2 Next, another team member follows the recipe as written, **varying the brands of ingredients** and **kinds of equipment**. Even the types of stoves we use are changed.

3 A third team member repeats the whole process **using yet another set of equipment** and **alternative ingredients**. By the time the recipes appear on these pages, they are guaranteed to work in any kitchen, including yours. **We promise.**